Believing in Order to See

Series Board

James Bernauer

Drucilla Cornell

Thomas R. Flynn

Kevin Hart

Richard Kearney

Jean-Luc Marion

Adriaan Peperzak

Thomas Sheehan

Hent de Vries

Merold Westphal

Michael Zimmerman

John D. Caputo, *series editor*

Perspectives in
Continental
Philosophy

JEAN-LUC MARION

Believing in Order to See
On the Rationality of Revelation and the Irrationality of Some Believers

Translated by Christina M. Gschwandtner

Fordham University Press
New York ■ 2017

Copyright © 2017 Fordham University Press

All rights reserved. No part of this publication may be reproduced, stored in a retrieval system, or transmitted in any form or by any means—electronic, mechanical, photocopy, recording, or any other—except for brief quotations in printed reviews, without the prior permission of the publisher.

This book was originally published in French as Jean-Luc Marion, *Le croire pour le voir: Réflexions diverses sur la rationalité de la révélation et l'irrationalité de quelques croyants,* Copyright © 2010 Parole et Silence.

Fordham University Press has no responsibility for the persistence or accuracy of URLs for external or third-party Internet websites referred to in this publication and does not guarantee that any content on such websites is, or will remain, accurate or appropriate.

Fordham University Press also publishes its books in a variety of electronic formats. Some content that appears in print may not be available in electronic books.

Visit us online at www.fordhampress.com.

Library of Congress Cataloging-in-Publication Data available online at http://catalog.loc.gov.

Printed in the United States of America

19 18 17   5 4 3 2 1

First edition

In memory of Robinson, whom we shall see again

Contents

Preface		*xi*
Translator's Note		*xv*

PART I: REASON AND FAITH TOGETHER

1	Faith and Reason	3
2	In Defense of Argument	14
3	The Formal Reason of the Infinite	30

PART II: WHO SPEAKS ABOUT IT?

4	On the Eminent Dignity of the Poor Baptized	47
5	The Service of Rationality in the Church	66
6	The Future of Catholicism	76

PART III: WHAT IS POSSIBLE AND WHAT SHOWS ITSELF

7	Nothing Is Impossible for God	87
8	The Phenomenality of the Sacrament	102
9	Transcendence par Excellence	116

PART IV: RECOGNITION

10	The Recognition of the Gift	*125*
11	"They Recognized Him and He Became Invisible to Them"	*136*
12	The Invisible Saint	*144*
	Notes	*153*
	Index	*169*

Preface

"Believe then! It doesn't hurt."

—Ludwig von Wittgenstein

I offer here twelve texts, occasional writings spread over the years 1979–2009.[1] There would be no reason to gather them together but for the fact that they share the same concern and the same quarrel, returned to each time according to the circumstances and the solicitations with a consistency that was perhaps pointless, and in any case little rewarded.

What concern, and what quarrel? To show that faith and reason, in the case of Christian and more particularly Catholic thought, not only contradict each other today less than ever, but that the very question of their supposed conflict has no meaning and should not even be raised. Maybe one can lose faith (as the strange received expression has it), but certainly not because one increases in reason. It could be that one loses faith because one imagines reason to be incapable of understanding a part—and a decisive or even the most decisive part—of what our life makes us experience. Very quickly, one cuts one's losses: Reason does not understand everything, and therefore we must accept that there are immense spaces that remain incomprehensible or irrational. We must abandon them to belief and to opinion, and very soon we give up definitively on thinking about what we have already evicted from the field of the thinkable. Various nightmares spring from this slumber of reason—ideological nightmares. Thus the separation between faith and reason, too quickly held to be self-evident and entirely natural, is born first from a lapse in rationality, from reason's capitulation without struggle before what is assumed to be unthinkable. But if, then, one does not lose faith from an excessive practice of rationality, it may well be that on the contrary one often loses in rationality because one too quickly excludes faith and the domain that it claims to open (namely that of Revelation). We lose reason in losing faith—and at least three reasons support this apparent paradox.

First (this goes without saying) by excluding on principle the domain that faith proposes to open, rationality not only shuts itself off from a field of experiences and concepts that are at least possible, but it also saddles itself with the negative work (or more exactly the de-negative, i.e., undoing work) of criticizing and even destroying that domain. And there is nothing more difficult than endless destruction (soldiers know something of this): it requires an unceasing, repeated expenditure of energy and a labor that is literally for nothing. Second, even when this unsaying [*dénégation*] is gratified with the very flattering title of critique (or deconstruction), it can only be fully realized by affirming that its proper limits, the famed and celebrated limits of *simple* reason, are not to be contested but instead benefit from an unshakeable legitimacy. Yet no one can establish limits except by transgressing them in some form or other and even quite often without assuming a dogmatic statement on the nature of reason: What does one assume when one speaks of *simple* or *pure* reason?—Finally, in this time of nihilism one must maintain faith in reason itself. Or more exactly, because nihilism is characterized by the fact that reason does not justify itself, precisely because it first needs justification, one must base rationality on the desire for rationality or, in other words, ground the will to truth on the will to power. In plain language, reason assumes that one has faith in it, and the most threatening irrationalism comes not from belief but from the failure of belief and confidence—in short, from the lack of faith in rationality itself, its power, and above all its legitimacy.

The question of the link between faith and reason hence does not concern apologetics, because it is not limited to the defense of the rights of faith (which only an already devalued figure of rationality can contest); rather, it concerns the defense of the rights of rationality (not abandoning entire fields of the thinkable). In my own regard, I have personally experienced that the opposite of faith is not so much doubt, disbelief, or unbelief, but bad faith. And we know that bad faith, like resentment, comes from a pathology that is at first philosophical and thus especially rational. Yet we also know that the opposite of rationality is found neither in irrationality nor in belief but in ideology. And we know from experience that ideology is fed by the illnesses of rationality. It is necessary, then, to articulate the connection between faith and reason rationally and with good faith. In fact, as Levinas said, "the relation between religion and reason is not a problem of the philosophy of religion—it is philosophy itself."[2]

I have attempted to clarify this connection—and it is only a matter of a sketch, taken from different angles and in various contexts—by following an ancient and traditional argument, but also and for that very reason one that is more in touch with our postmetaphysical or, if one prefers, postatheist, situation. Commonly, that is to say metaphysically, either faith takes the place of reason when reason can no longer establish plainly what faith then assumes in a simple holding-for-true, namely by belief and opinion: the hierarchy of the genres of knowledge authorizes the weaker one when the surer one falters. Or one will say that our faith (our adhesion by will to a statement) will increase to the very extent that it can be grounded on a clear and distinct knowledge of this statement, obtained by reason and its evidence: from a great light in the intellect there follows a great propensity in faith. Thus faith and reason either grow in inverse proportion or in direct proportion, but always starting from reason, which serves as the positive or negative condition of faith. Yet, another model can be found, one that St. Augustine, among others, put forward in exemplary fashion: "Understanding is the recompense of faith. Therefore, seek not to understand so that you may believe, but believe so that you may understand, for 'unless you believe, you will not understand.'"[3] What matters is not seeing, that is to say knowing based on rational evidence in the (sensible or intelligible) light of reason in order then better to believe (hold as true or affirm) but, to the contrary, believing in order to see [*voir*] and to conceive [*concevoir*]. How could seeing in this way depend on and result from believing without descending into fanaticism, which takes to be true whatever it raves about? By taking into account intentionality or, rather, the place of this intentional aim. The point of the aim (the objective, the intentional object) allows for reuniting and synthesizing the diverse data of intuition (or the multiplicity of lived experiences) and the really perceived outlines only if its signification fits them. Yet all significations do not fit all lived experiences or outlines, only certain ones or, at each time, one only. Knowing consists in freeing the correct signification or the least inappropriate one so as to end up seeing the phenomenon in its entirety. It is still the case that sometimes, by fact and often by right, the appropriate signification remains indeterminate or even completely unknown; the entire inventiveness of reason then consists in discovering or in inventing it, by a new theoretical hypothesis. It becomes the work of the inventiveness of reason to allow the appropriate signification to be given for the diversity of intuition and outlines. How can new significations come *before* the phenomena are constituted in full visibility? By provisional and *believed* assumptions. This (still natural) *belief* in significations that are still undecided and missing governs all the scientific revolutions, which is to say the scientific conversions.

But doesn't faith (in this case Christian faith) also operate like the assumption and the invention of significations, which are as yet unknown, unheard of, or at least not yet evident or available? Doesn't what one presents by habit and a bit quickly as dogmas that are assumed to be arbitrary and without rationality precisely operate like such significations? Aren't such significations the only ones in a position to constitute lived experiences or outlines (up to that point unintelligible) into full-fledged phenomena, phenomena that manifest themselves so much more visibly because a corresponding signification, come from elsewhere and given by Revelation, orders them and puts them on stage? In such a case, faith would fix (and actually would *give*) the only significations appropriate to what gives itself and demands to show itself—faith would fix significations to what, if these significations were missing, would give itself without, however, being able to show itself. Faith would thus become the condition of the phenomenalization of the given of intuitive lived experiences and of still haphazard sketches. It would become the condition of the intelligibility of certain phenomena. Which phenomena? Precisely those that remain the strangest to us, even as they most affect us, those that Pascal assigned to the third order, an order invisible to the first two (the bodies of the world and the power that rules over them, the intellectual truths of the knowing mind and the realm of the sciences or, more precisely, essences): namely, the order of the "heart," of charity and of holiness. In this order, one only sees if one has the sole appropriate signification available, charity itself. And one only has it available if one reaches it as it gives itself, namely by faith. In order to see, one must believe, but by believing one only accomplishes a work of reason. Of a "great reason" (Nietzsche) to be sure, and thus all the more of reason.

The texts that follow thus repeat a triviality [*une banalité*]. They are reproduced as they appeared with the mark of the circumstances (or even the very dispassionate polemics) that gave rise to them. I hope only that, brought together through the stake they share, they will be of use for some readers.

Jean-Luc Marion
Paris, November 2009

Translator's Note

As in my translation of *The Visible and the Revealed*, all previously existing translations have been retranslated from or heavily edited against the most recent French text, although credit is obviously still given to the original translators, and rights for existing translations have been procured. Translations of biblical texts have often been slightly altered to remain closer to Marion's text, always in consultation with the New Revised Standard Version and with the original Greek for New Testament texts. Slight mistakes in biblical and patristic references have been silently corrected. (Marion often seems to cite from memory and the printed French text has not always been amended.) Marion's use of capitalization (whether of pronouns for the divine or of such terms as Revelation/revelation, Church/church, Word/word, etc.) has been reproduced as it appears in the French. When it could be done easily and without distorting the original text, inclusive language has been adopted. In several chapters, however, the male pronouns (and "man" for "l'homme") have been retained because any changes would have been too extensive or too awkward. (The French text never uses the female pronoun, but often treats the male as inclusive of both.) One should also keep in mind throughout that most of these pieces were originally written for a Roman Catholic audience in France—many were first published in the Francophone version of the lay Roman Catholic theological journal *Communio*. There is hence often a slippage between "Catholic" (Marion never uses "Roman Catholic") and "Christian," which may well have been treated differently if writing for a broader or more diverse audience.

As Marion himself points out in the Preface, some of these pieces go back to the late 1970s. While this provides an opportunity to see both the continuity and the development of Marion's thought over four decades, some care should be taken not to attribute positions to him now that he has revised or significantly refined since their original composition. Several pieces included here predate the collection *The Visible and the Revealed*, which is in many ways a companion piece. The reader might also want to consult *The Rigor of Things*, a set of interviews or conversations with Dan Arbib, in which Marion provides much of the background for the articles in this volume and also elaborates on several of them, especially in regard to his views of the prospects for Roman Catholicism in France and the future of Christianity in the contemporary world more generally.

I am immensely grateful especially to Stephen Lewis, who not only helped me with several translation problems, including some distinctly "Catholic" questions, and gave very useful advice on several issues, but carefully went through the entire translation, corrected any number of mistakes, and improved the translation tremendously. His numerous suggestions and corrections were adopted almost everywhere. Any remaining mistakes are, of course, my own. Thanks also to Michael Dauber, who helped look up some of the medieval references in English translations.

While working on this translation, not a day—sometimes not an hour—went by when I did not think of Helen Tartar, who originally entrusted me with this translation: wondering how she would have put things, what advice she would have given, how to make the English sound just right. Beside her many other talents, Helen was an incomparable copy editor with an eagle eye for "false friends" and other common and not-so-common translation mistakes, a fine ear for the poetic possibilities of rendering a text in a new idiom, and a marvelous sense of language. She was also immensely supportive of younger scholars and unfailingly generous. Her kindness, infectious enthusiasm, admiration of and attentiveness to even the smallest instances of beauty, and her care for her books, their language, their spirit, their materiality, and their authors, are sorely missed, and this translation is dedicated to her.

Believing in Order to See

PART I

Reason and Faith Together

1

Faith and Reason

Faith and reason, believing or knowing, believing without certainty or knowing through definite science—what opposition seems more obvious? And if one adds that it is "modern science" facing Christian faith, then the dichotomy imposes itself beyond dispute, ready for all the weekly reports, for all the prefabricated debates and ideological arguments. Yet we should be on our guard against what is assumed to be so obvious here, for by a strange reversal in this commonplace dispute the argument from authority is today definitely found on the side of "science," which has become the object of the most unwavering faith for its devotees, whereas on the other side, "believers" guard the prerogative of doubt, of a critical sense, and an attitude of research (admittedly at times involuntarily). Actually, nothing is more fragile than this opposition, as the best philosophers of science have demonstrated. The first task of a merely honest and informed mind would be to show how artificial this opposition is, for faith has its reasons and scientific reason has its beliefs.

Christian Faith as Rationality

To begin with, Christians themselves should be the first to realize that their faith cannot and must not in any way do without reason; nor should they pride themselves on doing without it. Believing without reason actually amounts to scorning Him in whom we claim to believe. This is so, first, because as Saint Peter underlines, we must be "ready to make a defense (*apologia*) to anyone who demands an accounting (*logon*) for the hope that is in" us (1 Pet. 3:15). Believing without knowing how or what to believe does not increase faith but leads it astray, maybe even ridicules it. The point of "giving an account" here actually is not to quarrel with the interlocutor face to face, as in an ideological battle, but to do justice to Him in whom we say we believe, in Him and in his high reason. For the believer will have to "give an accounting (*apodidonai logon*) to him who stands ready to judge the living and the dead" (1 Pet. 4:5). We will have to answer to Christ for what we will have answered humans on his behalf and "for every careless word you utter, you will have to give an account (*apodōsousin peri autou logon*) on the day of judgment" (Matt. 12:36). What we will have said of Christ before humans, Christ will say of us before the Father.

This immediately raises another question: Why does God expect us to speak of Him with arguments, reasons, and rationality? Does God not know better than all of us that we can neither comprehend him nor even reason correctly about him, without taking into account our fear of those who do not accept him? Yet if God is God, he knows all that and more; thus if he asks us to speak with reason, without doubt he has good reasons for asking it of us. What do we know about these reasons? We know at least this: The Christian religion announces the death and resurrection of a human being who was and thus still is God. This man Jesus Christ is called the *Logos*, the Word and hence Reason. Even the paradox of his crucifixion, which contradicts "the wisdom of the world," remains a *logos*, "the *logos* of the Cross," which opposes a different *sophia* to the wisdom of the world, namely the "wisdom of God" (1 Cor. 1:18–25). When Saint Paul debates the Athenians on the Areopagus, it is in the name of the *logos* of Him who rightfully bears the name of *Logos*. And when he announces the foolishness of the Cross against the secular culture of the Corinthians, he still speaks according to a *logos*, because he speaks in the name of the *Logos* and according to the *Logos*. Even and especially when someone faithful to Christ confronts the rationality of the world, he or she confronts it with the reasons and for the love of wisdom. To witness can designate making an argument as much as giving one's life, to philosophize as much as to suffer martyrdom. Thus the first Christian to lay claim to the title of "philosopher," Justin, the Palestinian from Nablus who in the second century discussed so dispassionately with the Jew Trypho, was also a martyr, which is why he bears the admirable title of "philosopher and martyr." And the final giant among the Greek Fathers (also the most difficult), Maximus the Confessor, who in the seventh century brought to a close the brilliant christological and trinitarian synthesis begun by the council of Chalcedon, likewise suffered martyrdom: in order to silence his arguments, one had to cut out his tongue. Concepts can also bear witness.

The announcement of the Word come to reveal God in his humanity to humanity unfolds a new and superior reason, which can only be unfolded with reasons. The *logos* is not optional for Christians, because He from whom they take their name bears the title of *Logos*. For better or for worse, they had to take up again the knowledge of the Greeks, their *logos*, and hence their philosophy and their sciences (as also later the Roman law). Besides, as Saint Augustine firmly underlines, Christianity from the outset refuses to be compared with the ancient religions (the *theologia civilis* or the *theologia fabulosa*), agreeing only to a connection with the *theologia naturalis*, the pursuit of a rational knowledge of the divine via the study of celestial motions. And, facing the theological cosmology of the ancients, Augustine claims for his Christian faith the credentials of a true knowledge of the divinity as the only correct sense of the term *theologia*, which was pagan in origin and thus suspect. Because it is a matter of truth, "it is with the philosophers that the comparison must be made (*cum philosophis est habenda conlatio*)." Faith thus appears first of all as a matter of philosophy, which seems strange to us but obvious to him, because, he concludes, "the true philosopher will be a lover of God (*verus philosophus est amator Dei*)."[1] Of course the ultimate destiny of philosophy, the science of being that later became "metaphysics," will render its identification with the science of God impossible (although under the formulation of *philosophia christiana* it would endure at least until Erasmus). Yet one thing will not disappear: Christian theology's duty to rationality. At times it has even fulfilled this duty too well, at the risk of reducing the revealed Word to a system of concepts. Yet this duty has nevertheless permitted the development of a *theo-logy*, a knowledge about God through reasons coming from God. We take this accomplishment as self-evident, but all things considered, it is achieved *as such* only in the Christian religion. Both cases confirm that faith has a duty to reason in regard to itself.

Granted, one might object, but the issue is not faith's duty to reason in regard to itself, but rather faith's rationality in regard to reason itself, the type of reason that is displayed in the sciences. And how could one avoid thinking of several conflicts that have marked history, from Galileo to Darwin, to stick only with the most legendary cases?

This way of putting the question calls forth three remarks. First, the most obvious: No conflict could have broken out between some science or other and some decision or other of the Church's ordinary magisterium, if both had not been situated on a single shared ground, precisely that of reason. To the point that one must sometimes wonder whether this ground was really shared, whether the encounter was even legitimate. Did the magisterium have to defend a particular cosmology against a different one—and anyway is that really what happened? Did Galileo really have to contest the rules for the interpretation of the Scriptures—and did he do so with full awareness? Contemporary history and philosophy of science have made us much more prudent in regard to these questions than our predecessors were, and one can reasonably assume that the two camps themselves were lacking epistemological prudence.

A second comment follows from this: the history of Christian faith is remarkable less for its omissions than for its often decisive contributions to the birth and growth of the sciences, even if we restrict ourselves to the collection and transmission of ancient texts, the foundation of the universities, the emergence of the "arts" in these universities as independent from theology, the impetus given in the schools to mathematics, astronomy and physics, and so forth. Precisely because Christian faith first owed rationality to itself, it could not keep it for itself but expanded it into the world and human society.

Finally, even the conflicts or at least tensions that today oppose the magisterium of the Catholic Church to certain developments in biology and the neurosciences have their rational stake: how is one to reconcile freedom in regard to conception with the humanity of what has been conceived, how determine the humanity of a biological life, how recognize the end of a human life, how safeguard the identity of the individual against the threat of its reproduction? Without a doubt, these questions are vexing and will continue to be divisive. Yet who could disregard them and reduce them to irrationalism? To the contrary, they rather require us to complicate the models and the currently accepted technical protocols in order to reach a rationality that would be more sophisticated, more flexible, hence higher.

What Reason Thinks and What It Does Not Think

A higher reason—what does that mean? If we understand this as asking the rationality of the contemporary sciences to manage thinking the divinity, it is an absolutely unacceptable demand. Unacceptable first in regard to the sciences, which never claim (at least one would reasonably hope so today) to know the world absolutely or to understand its potentially divine dimension. Then in regard to faith, because God's transcendence would thus be insulted due to the fact that He is known only by not being known: for "man reaches the highest point of his knowledge about

God when he knows that he knows him not, inasmuch as he knows that that which is God transcends whatsoever he conceives of him—*illud quod Deus est, omne ipsum quod de eo intelligimus, excedere.*"[2]

But could we think this higher reason in a different sense, one that is more precise and rigorous? Perhaps by listening to one of Nietzsche's rather enigmatic remarks: "You say 'I' and are proud of this word. But greater is that in which you do not wish to have faith—your flesh and its great reason (*dein Leib und seine grosse Vernunft*): that does not say 'I,' but does 'I.'"[3] This strange formulation raises two questions. What is meant by "the flesh"? And how is it partially connected to a "great reason"?

Flesh does not mean the body that is perceived or rather sensed as it is extended in the space of the world; instead it means this other and unique body—mine—that alone senses the bodies of the world. My flesh senses the bodies that, themselves, do not sense. It can do so by virtue of another privilege: it only senses everything else by sensing itself sensing. But how could this flesh possibly surpass the "I" and its reason?

In order to understand this, one must consider what the "I" knows, the ego that makes modern metaphysics so "proud." It knows with certainty, because it retains from an experience only what it can keep of it and anticipate there, abandoning everything else as unknowable. Descartes identifies what offers such a grasp to reason as order and measure; today we would say models and parameters. Yet only phenomena of extension, of quantity and hence of exteriority offer such material to certain knowledge. We call "objects" the kinds of phenomena, for which intuition responds in advance to the expectations of the concept without overflowing it. To each science there hence corresponds a method of constitution and of production of objects. And modern rationality unfolds by ceaselessly enlarging the number and the range of such objects. Not only does it constitute them intellectually and realize them experimentally, but it produces and reproduces them technically, in such a way that a new world of technical objects has sprung up before our increasingly less surprised eyes. This new world covers up and replaces the ancient world of things more and more. This change has defined the common rationality of our reason and is extended to nature, whose "masters and possessors" we become.[4]

This success and uninterrupted process (for each scientific crisis becomes the opportunity for a new technological leap) nevertheless leaves us puzzled or even anxious. For we rather suspect that the world is calculated only via far away objects, only from afar and in the remote region where objects face us, precisely as the objectives of our aim. We really know objects as we produce them—at a distance. Yet because we also live among them, we sense them and in this way we inevitably feel ourselves first of all. And this felt immediacy, precisely the flesh, concerns what is the closest, whereas the rationality of objects concerns what is the furthest away. Just as in the immediacy of feeling we experience ourselves without distance, so the distant knowledge of objects no longer helps us at all: we do not stand opposite ourselves, but sense what we are and are what we sense in the closest, namely pain and pleasure, death and birth, hunger and thirst, sleep and fatigue, but also hatred and love, communion and division, justice and violence. From this, from what is closest, we know very clearly that the common rationality of objects knows nothing and is of no help.

In *this* sense, Heidegger could legitimately say that "science does not think." He should only have added that it has claimed this as its privilege: science does not think, it measures and orders in the form of modeling, of parameter and of objectification. Technology produces what is understood in this way and vice versa. In contrast, only the flesh reaches nonobjective phenomena, those where an excess of intuition saturates the limits of the concept already known and always foreseen—for example, it reaches the event that occurs unpredictably despite its supposed impossibility, the idol that fascinates the gaze by dazzling it, the flesh of this other who eroticizes mine through his flesh, the face of every other who commands my respect and asks me to spare his or her life. No one can claim to be ignorant about such phenomena and, even so, no one can conceive them according to the rationality of objects. In front of these phenomena, I cannot simply say "I," constitute them, foresee them, and hold them at a distance from me. To the contrary, these very phenomena saturated with intuition make me and unmake me. The flesh exposes me to what the "I" cannot constitute as an object. It surpasses my objectifying rationality. It really does point to a "greater reason."

Who can exercise such "great reason" today? That is a fair question, except that one should rather ask: Who has to exercise it and cannot do without it? Response: Everyone for whom the humanity of humans, the naturalness of nature, the justice of the city and the truth of knowledge still remain absolute requirements. That is to say, everyone, or at least everyone who believes these things still to be possible. Or more exactly that part of each of us that still wants to believe in them. For on top of the first difficulty (objectivity), we must confront a second one that is linked to it but is much more severe: nihilism. One often claims that it would be enough to round off the science of objects with a supposed "soul supplement." This is a simplistic illusion, because what one understood under the term "soul" has precisely been rendered inaccessible by objectivity: henceforth, what we can no longer know as a certain and hence remote object can only be thought as a "value." Yet in these times of nihilism, the highest values are being devalued. It serves no point to "defend" the vanished soul any more than it does the supposed values, for that amounts to recognizing the intrinsic weakness of what it is a matter of defending or attacking; as a value, it is completely dependent on whoever evaluates or devalues it. In every case, nihilism brings out its black sun by insinuating this disarming question into each of us: "What's the use?" What is the point of the humanity of humans, the naturalness of nature, the justice of the city and the truth of knowledge? Why not rather their opposites, the dehumanization of humans for improving humanity, the systematic bleeding of nature in order to develop the economy, injustice so as to render society more efficient, the absolute empire of information-distraction in order to escape the constraints of the true? These counterpossibilities are no longer fantasy or prediction, because the ideologies that have dominated history since the beginning of the last century have had no other plan than to turn them into reality. The ideologies are unaware of any flesh; thus they literally no longer sense themselves; and, no longer sensing themselves, they accomplish nihilism without even knowing it.

Reason, such as we know it, therefore suffers two limitations that are linked to each other and can become real dangers. To reduce experience to objectifiable phenomena and to ignore our flesh can lead to the devaluation of all values and to succumbing to ideology. Thus it is today no longer a matter of saving reason from obscurantism or from superstition, but of saving it from its own dangers. It is no longer a matter of reasonably justifying all things [*rendre raison de toutes choses*], but of justifying the reason of rationality [*rendre sa raison à la rationalité*]. In this situation, one must no longer wait for a miracle or for a "god" to save us (as if he had not already come). Rather, it is necessary that all those who can act, that is to say, first those who can think and think otherwise, do so.

The "Great Reason" of Love

With our reason in such a situation—for there is only one single reason, which is shared and not optional—what can we do? All who think can contribute in their own way to justify reason its reason [*rendre sa raison à la raison*], scientists as well as poets, wise men as well as politicians, the poor as much as the rich, all religious traditions and all cultural heritages, each their original and indispensable share.

What kind of contribution can and should Christians make to this common effort? Here as in any other case, Christians cannot bring anything other than what they have received: Christ. "For I received (*parelabon*) from the Lord what I also handed on (*paredōka*) to you, that the Lord Jesus on the night when he was betrayed (*paredideto*) took a loaf of bread, and when he had given thanks, he broke it and said: 'This is my body [given] for you, do this in remembrance of me'" (1 Cor. 11:23–24). He who gives and delivers himself as our bread belongs to all. Christians do not own Christ as a property, but as first recipients they must in turn hand him on to others, at least to those who really want him (for people do not love God very much). Receiving the glory of Christ, that is the weight and test for all, not only for the "Christianity" understood as an avant garde of humanity's proletariat; every one of us, without exception and in some way or other, has had, must, or will have to justify him- or herself to Christ, whether believing in him or not. Not to believe in Christ is already to respond to him. The contribution of Christians to "great reason" thus will not come from them, but from Him from whom they draw, like a nickname, even their own name. What does Jesus Christ then deliver to all, everywhere and always?

He gives a nonobjective and saturated phenomenon without equal, one that would remain inaccessible without him—love or the erotic phenomenon: "God is love" (1 John 4:16) and "You shall love the Lord your God with all your heart, and with all your soul, and with all your strength and with all your mind; and your neighbor as yourself" (Luke 10:27, citing Deut. 6:5 and Lev. 19:18). In this way those who love God live in him, namely those who love each other (1 John 4:20). This announcement becomes good news for us for countless reasons, and all the time in the world will not be enough to say or celebrate it.

Yet one of the reasons is this: only this love can give access to the "great reason." For the love revealed by the Word, hence by the *Logos*, unfolds as a *logos*, thus as a reason. And it is a reason by full right because it allows us to reach the closest and the innermost phenomena, those experienced by the flesh and those that intuition saturates. If the Revelation of Christ had shown only this, namely that love has its reason—a forceful, original, simple reason that sees and says what common reason misses and does not see—it would already have saved, if not humans, at least their reason. But Christ has not only shown the logic of love, he has demonstrated and proven it in deeds and actions by his passion and his resurrection. Since the coming and the presence of the *Logos* among us, love has not only found its logic, it has accomplished it "all the way to the end—*eis telos*" (John 13:1). For "charity and truth are born in Christ Jesus" (John 1:17) and we have seen him, see him, and will see him, at once and indissociably, "saturated with love and with truth" (John 1:14).⁵ Love not only gives itself in truth in the gesture of Christ, but we must go to the point of turning this proposition upside down: in Christ, love is manifested as the last and first truth, the one that makes all the others possible and recapitulates them all at the end of ends: "I am the way, the truth" (John 14:6). One can challenge this claim as an illusion without future, denounce it as presumptuous delusion, or even fear it as a corruption of the young. In any case, Christians have nothing else to say than this, because they have received it as it is.

What kind of reason does the logic of love unfold? Let me limit myself here to indicating some of its laws. First, certainty. For love "bears all, believes all, hopes all, endures all" (1 Cor. 13:7). This means that love always loves without condition, never on condition, in particular not on the condition of reciprocity. Love does not require a return on its investment in order to love, because it enjoys an unprecedented privilege in regard to any economy: a love one refuses or scorns, in short a love that is not returned, remains no less a perfect love accomplished without remainder; a gift refused remains no less a gift given. Actually to love thus depends only on love. Creation follows from this as the unconditioned and unilateral precedence of love over being.

Second, possibility. For nothing is impossible for love, especially the ability to love without regard of persons, to the point of loving one's enemy (Luke 6:27–35), precisely because love requires only itself in order to love. God is characterized by the privilege of the impossibility of impossibility; it is even one of his properties, a privilege comparable to no other: "What is impossible for mortals, is not impossible for God; for God all things are possible" (Mark 10:27). Yet Christ adds immediately, that the one who believes shares fully in this privilege, provided this belief is by love and in love: "If you are able! All things are possible for the one who believes" (Mark 9:23). The resurrection of Christ proves it, and hence our own becomes possible.

Third, self-knowledge. For we have seen that if our "I" wants to be grounded on thought, this existence performed by *my* thought is still exposed to two threats: either the illusion of thought ("What thinks in me?"), or the suspicion of nihilism ("What's the point?"). And thus, says Saint Paul, "anyone who claims to know something does not yet have the necessary knowledge." Yet how must one know, in order to know oneself assuredly? One must let oneself be known by God, and for that one must love Him: "Anyone who loves God is known by him" (1 Cor. 8:2). To know oneself by thought, yes, but not by *my* thought, instead by that of Him who thinks (me) in loving me and only makes himself known to whoever loves him. One must "have come to know God or rather to be known by God" (Gal. 4:9). Hence the other, who loves me, reveals himself to be more interior to me than I am to myself. The grounding ego because grounded.

Fourth, alterity. For love alone achieves knowledge of the other, because it supremely believes in the other. Indeed, in order to know what it loves, love has no need to represent or conceptualize it, that is to say, to reduce the known to itself. Or rather, what it loves will appear to it to the exact extent to which, by loving it, it will aim at it, and, by aiming at it, it will move itself into it. Only love can know beyond itself because it alone displaces itself outside of itself and can "know the love of Christ which surpasses all knowledge" (Eph. 3:19). Such a knowledge by transfer into the known, actually into the beloved, is called communion. It alone allows via love attainment to the incomprehensible transcendence of the other.

Henceforth nothing accomplishes better than love the earnestness, the work, the patience, and the pain of the negative, precisely because only for love is it not a matter of the negative but of kenosis, of the self-emptying and the abandonment that is characteristic of its positive nature. Love hence has a full and entire right to resume charge of what philosophy, still without really knowing what it wants to say, has laid down for these fragile virtues. "The love of truth" (2 Thess. 2:10), in other words, that of the *Logos* become flesh and hence master of any proximity, christologically resumes the very definition of philosophy as the "love of truth."

Faith hence does not lack rationality, at least if it presents itself as it must be thought—as faith in the sovereign and poor power of love. And faith then will not lack assurance: for, as faith in love, it loves *already*, thus *already* unfolds the logic of love. It is not faith that is defined as the "shadow of future things" (Heb. 10:1), but the promise of the Law. Faith itself *already* attains "the reality of things hoped for (*pistis elpizomenōn hypostasis*)," because it finds, in its practice, *already* "the conviction of things not seen (*elegkos ou blepomenōn*)" (Heb. 11:1). And what kind of invisible things become definitively accessible by faith in this way? Saint Augustine has shown them: all the phenomena that are closest to my flesh, like "the good will of your friend for you," or rather, "the good faith, by which you believe what you do not see in him," or in short, "the love of those who love, which we do not see."[6] One should not object that it is a matter here of the knowledge of the other [*d'autrui*], and not that of God. For knowing signifies loving and love cannot be divided.

Reason so far has been content with interpreting the world, hence with transforming it into objects that it masters. It is time for it to begin to respect them. Respecting the world means seeing, hence envisioning the face of the other human being. And that is only possible in the figure of love, following its logic and in the light of its glory. Christians have nothing better to propose to the rationality of humans.

2

In Defense of Argument

Why should one subject reason to questioning? Why not turn it, as would seem suitable, into the immovable rock from which to question everything else? What reason would incline us to reason about reason, instead of allowing reason itself to reason on its own basis? Even more, why wonder about reason from a theological point of view, as if the distinction between fields, which began as a distinction within Christian theology before it moved to secularism [*laïcité*], were no longer self-evident? In this indiscrete concern for reason, should we not fear the hegemonic designs of a "fundamentalism" threatening "pluralism"? Moreover, how should we understand the fact that Christians, who are more familiar than others with totalitarian oppression because they have suffered it more continuously than others, find themselves turning this fear into an accusation far more often than would appear reasonable and rational?

I

The answer, assuming it is accessible, requires an indispensable but elementary (even simplifying) detour through philosophy. In fact, for at least a century, whether we like it or not, we have been living in the situation that Nietzsche diagnosed as nihilism. Nihilism is defined by an event; the highest values are devalued. And the gut reaction, which would consist in defending these highest values more vigorously the weaker they become, reinforces nihilism all the more because it thereby proves that these very values are only values, without any other value than the power of affirmation that upholds them from the outside and thus unveils them as intrinsically dependent on the will to power and transferred over to its empire. In the end, it matters little what values are affirmed or even whether they are affirmed or denied; the only thing that counts is the degree of the will to power that appears through them. As just so many symptoms without intrinsic authority, they are all reduced to the dishonorable status of pure and simple ideologies. More exactly, they become all the more ideological as they develop in an impure and complex fashion—or, which comes down to the same thing, claim to be "scientific."

The event of nihilism defines postmodernity (let us allow this still very vague term as an hypothesis, in order to contrast nihilism with the positively rationalist modernity of the sixteenth to the nineteenth centuries). What under the blow of nihilism succumbs to or at least enters into a long and rich crisis is first of all the metaphysical definition of reason. Before and beyond the "death of God," which only results from it, Nietzsche deconstructs the foundations of rationality—and first the possibility in general of any primordial grounding. He thus puts the two fundamental principles of rationality in question: first, implicitly, that of non-contradiction (a thing cannot be, within the same relationship and in the same instant, other than itself), formulated since Aristotle; then, explicitly, that of sufficient reason (everything has a cause that makes sense of it), developed by Leibniz. Admittedly, Nietzsche announces in grand style another, a "greater" reason. But he did not manage to capture it, even in his utmost progress, as was also the case for the "new gods." To the contrary, what became established was the crisis of grounding. And we are still there.

The crisis of grounding manifests itself by an almost unique symptom: Rationality continues to expand, but it can no longer directly vouch for its truth value. Let us once more give a name to this situation: it is called ideology. The features of such a rationality without radical grounding, thus with neither reference nor pretension to truth, are well known. (a) Instrumentalization: it is no longer a matter of naming the essence of things in themselves (not even the essence of "well-founded phenomena"), but of describing the process that would allow an anticipated result to be obtained regularly and without fault, even if we cannot justify it intrinsically [*en rendre intrinsèquement raison*]. (b) Plurality follows: several concurrent and even theoretically contradictory processes work equally toward a result. (c) The competition between processes thus cannot be decided by a single crucial experiment, one that would be tried and true in itself; therefore, the competition will be judged by the clash between rival interpretations of the same phenomenon, that is to say, the clash among the powers of affirmation (argumentative or possibly more violent—for example, political and institutional). (d) The inevitable conflict that results from this can either be radicalized into a forced, or in the worst case, totalitarian hegemony, or, in the best case, be institutionalized in a well-understood pluralism.

This situation, which is our situation, likewise pertains in regard to the three transcendentals. First, of course, in the realm of the true, where the ideological situation is patently obvious in the humanities and the social sciences: each doctrine must straightaway be subjected to an interrogation about the one or the ones that support it (thus the sinisterly celebrated question "From where do you speak?"), which explicitly ignores truth itself, in fact or in theory. But it is no longer absent even in the "hard sciences," where the "complementarity" first hatched in fundamental physics is extended quite legitimately into the confrontations between schools, between journals, between laboratories, between research programs—confrontations that are regulated less by an unattainable "truth" than by provisional agreements. These agreements themselves owe their regulation to political considerations; not, in a pejorative sense, to a "politicized" politics, but to an economic, financial, industrial, and even military politics. A recent example was supplied by the judicial investigation to determine who discovered the AIDS virus, which was officially settled by two political leaders at the highest level on the basis of a juridical-financial agreement, leaving the fundamental scientific question perfectly undecided.

In the realm of the beautiful, the strictly aesthetic criterion of something beautiful as such has for more than a century given way to the successive or simultaneous examination of all the possibilities of production of the object, for the subject's pleasure (or not). Thus in painting, through the transgression of the limits of the picture, as well as its objectivity, its unilaterality, its privileged social status, and so forth, artists have set out to make appear either what had never appeared or, on the contrary, what cannot appear. In such a situation, the legitimacy of each attempt lies less in its visible results or in universalizable aesthetic pleasure than in the theoretical (conceptual) justification that supports them, and thus in the power of the corresponding ideology. Or—and this is not a contradiction—it lies in the simple economic result of a speculation about the artistic object. The emergence of an art market, standardized by the market and not by the art, simply indicates that art itself has been devalued to the point of functioning as value.

But it is of course in the realm of the good, and especially in that of politics, that this crisis of reason has unfolded most markedly. The matchless example comes from the Marxist movement, which spanned three quarters of the century. Regarding the collapse of the Soviet empire—for one forgets too quickly that it collapsed to the benefit of terrors more cowardly than clear-sighted—I will make really just one comment: Its end began, slowly, when little by little it became obvious that its supposedly scientific reason was based only on itself. Ideology's lie consists precisely in that it is an ideology and neither science nor reason, as it claims to be; thus it does not provide reason [*ne rend raison*] for anything, neither for itself, nor for reality, and especially not for reason. Marxist ideology began to weaken and then to crumble away when it allowed its status as ideology to appear, hence its inclusion in the common rule of nihilism where the supposedly scientific "truth" essentially depends on the will to power that affirms it. Truth, at least the truth that ideology never has the status of truth, has uncovered ideology as such, which has thus given way under the weight of its own lie, the one nihilism had produced. Military, police, and political power did not sustain it, precisely because it was the ideology that sustained it. And ideology has silently collapsed before the evidence that it was a matter of pure and simple nihilism. A defeat, not of reason, but in front of reason and absent reason.

II

Reason thus passes through nihilism. This crisis comes from afar and will probably last a long time. It is not enough to invoke here, as Heidegger did, another thought still to come and a "god" to be awaited silently, among the death throes of the "end of metaphysics" or the supposed lifelessness of an "end of history." For we live within nihilism every day, and thus we must make up our mind about it without delay. We must endure it. But without taking two easy ways out—tempting for all minds, but especially for Christian minds.

The first would be to imagine that we have to condemn nihilism. Nihilism is not the result of an intellectual fault or a "theoretical original sin," for which it would be advisable to expose those responsible, whether philosophical (Descartes, as Maritain said) or religious (Judeo-Christianity, as Nietzsche said). There is only one original sin and that's really quite enough for our misfortune. Maybe nihilism still belongs to reason, or at least to its metaphysical era, out of which strictly speaking it draws the theoretical consequences. It manages a bankruptcy, but causes no harm in itself.

Conversely, the second temptation would be to claim to overcome nihilism by an even greater affirmative power. This would be a mistake, precisely because such a voluntarism would just assert a further ideology and would hence obey the logic of nihilism all the more strictly. Once again, nihilism is a fact and a fact of reason itself; we are neither responsible for it nor are we its adversaries. Christian thought has lost far too much energy by demonizing modernity (traditionalism) or by making itself feel guilty over it (progressivism): may it not repeat this disastrous tactic when faced with postmodernity!

III

So then, what attitude shall we take in front of the crisis of reason? This question is asked of us in two respects—as political individuals endowed with reason and as Christians invested with the Revelation of the Word. Even so I will consider them simultaneously.

A first point should go without saying. Christianity rests on the Revelation of God, through himself and in person, as triune and as one. On the basis of the Father and as the absolute gift, the Trinity unfolds the Word as *Logos*, that is to say, as first and ultimate reason of all things that were created in Him, according to the communion of the Holy Spirit, namely by the charity he allows, according to a unity that reinforces the singularity of individuals sanctified in God. Consequently, the Word, in whom everything receives being, life, and movement, displays reason. Not a reason [*une raison*], but reason [*la raison*] in its fullest meaning. This reason obviously does not coincide (at least not essentially) with the speculative reason of metaphysics or with the calculating reason of the sciences. It reveals the more powerful, but also more secret and more paradoxical, rationality of charity. Nevertheless reason never contradicts reason. Nor does the truth contradict truth.

The Christian tradition, and more specifically the Catholic tradition, has paid a steep price to end up admitting this principle concretely and historically. First, in regard to the question of the relation between faith and science: today we know why and how contradiction is just as impossible as strict harmonization. Next, in regard to the relation between philology and the Scriptures: today we know why and how the so-called scientific exegesis confirms biblical Revelation, whether it wants to or not. Our God always reveals himself as the underlying reason. And he exceeds our comprehension only in the name of a more exacting reason. This is why we are not Manicheans: the same God who has created the world also saves it. God's reason reveals itself, hence surpasses and confirms natural reason without contradiction. This is why we are not Gnostics; it is not a better knowledge that saves, but "the knowledge of the love of Christ, which surpasses all understanding" (Eph. 3:19). When we do not understand some aspect of the world, it is because we do not work at it enough. If at a given moment a result of a given science contradicts at that instant the received interpretation of some article of faith, it is either because this science remains partial, or because it extrapolates one of its provisional results in an unscientific manner, or (and often enough) because we have not sufficiently reflected on the article of faith in question—thinking that revelation has the same limits as our blind zeal or our narrow-minded hermeneutics. Reason does not contradict reason on principle [*par principe*]—due to the principle [*par le principe*] that the world was created by the originating Principle [*par le Principe*].

Thus nihilism is no sin (nor is postmodernity). That's nonsense—a stupidity evenly shared among Christians and others. But it's more serious in Christians because they are responsible for the Word. Thinking as a consistent rationalist is thus a strict duty for any Christian. The only question is whether we still think with enough coherence to remain rationalists all the way to the "amen" of the Credo. Yet a second question immediately comes up: Does human reason know, at any given moment, how to remain sufficiently reasonable to do justice to all the facts and all the conceptual requirements, including those of Revelation? Our duty to remain strictly rationalist hence immediately involves the duty to criticize all the unjustified limitations that the rejection of God can claim to impose on reason. For if, in the last analysis, reason belongs to the Word because it comes forth from it, then we are not its "masters and possessors." We must often go beyond the limits of the thought of understanding, toward the unknown lands of speculative reason (Hegel remains a model here). Speculative reason in no way means a frenzied reason that would want to speak of what it knows nothing about, but a reason that is able to criticize itself so that it would end up admitting the extent and the dimensions of what it can (and therefore must) reflect in a mirror, sometimes darkly. Thus the question never comes down to a decision for or against reason—for we are rationalists by virtue of baptism—but of specifying what kind of reason can, according to the things themselves, reach what gives itself to be thought. We should never humiliate or criticize reason (as traditionalism has never stopped claiming to do). We must criticize the unjustified limits on reason in the name of the reason revealed by and in the Word (against all kinds of positivism, the experience of which has sufficiently shown that they betray rationality by claiming to limit it). We have a duty to rationality in the name and from the point of view of the Word. What's more, it is the greatness of the First and later the Second Vatican Council to have strongly confirmed this.

Once this decision is made, it remains to apply it. What model of rationality do we have available in the situation of nihilism? We have something that could be called, without any polemic, as we shall see, a zero degree of rationality: the kind of reason that together with Jürgen Habermas I will call "communicational."[1] That is to say, the statement that the declarations, all claiming to be rational regionally, enter into competition, even into conflict, precisely because none of them can claim an absolute grounding, and hence an unconditional status of truth: from now on, reason can no longer impose itself in the name of a grounding and can only result from a contractual negotiation. This agreement is not summed up in a simple (political or ideological) compromise, but instead searches for a *consensus* that is itself rational. Renouncing any argument from authority (drawn from its own tradition, from its "identifying" identity), each of the opposing parties must enter into a rational *disputatio* with all the other parties. Rational here means proceeding only by arguments that would be intelligible and thus possibly convincing for all the participants, admitting the arguments of other parties, when these prove themselves to be actually rational and hence potentially convincing. Reason is here no longer exercised foundationally ("vertically" from a thesis to an absolute grounding), but rationally by procedures, or rather communicationally ("horizontally," by the more or less wide-ranging conviction of some by others). Truth no longer comes from a declaration's rationality per se, but from the agreement reasonably acquired by those declaring it. It is a matter of a zero degree of rationality because truth no longer precedes reason in order to regulate it (by an adequation of the understanding with truth, in whatever sense one might understand it), but inversely so that reason, reinforced through debates and arguments, precedes and produces truth. Or at least what takes truth's place. This model of rationality develops its zero degree because it presupposes no unhypothetical grounding (empirical or a priori), nor any self-showing truth (as in phenomenology); in short, there are no preliminaries. Indeed, this is why it can be exercised even in the situation of nihilism. Its formal poverty coincides with its privilege.

It would be serious foolhardiness for Christian thought to refuse from the outset this model of rationality, strong by its very weakness. Admittedly, it does not achieve any absolute foundation. Admittedly, it only reaches a pragmatic reason, measured each time against the debate and the arguments that are brought together. Admittedly, by definition it implies the calling into question of its draft agreements. Yet, in the situation of nihilism, no absolute foundation, no universal truth, no definitive result still remains possible. The communicational model of rationality offers, in contrast, a noteworthy double result. First, it straightaway abandons any ideologization of rationality because it publicly unfolds its argumentative procedures, and thus experiences at the same time their limits and validities. The ideological temptation—to impose an (apparent) rationality according to the unjustified authority of "science"—finds itself on principle excluded right away, both by its totalitarian ambition and by its refusal to present potentially refutable arguments. Second, and consequently, the communicational model of rationality condemns as a nonargumentative violence the tactic of suspicion and of intimidation, which always asks before any argument of the adversary and in order not to listen to him or her: "From where do you speak?"—which amounts to telling him or her to be silent. Thus the intellectual versions of terrorism by hypothesis would have to give in to the confrontation of arguments, which have no other limits than their rationality.

It goes without saying that the communicational model of rationality offers two opportunities to a Church always exposed to the risk of history and the world through its originally missionary and testimonial vocation. It frees it first from the ban on speech practiced by any ideology, hence by any totalitarianism; from now on Christians can on principle speak out.[2] But they also must do so. For it is not just a matter of speaking but of speaking according to reason, that is to say, of arguing.[3] Faith is not shouting. Let us admit that in the recent past it was more a shouting than a convincing reasoning. The discredit that modern theology has brought on apologetics is too massive for the even merely formal adoption of a communicational model of rationality not to have to modify the priorities and the methods of theological work profoundly. But in doing so, theology would nevertheless only return to one of its most primordial functions: "being always ready to give an account (*apologian*) to whoever demands reason (*logon*) from us concerning the hope that is in us" (1 Pet. 3:15). The kerygma itself requires and, moreover, accomplishes the setting forth of arguments. For the Word itself, when it speaks with authority, turns itself directly into argument, indeed an argument provoking the contradiction of its contradictors. In a prominent sense, one would even have to reread all the accounts of the passion as exchanges of arguments where Christ ceaselessly confuses his adversaries with reasons. He does so especially by making them say themselves what they had certainly not wanted to admit: that He Himself, "the man," is the innocent one who has "not done anything," "the king of the Jews," "the son of God." There is probably no contradiction between the logic of testimony and that of argumentation. In numerous cases they become indistinguishable. It is even possible that radical testimony—martyrdom—could still be exercised as an argument, provided that it does not amount to a military act but is offered as an effect of the Spirit.[4]

IV

This new situation created for rationality by its communicational model obviously does not offer only opportunities to theological reason. Far from it—there would be some naïveté or some cunning in presenting it in this way. This model suffers from at least two uncertainties, indeed two intrinsic insufficiencies, and it allows for yet another new ideological drift. The first uncertainty is due to the principle of the absence of any presupposition. Thus, in principle, each interlocutor must enter into debate in a rational posture, that is to say, by disregarding any nonrational presuppositions (and above all any arguments from authority drawn from his history and his tradition). But does not this approach itself presuppose at least one common presupposition? Namely, the fact itself that all enter into the debate by adopting this position of disregard, by committing themselves to unfolding arguments (and not threats, seductions, historico-hermeneutic justifications, etc.).

One can really only respond to this objection in three ways. (i) There is indeed an ultimate foundation, exterior and anterior to rational debate, because it makes it possible: namely, the meaning itself of reason as single norm (K. O. Apel). (ii) There is no ultimate foundation, but it is the debate itself that, by regulating itself, finally constrains its interlocutors either to recognize argumentative rationality as rule, or to exclude themselves from the debate (J. Habermas). (iii) There is indeed a rational self-founding of debate, but it comes down to the confusing of the conditions of the debate with the most positive (and hence rare) results of such a debate: transparent rational agreement. Now, in practice, in real debates, the discussion always unfolds between participants who precisely do not respect the requirement of the rationality of the arguments given and the rationally honest recognition of the arguments received (R. Boudon). Certainly we are not forced to take sides in this elementary but important discussion. We only have to pay good attention to an essential weakness of the communicational model of rationality—precisely that it presupposes rationality to be already recognized, in some way or other. This allows us to risk proposing a paradox: by its claim to a transcendental and at the same time historical legitimacy, the Church is in no way excluding itself from (or at the least lending itself with difficulty to) a rational and argumentative debate. Rather, its claim to a grounding in the Word obtains for it (and imposes on it) the double presupposition of any debate—

namely, that the rationality of an argument is enough to assure it a constraining authority for any interlocutor, an authority it can only eventually yield to a rationally more powerful argument. Christians might well be inspired to wonder whether and to what extent the communicational model of rationality has not already functioned in a paradigmatic manner inside the Church, for example, at the time of the first ecumenical councils, in the scholastic method, or even in the modern encyclicals of the ordinary magisterium—so strangely rationalist in tone and manner.[5]

The second uncertainty is due to the renunciation of any normative ambition, which is essential for a communicational model of rationality. One can probably claim that the rationally argued results maintain an obligatory validity for a given situation of debate and can end by being imposed at least on a majority of its participants. But this constraint, which can become a *consensus*, even if it is exercised by law or by regulation, could not reasonably claim to reach the level of an ethical norm. Besides, all the ethics boards completely agree on this. It is on this condition that, for example, abortion legislation can be politically timely, and can avoid becoming a morally illegitimate oppression of the consciences that challenge it in the name of a reason recognizing different norms. Of course the difficulty lies elsewhere: If one must renounce, strictly speaking, the decreeing or recognizing of norms through rationally argued debate alone, must one then also renounce absolute norms in general? Can a society do without indisputable and in principle unquestioned regulations, even if it actually transgresses them sometimes? Without entering into particular discussions and without assimilating them to each other, can one maintain the prohibition of incest, the ban on homicide, *habeas corpus*, the declaration of human rights, and so forth, as debatable, even in a strictly rational and reasoned debate? Moreover, in the facts of the matter, do the discussions today ever concern the validity of these regulations even when one discusses their foundation and their limits? That would mean that the communicational model of rationality, precisely because it shows itself to be operating in certain cases, could not, as the zero degree of reason in the situation of nihilism, decide in the radical matter of ethics—that is to say, decree norms. Those would require, by definition, an unconditioned truth that nihilism makes impossible and which the communicational model teaches us to do without. Of course, from the point of view of this model, it can seem illusory and fantastical to claim to reach grounded norms, and to reach them absolutely.

But this point of view cannot decide about this, because, by definition, it does not have the means to do so. It can only claim a single, already quite ambitious requirement: that those who suggest (first of all to themselves) such norms, supposedly absolute and grounded in truth, must establish via rational and acceptable if not always convincing arguments that they are not against rationality and its procedures. Similarly, according to this second degree, Christian apologetics must also unfurl its efforts. The least one could say, when for example we consider the ordinary teaching of the magisterium in the matter of personal ethics, is that this work has not been carried out very far or very effectively by contemporary moral theology. For here, the systematic critique and the repetitive acceptance of commonly received positions offer only the two faces of the same collapse.

V

These two deficiencies also clear up a certain vagueness. This vagueness makes a new ideological drift possible (though in no way certain!). It bears precisely on the conditions of entry into the debate about rational argumentation. On principle, participation is open to those who are inclined to proceed only by rational arguments (without recourse to authority, even that of opinion or of diverse powers) and, reciprocally, to recognize the possibility of being convinced by arguments advanced by other participants. So far no major problem. The difficulties begin when this (again, perfectly rational) attitude of renunciation of arguments from authority is clarified into a ban on the traditions proper to each of the participants. In that case, the Christian (like the Jew, the Muslim, or any other believer, sage, or religious person) would, in order to enter into rational debate, have to bracket his tradition and his convictions, that is to say, would have to argue methodically as if they were no longer available to him, exactly like a non-Christian, a non-Jew, a non-Muslim, a non-Buddhist, a non-Taoist, and so forth. Rational discussion would then only be possible between rationalists. This rationalist drift seems to me *rationally* untenable for four reasons.

(i) First, the real conditions of entry into debate would in this way also define from the outset the final result of the debate, if there is one. It would then be a matter of an ideological radicalization of the first theoretical deficiency that we had pointed out above: the confusion between the formal conditions and the result of the debate. We would find ourselves again facing a repetition of the tyranny of a single party through what Péguy branded so prophetically as "the intellectual party": a certain group assumes the right of opening the debate and, with the same gesture, of closing it to others—rationality by co-optation, the Jockey Club of reason, or in the words of Armande, "We'll show that only we and our friends have wit."[6]

This drift has not yet become irreversible. Let us nevertheless recognize, without descending into paranoid polemics, that it has at times already appeared.

(ii) Second, this bracketing of all the convictions stemming from tradition implies a first dogmatic thesis, contradictory to the very principle of communicational reason: an extremely strict anthropology, determining (paradoxically in the manner of second scholasticism!) a "pure nature," historically never realized, yet posited as the blueprint of credentials for any admission into humanity. This strictly rational demarcation of the humanity of the human has always led (even in thinkers as much above suspicion as Kant and Husserl) to an inevitable exclusion of certain people outside of full and "European" humanity (for example and to begin with, the Eskimos and the Gypsies).

(iii) Third, this bracketing also implies that one could define the criteria of rationality before the debate begins, that is to say, before communication is engaged, even though communication alone was authorized to release rationality. A fatal sophism ensues: communicational reason would precede communication and reasoning; it would claim to know itself before the debate that generates it, hence before itself. In short, communicational reason would drop below itself, into the dogmatism that it had as its sole legitimacy to claim to surpass.

(iv) The very criterion of the rationality of an argument becomes ambiguous within this context. It can in fact be understood in two quite different senses, depending on whether it is concerned with the meaning or the origin of this argument. Therefore it seems perfectly defensible that an argument borrowed from a religious or even a revealed tradition could be formulated as such without thereby contradicting rationality. The best example perhaps comes from the principle of the "golden rule": "In everything do to others as you would have them do to you; for this is the law and the prophets" (Matt. 7:12). Would it be rational to disqualify this argument because it is given according "to the law and the prophets"? Does this historical origin and its belonging to the Jewish and Christian tradition diminish its rational validity and forbid it to function as an argument? Must this argument reappear in the *Groundwork of the Metaphysic of Morals*—"Act in such a way that you treat humanity whether in your own person or whether in that of any other always at the same time as an end and not simply as a means"—in order for it to become all of a sudden rationally valid, by an *irrational* change of status rather than by a change in meaning? Even admitting that the metaphysical formulation adds a stricter formality to the Gospel precept, does not the latter in its very "naïveté" retain a rational validity of argument?[7] In this respect, the very fact that the communicational model at times claims to surpass the "golden rule," including in its Kantian formulation, leaves a serious ambiguity hovering over the unjustified restrictions applied to rationality by communication. Be that as it may, this privileged example is enough to mark the reasonable conditions under which the participants can be admitted to the table of debate opened by communicational reason: regardless of origin, their arguments must be formulated and appreciated only inasmuch as they remain rational, that is to say, correctly constructed and endowed with meaning that is universalizable and open to refutation. These conditions permit the elimination of affirmations without arguments, but they allow all the participants to speak, provided they reformulate their traditions and their history according to these minimalist rational conditions.

They suffice also to impose on the believers of any confession a salutary test in the encounter with truth: When they defend a principle or claim a right, they should always first ask themselves what they thus mean to say, which arguments support their discourse, which rationality they can themselves grant to it, a fortiori what sort of validity their interlocutors, with (possibly) the best will in the world, would be able to acknowledge on their behalf. Before opposing abortion or contraception (and in order to do so), before claiming rights to free schooling or access to mass media (and in order to do so), it would be high time for Christians and especially Catholics to ask themselves what rationally acceptable, convincing, and general interesting arguments they have available—in plain language, what sort of conceptual work they have undertaken in order to have them available. The role of the ordinary magisterium of the Church does not exempt them from this effort of reflection, of argumentation, and of persuasion. The success of such a work of explication is always more or less difficult; obviously less so for the appeal to solidarity with the most destitute or for the defense of free schooling than for the questions of personal ethics, of immigration, and of religious tolerance; thus it is necessary to invest that much more argumentative effort in these domains that present greater difficulties. In the situation of at least potential cultural conflict, as is the case in Europe between the Catholic Church and at least some part of public opinion, the right attitude consists neither in the abandonment of difference nor in a defensive turn, but in a serious, patient and continuous effort to construct rational arguments corresponding to each of the recommendations of the ordinary teaching of the magisterium.

This attitude assumes considerable intellectual and cultural means, and it is not certain that the Church in France has really taken their full measure. Unfortunately, this deficit of reasoned rationality leaves the field open to prophecy—sometimes inspired, often grandiloquent, sometimes judicious, often corrupted—and, more often, to silent or wordy rejection. Rare are those who see the true difficulty and attempt to work on it. On this point many of us have to challenge ourselves.[8]

VI

Some Christians might object that this position betrays a lot of naïveté or even otherworldliness. Is it not obvious that, among many of those who want to hold onto communicational reason, the intention is to conduct battle against any revealed religion by disqualifying it, via the old Leninist ruse of mixing things up, so that under the label "fundamentalism," the "religious" is conflated with "irrationality," John Paul II with Khomeini, Lustiger with Écône? The attempt is in fact obvious, although happily marginal. It calls for several remarks.

First, once again, this campaign develops more easily to the extent that Christians, and especially Catholics, do not propose serious counterarguments. Second, and more widely, all potential parties to the debate should admit that there is no shame in the minority position; rather, they should admit that it becomes very honorable, provided it can define with reason and arguments what separates it from the majority or from the minorities collected together on an ad hoc basis into a chance majority. The difference is not only a right but an essential, even vital component for rational debate: without it, and hence without those who put up with assuming the minority role on some subject or other, in some period or other, the *consensus* can always turn to tyranny—and a soft tyranny remains a tyranny; a conformism claiming to be progress quickly becomes a simple progress of conformism. Besides, as regards the majority of ideas, there is never a majority and a minority, but, following the questions and as is logical, some move from the majority to the minority and the reverse. The Church was a minority when it condemned Bolshevism and Nazism in the same year 1937, but a prophetic minority that the events ended up turning into the majority in 1945 and then in 1989. The encyclical *Populorum progressio* for a time put forward a minority view that linked peace to development and then to human rights, but this was a very inspired minority view because today nobody would openly risk claiming the opposite, even in the sanctuaries of capitalism and in the prudent chanceries. Admittedly, *Humanae vitae* has provoked a fracture and a rather wide rejection, but who can foresee whether, in a few decades or less, under the irreversible pressure of ethical problems in medicine and biology, it will not seem the courageous anticipation of an ecology of the body [*une écologie du corps propre*]?[9]

The future belongs only to God, even if it depends only on us. The debate is thus never closed, the positions are never set, the contractual agreement never definitive. The ordinary teaching of the magisterium must be taken for what it gives itself to be, as a teaching. Faithfulness to a teaching does not mean, here as elsewhere, to repeat it, but to think it—to discuss it argumentatively.

Third, and finally, please allow me to suspect a level of immaturity in a number of Catholics (or else an ambiguous nostalgia for "Christendom," which probably never existed as imagined). They would almost think Revelation to be threatened or definitively destroyed just because they can exercise neither the intelligence, nor the culture, nor above all the work and the courage sufficient for convincing their contemporaries of that of which they themselves are often deep down and to begin with so little convinced. Catholics, my brothers, my fellows, have we not in recent history committed enough follies to have merited this minority position a bit? Maturity would mean first that we notice our mistakes, and then that we work toward providing society with arguments and useful analyses to face the problems that confront us all—a society that expects these arguments and analyses more than it fears them (or fears them because it expects them). The common good requires that we offer to all what Revelation has given us—and has given us to comprehend. Today, intelligence becomes a duty of charity. It is up to us, to us and to no one else, to transmit the light that we claim to have received—in vessels of clay, yet we really have received it. When a Church dies in a nation, it is never primarily its adversaries' doing, but that of its members, who lose courage and faith, and thus intelligence.

Of course, a Church can find itself—but this is certainly not our case—in a constant minority situation in front of civil society, or even in the situation of an institutional marginalization in front of an unjust state. But even that should not surprise because it would be an illustrative case where "witness" has to be said in Greek as "martyr." This extreme situation, which others have known and will know, should illuminate ours, which is much less extreme: the Christian Church received the promise of perenniality and universality (and sees it realized, at least potentially), but never the promise of being the majority, nor of *consensus*. It always started by gathering communities that were in a minority position; it has lived through centuries in a minority position; it continues to work at the humanization and the deification of people who are in a minority position. Besides, what would it have to gain from reaching a majority position, other than succumbing to the temptation of imperialism, of the perfect city on earth, in short, the dream of the Grand Inquisitor? All appearances indicate that Christ was in a minority position on the Cross. The only real minority that we must fervently get beyond is that of the Holy Spirit in us, who is most of the time spread through only a minority share of our heart.

VII

Reason, then. It finds itself in the situation of nihilism, for everyone, including Christians. It can at least be practiced according to the model of communicational reason, as the zero degree of rationality. From now on, reason passes from foundation in truth to agreement through arguing. This figure of reason forces Christians to take up apologetic work again—this time in the best sense of the term, that of the apologetic Fathers, of whom the "martyr and philosopher" Justin remains the emblematic figure. In so doing, Christians will not labor only in the "rational service" (Rom. 12:1) of Revelation, nor for the common good by giving everyone a little bit of what has been given them to know, but they will reinforce reason itself, which has become almost problematic in this time of nihilism, where it seems to stagger under the weight of its conquests. If reason, in the crisis of grounding, cannot prop us up to say the Word, then maybe one must work toward the Word giving reason back to itself. That was Hegel's ambition when speculative reason seemed to be at its summit of power. This must be the ambition of Christians, at the moment where reason seems to have become frantic over itself. In order to guard reason, in all the senses of the term, it is necessary henceforth to receive it from the Word. A certain poverty is thus required. For poverty alone can receive the Word, which gives itself, like time, from day to day, "mercifully" (Hölderlin).

3

The Formal Reason of the Infinite

The Infinite in Reason, Reason in the Infinite

The use of reason first of all requires us to practice the infinite, as one practices an unmanageable but essential instrument, in order to improve our rational capacities by applying them not to some delimited object, but to that which, by definition, will always resist definition. More than this: reason also consists of exercising the infinite, as one exercises a political, administrative, or financial responsibility—because it is very necessary for us to assume its crushing but indispensable burden. This is also the case because the supreme task, that of thinking the infinite, fascinates, attracts, and captivates the minds of those who are, so to speak, most endowed with reason. Man is a privileged being, not only because there is Being at stake in us, but also because the infinite is at stake in us even in regard to Being. For us, to arrive at truly thinking, in one way or another, in any field of knowledge, depends on our picturing the infinite, on our thinking of the infinite. But this depends less on our picturing the infinite in a positive manner than on our applying our reason to the infinite for some question or other. Therefore, the infinite is first of all not called transcendent, but is given a transcendental status—that of the very condition of exercising reason. A form of reason that would not think about the infinite—not only about it but also in accordance with its requirements—would be deficient in itself. There is no rationality without turning to the infinite.

It must be stressed that this is first of all not solely a requirement of philosophy, of speculation, of desire, or of religious belief. It is a requirement above and beyond a narrow practice common to all the sciences. For us nowadays, each of the sciences actually has dealings with the infinite, in one way or another. The formal infinite of mathematics, the real infinite of space (of extension) in physics, which itself encompasses, to paraphrase Pascal, the "infinitely small" of particle physics, of biology, and of the life sciences, and the "infinitely great" of the sciences of matter, of astrophysics, and so forth; and again, or even above all, the infinite by accumulation which is generated, at its risk and at our peril, by industrial production and its imperialistic interpretation of the world; and we can't omit the infinite by projection and classification, which is engendered by the parameters of statistical science. For us, a science that would never have dealings with the infinite would not be a science because it would not possess two necessary characteristics of scientific rigor: first, a proper method that would open up entirely new types of subjects to it, and second, free scope for progress without assignable boundaries.

It goes without saying for us that all science must practice the infinite and must even exercise the infinite within its domain, but this was not so for the Greeks. In fact, according to Aristotle, every science was assigned to its place, without anyone being able, or at least having the right, to move from one to another, so that the homogeneous space of the *mathesis universalis* did not have to be and, in fact, did not succeed in being organized by the Greeks, but had to await the new Cartesian beginning. The only universality admitted by Aristotelian thought and its final heirs in the sixteenth century related solely to mathematics, where quantity in general eventually enabled the grouping together of arithmetic, geometry, astronomy, music (and other applied mathematics) into a general form of mathematics (*mathematikē pasōn koinē kathólou*,[1] *mathematica universalis*), which was scarcely outlined historically. Yet, this restriction was based, as much for Aristotle as already for Plato, on an even more radical argument, which in turn was evidence of a fundamental theoretical decision: namely, that knowledge requires the delimitation of what is known, that the act of knowing requires that what is known also be in act and the first to be delimited: *entelechy divides*.[2] The undivided, the unlimited, or, in short, the infinite negatively understood as the indefinite (*apeiron*), renders the human incapable (*hō apeiros*) of knowledge, according to Plato's telling play on words.[3] Logically such an indefinite, unlimited, and undivided infinite culminates in matter—and culminates less in materiality as such than in the imprecision that it imposes on form, on its effort of delimitation, and therefore of intelligibility. Even Plotinus, in the name of the entirety of

Greek thought, did not hesitate to conclude that matter is equivalent to the indefinite.[4]

This constraint—that to know excludes the infinite because it implies indeterminacy and therefore contingency—has been transgressed by modern thought. Indeed, modern thought has established itself only by transgressing this restriction. We could think here of Duns Scotus, Nicholas of Cusa, and Kepler or Galileo. We shall stay with Descartes, who lucidly met the Greek objection with: "And I must not think that, just as my conceptions of rest and darkness are arrived at by negating movement and light, so my perception of the infinite is arrived at not by means of a true idea but merely by negating the finite. On the contrary, I clearly understand that there is more reality in an infinite substance than in a finite one, and hence that my perception of the infinite, that is God, is in some way prior to my perception of the finite, that is myself."[5] Consequently, and definitively, the infinite appears as primary. This does not only mean, nor does it primarily mean, that it is established as a metaphysical name for God (although it is just this since Duns Scotus and Suárez), opening the way to a rational theology of the infinite being who is infinitely perfect, the privileged provider of a future "ontological argument." More profoundly, however, this reversal means that the infinite precedes the finite—human thought, what organizes and deploys its sciences—like a horizon that is always already open in advance to welcome its progress and its desires. It is here, since Descartes, that the infinite has become established as the ultimate transcendental, even more than as the first transcendent. Kant recollected this, writing that "the infinite is not the specific objective concept of a size in its relationship to others, but *being brought into effect subjectively*, it surpasses in magnitude anything else that we might put forward, even though this would not be the result of every understanding."[6] In short, it is such that it will always be possible to conceive of something bigger. But this transcendental priority, which determines the conditions of possibility of all knowledge (including, first and foremost, scientific knowledge), has a price: if the infinite precedes and makes possible the finite, the finite cannot, by definition, include this infinite within its comprehension because it is precisely the infinite that makes the finite possible; the conditioned cannot comprehend the unconditioned that conditions it. It is therefore necessary to admit this impossibility as an a priori necessity, or rather to admit this a priori as a necessity: "It does not matter that I do not grasp the infinite, or that there are countless additional attributes of God, which I cannot in any way grasp, and perhaps cannot even reach in my thought (*nec comprehendere, nec forte etiam attingere cogitatione*); for it is in the nature of the infinite not to be grasped by a finite being like myself."[7] Paradoxically, an incomprehensibility such as this does not imply any ignorance, nor the least regression toward the unknown, for, absolutely as a first idea, or we could also say as horizon, the infinite quite rightly imposes itself on my mind as "the most clear and distinct idea" and the "most real idea" of all.[8] It is precisely because it is infinite and the transcendental condition for all the others that this idea surpasses them epistemologically, so that the impossibility of understanding it as a finite object precisely coincides with its perfect clarity and distinction, its incomparable truth.

Yet, a paradoxical conclusion follows from this, from one of those paradoxes that provide reason with its most unshakeable points of support: "For the idea of the infinite, if it is to be a true idea, cannot be grasped at all, since the impossibility of being grasped is contained in the formal definition of the infinite—*idea enim infiniti, ut sit vera, nullo modo debet comprehendi, quoniam ipsa incomprehensibilitas in ratione formali infiniti continetur.*"[9] Let us give attentive consideration to this fundamental statement. (a) It of course explains the title of our subject: the formal reason of the infinite precisely consists in its incomprehensibility. (b) It not only shows that incomprehensibility defines the infinite (in the obviated sense of *ratio formalis*), but above all that reason (the primary meaning of *ratio*) does not constitute a limit of intelligibility but formally includes the incomprehensible when it is a matter of thinking the infinite. Incomprehensibility constitutes the epistemological reverse side of that for which the infinite provides the ontic obverse. The same coinage has an ontic face (the infinite) and an epistemic face (incomprehensibility). (c) Incomprehensibility must also be thought in such a way that in principle it belongs to reason, in the situation where it has to do with the infinite and must understand it (*intelligere*). Taken in this sense, the incomprehensible does not go beyond the borders of rationality, but designates its furthermost area, or even its most strategic borderland; for, by losing incomprehensibility, reason would risk losing all its legitimacy, and thus its entire realm.

To Know the Incomprehensible as Such

Yet, even according to Descartes, this paradox is only valid on one condition: that reason's task is to think God. Two objections follow from this. (a) Does not this condition assume that what is to be proved has been established—namely that reason can always claim to think God, whether he exists or whether knowledge of him exceeds the theoretical powers of reason? And does not the Cartesian solution—namely, that to think the infinite is equivalent to thinking it as incomprehensible—precisely confirm that reason does not have the means to do so? (b) Another objection can be added to this: Although it would be possible to think the infinite as incomprehensibility in the, by definition, exceptional case of God, what result is to be derived from this? What other use of incomprehensibility could this offer in other cases, where it is only a question of a finite being and, most often, of synthesized objects, which are constituted and finally produced at will, and which are all perfectly comprehensible? The incomprehensible is therefore exposed to two rebuttals: its noetic impracticability and its marginal character within the actual use of reason. I will examine the first in this section, then the other in the subsequent section.

First, can the thought of the incomprehensible take the place of authentic knowledge? We cannot evaluate this thought without connecting the position taken by Descartes to an unwavering tradition, even though he was probably unaware of it. In fact, his wording echoes that of others. (a) The problem is clearly formulated by Saint Anselm: In regard to God, it is a question of "rationally comprehending that he is incomprehensible."[10] The rationality that this oxymoron ("to comprehend the incomprehensible") is capable of surmounting (or accomplishing) remains to be defined. Indeed, is it not sufficient to renounce argument in order to return to holiness, as Saint Bernard points out: "It is not debate but sanctity that comprehends them, if, however, what is incomprehensible can in any way be comprehended"?[11] Indeed not, since then the comprehensibility of the incomprehensible would remain doubtful because holiness does not first have a theoretical vocation.

(b) Because in these two cases one encounters the head-on opposition between comprehension and the incomprehensible, what would be needed is an attempt to organize these within a relationship that is itself rational. This was attempted by Saint Augustine: "We are speaking of God: What marvel, if you do not comprehend? For if you were to comprehend, He would not be God."[12] The paradox regains its full intelligibility here: it is no longer a question of placing comprehension in opposition to incomprehensibility in the same field, but of constructing a hierarchy for the whole of comprehension in general in relation to an exceptional thought, in which this concept, and only this concept, *must* remain incomprehensible in order to remain rational; this is what Descartes calls the infinite. Consequently, incomprehensibility is perfectly capable not of suspending knowledge but of supporting it, because it provides it with a theme that is out of the ordinary. It is not a question of abandoning knowing, but of knowing what, as such and by positive privilege, exceeds comprehensibility; and in order to know this, it is rightly only a question of recognizing the excess therein. Going forward, the experience of thought of its (subjective) incomprehensibility becomes the (objective) experience of the infinite. Between Augustine and Descartes, Montaigne can be heard among others: "It is through the mediation of our ignorance rather than of our knowledge that we are knowers of that divine knowledge."[13] Therefore, ignorance is worth nothing less than the only mode of knowledge that is paradoxically suited to the knowledge of the infinite. Several thinkers have clearly emphasized this: Saint Augustine: "the Most High who is better known by remaining ignorant,"[14] and Thomas Aquinas: "wherefore man reaches the highest point of his knowledge about God when he knows that he knows him not,"[15] and even Dionysius: "God is known through knowledge and through unknowing. . . . And yet on the other hand, the Divinest knowledge of God is received through unknowing (*di agnōsias*)."[16]

(c) Yet there is more: Incomprehensibility, as an ordeal that cannot be grasped, does not only have a negative function (the apophasis of transcendence); it can also, by the same function, give access to a real and positive experience of the infinite. Basil of Caesarea does not hesitate to speak of anything less than a *sensation* of incomprehensibility: "The knowledge of the divine essence is only the sensation of its very incomprehensibility."[17] The infinite is manifested positively to the extent that even its incomprehensibility is vouched for positively in an epistemic register. Admittedly, we obviously do not understand the incomprehensible, but we experience this incomprehensibility not as a denial of evidence, but truly as evidence that affects us by right, or in short as a mark of the infinite's affection. We comprehend that we do not comprehend and that we do not have to comprehend the infinite, and that it will be henceforth by this sign that we will know or (re)cognize it—as what certainly never allows itself to be reduced to the a priori conditions of knowledge of an object. In other words, according to Gregory of Nyssa, "This is the true knowledge (*eidēsis*) of what is sought" (i.e., the incomprehensible God, *akatalēptos*): "this is the seeing that consists in not seeing (*to idein en tō me idein*)."[18] I conclude: Incomprehensibility does not epistemologically disqualify the infinite, but designates what we can grasp of it without striving in vain to understand it like an object. "Everything that is incomprehensible does not cease to remain incomprehensible."[19] The infinite remains among us, not in spite of, but indeed because of the sensation of the incomprehensible.

Yet, one could retort, is this simple sensation of the incomprehensible really accessible to us? Even if one recognizes here an inevitable appearance of reason in a Kantian mode, must one for all that also grant its full-fledged phenomenality? Is it not a question of a result of perspective, admittedly impossible to eliminate, but nevertheless all the more illusory? An additional hypothesis may—we do not say must—intervene here, which in the end responds precisely to the implicit question of the conference ("Certainly two thousand years, but after what?"):[20] If in the form of incomprehensibility the infinite has for almost forever remained among us in accordance with the constitution of our finite experience of the infinite, then what is more, for two thousand years this very same infinite has "pitched its tent among us" and "has become flesh" (John 1:14); in short, it has taken on our flesh.

One can all the more refuse to conceive this unprecedented event because it is effectively inconceivable and only matters as long as it remains so. One may well reject its viewpoint, but one can dispute neither its logic nor its consistency or its rationality. One can also not dispute the fact that for two thousand years an uninterrupted and still deep-rooted religious tradition has been built on the belief that the infinite has taken flesh—flesh, blood, and bone—among us, and has become one of us to the point of sharing our death and in the resurrection that he inaugurates. In any event, whether one rejects it or whether one assumes it, it is not optional to ask what this claim means. It signifies at least two paradoxes. First, it does not imply that the infinite henceforth becomes comprehensible in Christ (which would be equivalent to the "fanaticism" of the *Schwärmerei*) but, on the contrary, that the incomprehensibility of the infinite becomes the flesh of our flesh for us. Indeed, if the infinite has become incarnate and if the incomprehensible "has assumed human likeness, and being found in human form (*en homoiōmati anthrōpōn genomenos kai schēmati euretheis hōs anthrōpos*)" (Phil. 2:7), what do we see on this face? On the one hand, while seeing Christ, we of course see the Father ("Whoever has seen me has seen the Father. How can you say 'Show us the Father?' Do you not believe that I am in the Father and that the Father is in me?" John 14:9–10). On the other hand, unless there were a regression this side of the Mosaic revelation, it remains established that "no one has ever seen God, but God the only Son, [he who is] turned toward the Father's heart, he has made the exegesis of God" (*ekeinos exēgēsato*, John 1:18). Therefore, on Christ's face we still see the incomprehensible, but this time we see it definitively as such—in the authorized and definitive exegesis of his filial otherness, insurmountable because carnal. It is inescapable, insoluble in its objectivity, the face of faces, the other par excellence, the perfect immanence of transcendence. Immanence and transcendence are henceforth reconciled with each other. The incomprehensible has sided with us.

This leads to the second paradox. This infinite has assumed and still assumes our flesh in its integrity without remainder. The incomprehensible infinite has therefore taken flesh in our reason. Our reason is henceforth to be found serving as a dwelling place for the infinite. It has therefore taken on a dimension that definitively and infinitely surpasses us. It henceforth ranks as the infinite, despite our finitude, or rather thanks to it; in this sense it therefore appears to us as incomprehensible to us. Not because we no longer comprehend our reason, but because we suspect, and indeed we note, that it henceforth extends infinitely further than our representations, our calculations, our wishes and our desires. It conceals a power of intelligibility whose limits escape us—or which at least cannot be reduced to what we imagine about it even in the most extreme way. When we speak of the endless progress of science, we suspect that what is at stake is much more than progress and science. At stake is the right of the infinite to make itself, endlessly, without respite, without rest, without attributable end, the official passenger of our poor, lurching rationality, which is henceforth in charge of a stake of reason that infinitely transcends what it could ever imagine.

No one should object that a commitment of this sort could weigh down our reason with pretensions and irrational pressures, leading it astray into an ideological or imaginary delirium of an illusory as well as dangerous "new age." For what has taken flesh in our reason, the infinite in the form of the incomprehensible, has laid claim to a name—namely that of the *logos*, the very term that the wisdom of the Greeks assigned to the rigor of thoughts and the meaning of things. The infinite, which has taken flesh in our finite flesh, lays claim to the very name from which our reason emerges. Reason has taken flesh in our reason. Only this *logos* can claim the otherwise corrupted title of the "Great Reason." And in its way, philosophy has never ceased to justify this claim, by basing itself on it in order to detect rationality in history, even in its most obvious contingencies and by practicing the work of the concept there. Our *logos*, including its formal logic, its mathematical computations, its quantifications and models, its hypotheses and even its ideological deliriums, remains haunted by the infinite *logos* within it, which is henceforth incarnate in our reason. If we bear in our rationality not only the comprehensible but also the incomprehensible, if we are henceforth no longer able to keep it within the limits of what we comprehend in the mode of objects, if it does not cease to make us yearn for all ambitions, for better or for worse, that is because our *logos* remains, whether we want it to or not, inhabited by the *logos* to the point of obsession. One ought to have the lucidity of concluding from this that christology is a matter, among others, of epistemology. Historians of the sciences have abundantly verified this. It remains for contemporary philosophers to admit it.

Man as Incomprehensible to Himself

We can now approach the second question: Although the infinite could be thought of as incomprehensibility in the case of God, by definition an exceptional case, what consequence can be derived from this? What domain of contemporary rationality would still have need of these kinds of considerations, which are of admissible rigor when approaching its outer limits, but which are of no use when the preoccupation is with a need for substantial reinforcement in research programs in what are termed the "hard" sciences? What science would need to take seriously the epistemological face of the incomprehensible, whose reverse is the ontic face that is called the infinite? Returning to our starting point in the first section, it could be replied that all sciences worthy of their respective methodologies have to do with the infinite. But the question here concerns something else—the incomprehensible. Yet, the progress of every science takes place in the line of battle where it confronts what up to this point remained incomprehensible in order to render it comprehensible. It is therefore only a question of a heuristic incomprehensible, one that is provisional and in the end always assumed to be reducible. What does the definitive incomprehensible matter, for what can we say about it except that it does not belong to the rational domain and must disappear into the outer darkness, where there will be wailing and gnashing of teeth? Or rather, where there will never be any sound, lost as they are in the silence of infinite spaces.

Yet things are not that simple. If, as we have seen, the infinite remains in us and constitutes us as such, then the incomprehensible also inhabits us—it has become us. We are ourselves the incomprehensible closest to ourselves. There is actually nothing astonishing in this paradox: the nearest remains the most difficult to access, the furthest away. This is first of all because our incomprehensibility to ourselves results directly from the incomprehensibility of the infinite, where God reveals himself in our flesh. Indeed, according to Gregory of Nyssa's flawless argument, if one admits that God created us, we humans are nothing less than "in his icon and his likeness (*kat' eikona kai homoiōsin*)"; if, on the other hand, the divine essence remains by definition "unknowable (*to akatalēpton tēs ousias*)," then our own "proper nature in terms of our mind" must also "escape knowledge (*diaphengei tēn gnōsin he kata ton noun ton hemeteron physis*)."[21] In short, the honor of receiving its essential definition from an iconic reference to the infinite implies human incomprehensibility—and for a twofold reason. It does so, first, because an icon of the infinite bears the mark of the infinite by resemblance, and therefore becomes incomprehensible. It is in this sense that Descartes recognizes in himself an infinite will, which is therefore unintelligible to his own finite understanding, because he admits "that I bear in some way the image and likeness of God."[22] Human incomprehensibility therefore results first from our likeness to the infinite. Second, our incomprehensibility follows from the fact that no finite image can equal its infinite model; or, to quote Dionysius the Areopagite, "Man is never like his icon,"[23] and our incomprehensibility results from the fact that by definition we cannot faithfully resemble the infinite. In short, as a necessarily inadequate image of the original infinite, humans first become incomprehensible because we receive its excess, then because we fall short of it. Even so, what matters here are not the vicissitudes of the *imitatio Christi*, the salvific concern only of Christians, but the quasi-transcendental stamp with which the infinite marks the finite. How do we recognize that man is a god (in the sense in which a painting is immediately recognized as being "a Cézanne" or "a Piero della Francesca")? By its incomprehensible character, the signature of its original icon, the infinite.

This result—our reason includes incomprehensibility because our essence bears the image and the likeness of the infinite and therefore of the incomprehensible—leads to the elucidation of several difficulties. It first becomes clear that no anthropology could ever render an account of human nature. Pascal said, "If he exalts himself, I humble him. If he humbles himself, I exalt him. And I go on contradicting him. Until he understands that he is a monster that passes all understanding"[24]—thus a phenomenon that cannot be grasped. We can also understand this from other voices: what metaphysics has increasingly constructed under the title of "man" probably only achieves the status of a drawing sketched in the sand and erased in the rising tide of nihilism, as we may suspect together with Foucault.[25] For even rigorous knowledge achieved by the "human sciences" can, by the very definition of scientificity, only have bearing on the objects that the respective methods of these sciences produce each time. Yet these objects—models of logic, principles of linguistics, psychic drives, decision-making processes, laws about the genesis of representations, and so forth—even when generously granting them an apodicticity that is all the same problematic, can at best only ever attain what can be universalized, modeled, and measured by man. In short, he can only reach the thin, albeit indefinite, layer of what can be objectified in me or in you, but which is neither you nor me, nor, incidentally, anyone who is genuinely human. All that the human sciences will teach me (and they instruct me more every day) will always relate to the object, which can be universalized, constituted, and reproduced and which, admittedly with increasing subtlety, they will have substituted for me and my irreducible and unrepeatable ipseity. An impassible chasm stretches between this *I* who I remain, alone with itself, and all these objected and objectified selves (*moi*), a gap that Husserl called "the intrinsic differentiation in the manners of being . . . , the most cardinal difference of all, that between *consciousness* and *reality*"; in short, between the incomprehensible *I* that I am and the things that I understand.[26] We recognize the stamp of the incomprehensible in us, which witnesses to our consubstantial infinite.

Therefore, it is not only a matter of admitting, with John Chrysostom, that "we do not even know well (*kalōs*) the essence of our own souls; rather, we do not have any knowledge whatsoever of that essence (*oudeopōsoun*),"[27] which is a simple acknowledgment of an empirical difficulty, which might perhaps be surmountable by a more rigorous science. It is a matter of drawing a conclusion from the grandiose but fruitless effort of modern metaphysics to indicate what I really think when I utter the words "I think." This impossibility holds not only for the move from "I think" to the potential certainty that "I am"—which is another, even more problematic ambition—but from the simple intellection, or even the representation, of the being that is limited to uttering only the apparently simplest and most paltry statement, "I am." Following Descartes, who calls it a "thing" without succeeding in establishing that it is indeed like a substance,[28] and Spinoza, who confines it to the body where it remains without further thought,[29] Malebranche will admit without quibbling that we have no idea of our soul.[30] From this Kant drew the inevitable conclusion: concerning the nature of our thinking essence, "We can assign no other basis for this teaching than the simple, and in itself completely empty, representation 'I'; and we cannot even say that this is a concept, but only that it is a bare consciousness which accompanies all concepts."[31] In short, it is an accident of objectness. By introducing the unconscious at the heart of this consciousness that is already incomprehensible in itself, psychoanalysis only brings this paradox to its head.

This sort of incomprehensibility of man to himself often passes either for a deplorable defeat of metaphysical reason or for the applauded liberation of postmetaphysical thought. This kind of alternative most probably misses the essential stakes: The final undoing of any representable idea of the *I* is not first of all a fortunate or unfortunate success achieved by metaphysics, but the forced or spontaneous recognition of the rational fact that incomprehensibility determines reason itself from top to bottom, exactly as it is put into operation by any *I* worthy of its humanity. And in this incomprehensibility (or even in our incomprehension of this incomprehensibility), we must recognize that we can only and must only think within the infinite, where we are, live, and breathe. And if ever we dreamed of knowing ourselves (of representing ourselves and therefore of grasping ourselves as an object), then we would come up against Paul's freely offered warning: "For if those who are nothing (no being, *nihil, tis einai*) think they are something (of being, *aliquid esse, tis einai*), they deceive themselves" (Gal. 6:3).[32] We are not a being, even a privileged one, because we come from the icon of the unknowable, beyond all being and beyond all beingness, and must return there in order ultimately to become ourselves. We must finally take seriously the fact that "I is another."

We can discover this incomprehensibility consubstantial to a reason saturated with the infinite in other cases, which are just as intimately distant from us: the other as my neighbor, the temporality of my birth (even more than that of my death), also the splendor of the visible and the tenderness of this world of flesh. Indeed, shouldn't one have something to say about the fact *that* something simply is—in short, *that* this is the case, this *that* itself, rightly called the mystical (*das Mystische*) by Wittgenstein?[33] Undoubtedly, we can say nothing about it if language only speaks of objects in the objectivity of predication. Yet perhaps we must learn to speak and therefore to think otherwise than according to objectivity. For surrounded by the infinite, our reason could also with care, prudence, and reverential fear perhaps "address mystical things in a mystical manner and holy things in a holy way (*mystikōs ta mystika phthengesthai kai hagiōs ta hagia*)" (Gregory Nazianzen).[34] For what is more holy in us than the fact that we are ourselves incomprehensible?

Resisting Human Self-Objectification

There remains a final objection, in the form of a common sense question: Why desire to think the incomprehensible at any price and on its own terms? What is to be gained by it? Can one even genuinely attain this, or is it an illusion of the bad infinite?

A first answer, at least, goes without saying. Short of thinking the incomprehensible—hence, of thinking it by the only path possible, "the very sensation of incomprehensibility"—reason closes off any access to God, if only as the final question of our infinite horizon. For the danger with regard to the knowledge of God never resides in his incomprehensibility, this inevitable effect of the ontic infinite in the epistemic, but resides in the nonsensical illusion of claiming to understand him. Indeed, to postulate that "the human mind has an adequate knowledge of the eternal and infinite essence of God,"[35] comes down to corrupting access to the incomprehensible into a commonplace conceptual idol. This is a basic case of the recurrent temptation of metaphysics: encompassing the given within the grasp of the concept so as to transform it into an object.

Yet, this first answer immediately puts us on the route to another, more general answer. If instead of denying access to the knowledge of God, "the sensation of incomprehensibility" opens up this access, this is because it keeps us from comprehending him like an object and prompts us to approach him without comprehending him, to see him without subjecting him to the attention of our gaze (*intuitus*).[36] This attitude of nonobjective knowledge—real knowledge, but not of an object or even of a nonobject—is moreover not only suitable for the question of God, as we have seen above, but is appropriate in the same way for the question of the other. If knowing the other requires treating him or her as another self, then, precisely in order to approach others in this manner, I must forgo transforming them into an object. As another *I*, the other is not objectified but possibly objectifies the remainder of what is knowable. In order to know the other as another *I*, I must recognize him as an exception to objectification because I myself only make myself felt as an *I* by excluding myself from the objectification I carry out. Consequently, the other, exactly like God, only becomes accessible to me as an exception to the objectification that is elsewhere always possible and is sometimes desirable. The other shares with God the privilege—which is by no means a fault—of only opening up to a "sensation of the incomprehensibility" of the object.

Therefore, considering these two occurrences of the privilege of incomprehensibility, why not consider the possibility of a third? Am I not, myself, threatened with the possibility of understanding myself as an object? In fact, the so-called "human" sciences, just like those called "hard" sciences, never stop proposing increasingly more powerful, more coercive, and therefore more attractive attempts finally to know myself as an object—by formal linguistics, by the "sciences of the mind," by the theory of action or decision, by experimental psychology, by neurology, by genetics, by economics, or by sociology. Certainly any reader of Kant knows how to counter this: The determination of the empirical me will never allow the transcendental *I* to be attained and even less to be known. It alone precisely thinks as a thinking thought [*pensée pensante*] upstream from a thought that is thought [*pensée pensée*]. But this correct and apparently definitive answer can scarcely resist the prestige of the science that makes and proclaims itself. Moreover, at stake is neither the right of prestige of models nor of ideological intimidation. The rise in power, which has only begun, of human self-objectification, that is to say, our self-degradation in the public space to the rank of an object among others, would quite simply remain unintelligible or even derive from a demoniacal excess of self-hatred if it were not governed by the metaphysical accomplishment of the principle of sufficient reason, as is definitively put to work by the essence of technology. There is nothing that reason cannot and must not account for, without exception, including the human. Man must render an account of man himself in the name of reason reduced to the principle of reason and therefore reduced to universal calculation. Without doubt this stands in contradiction to what thinking thought itself calculates as a thought that is thought as an object. Yet this concerns the same contradiction involved in defining God as *causa sui*, because nothing can differ from itself in order simultaneously to become both its effect and its cause. And yet Descartes did not hesitate to defy this formal contradiction (which he lucidly admitted) in order to extend the principle of causality (the tangential anticipation of the principle of reason) even to God. If the infinite, God himself, at least in his metaphysical meaning, was at the time not authorized to be exempt from the *principium reddendae rationis*, how would the finite, man, be able to elude this today? This question, like a threat that has come from the depths of modernity, overhangs what we call, more in imprecise hope than with guiding criteria, postmodernity—in other words, what is unfolding at the turn of this millennium.

What position shall we take in the face of this expanding empire of the *principium reddendae rationis*? There is only one: to contest radically that providing reasons [*rendre raison*] constitutes the highest degree of reason. Reason also and above all remains without any other reason that it could provide (and to whom?): Reason remains without why. We must insist on the fact that reason, taken in its formality, namely in its infinity, surpasses its ambition to provide reasons for objects by reducing all that can be known to what can be objectified and wholly synthesized or constructed, in short, to what is comprehensible. In a word, we must think of the infinite as being consubstantial with reason, which gives it the right to attain even to the incomprehensible. It gives it the right and therefore the duty. In certain cases of knowledge, reason has the duty, because it has the right, to know in the mode of incomprehensibility. In which cases? We have already encountered them: God, then—valid even for those who are troubled by the question of God—the other and the *I*. No one can be forced to consider seriously the question of God if he denies the question. But no one can shirk the questions of the other and of the *I* as optional. And, at least this is my thesis, no one can approach these questions with the least hope of making one step of progress without admitting that reason in these cases confronts what cannot be objectified, what is therefore incomprehensible. Incomprehensibility, the formal reason of the infinite, stands as the sole rampart against the deadly imperialism of sufficient reason—sufficient reason, whose sufficiency can only limit reason and forbid us access to ourselves.

"Know thyself!" enjoined the Oracle of Delphi. But it was obviously not asking us to know ourselves like objects according to the principle of sufficient reason. Perhaps, as in the anticipation of another *logos*, it was already suggesting that we ourselves must know the incomprehensible who henceforth lives among us.

The formal reason of the infinite would then state that "man infinitely transcends man," and therefore, "but for this mystery, the most incomprehensible of all, we remain incomprehensible to ourselves."[37] Undoubtedly the time has come, after the two millennia since the infinite has joined us, to admit the incomprehensibility in us.

Originally translated by A. J. Wickens

PART II

Who Speaks about It?

4

On the Eminent Dignity of the Poor Baptized

When the Church devotes its best efforts to analyzing itself, on the pretext of improving itself (as if that depended on itself alone), one might fear that it hides the aims involved in favor of a vague examination of intermediaries.[1] And when this questioning is focused on the "laity," one must fear the worst: the ecclesiastical body's turning in upon itself—the epitome of clericalism. For the layperson does not exist. Or rather, he or she only appears at that instant when the Church, instead of looking to Him who constitutes it, thinks that it can define itself on its own terms, as a religious society. Doubtlessly trying to mirror civil societies, it becomes organized around a central power, surrounded by concentric circles of bodies invested with lesser power, all the way to the outskirts where to some extent one can no longer clearly determine whether one is outside or inside. Yet from Christ's point of view, there are neither laypeople nor laity: there is only one people of God whose election is confirmed by their baptism, which is sufficient for ensuring their identity. It is most probably not a coincidence that the term "lay" (*laikos*) never appears in the New Testament, while that of the people of God (*laos tou theou*), which could easily have engendered it, is used abundantly. The reason for this absence is obvious: The people of God are only gathered together through the call of Him who saves them (Matt. 1:21, 2:6; Luke 1:68, 7:16, etc.). He who saves them has the name of Christ. Thus those who belong to the redeemed people are given the name "Christians" (Acts 11:26; 1 Pet. 4:16). One can gain the name "Christian" only by receiving baptism: "Christian" means baptized. It is the baptized who constitute the people of God and not the laity. What's more, at the very moment when Vatican II's constitution *Lumen gentium* seems to sanction the term "lay," it defines it, not without some embarrassment, with reference to baptism: "The term laity is here understood to mean all the faithful except those in holy orders and those in the state of religious life specially approved by the Church. These faithful are by baptism made one body with Christ and are constituted among the People of God; they are in their own way made sharers in the priestly, prophetical, and kingly functions of Christ; and they carry out for their own part the mission of the whole Christian people in the Church and in the world" (§31).[2]

"Come You Baptized, One More Effort to Become Lay People!"

All the same, one should be surprised at this definition, theologically so rigorous and pregnant with meaning: In no way do we find here what we have come to recognize over the last several decades under the label of the "layperson." We have learned to measure the gap between baptized and laypeople. The baptized belong by right to Christ, who frees them from themselves. Even so, they are always tempted to cast aside the freedom that deifies them and to return to the slavery that alienates them. A baptized person is a sinner late for conversion, someone selfish yearning for love, someone miraculously cured who tries not to regret his or her healing. After baptism almost anyone can be and remain a humble baptized, because where sin abounds grace abounds all the more. Nothing is more ordinary.

In contrast, there is nothing ordinary about the layperson. Understood as an accomplished condition, it seems to satisfy three requirements: militancy, an ideological doubling of reality, and clericalism.

1. *Militancy* understands conversion quite differently than being conformed to Christ, which is an end in itself and enables us to help and to love our neighbor and to bear ourselves. Militancy sees in conversion instead an ascetic and preliminary (possibly "mystical") means for a huge undertaking to conquer or to reconquer the world. Personal conversion belongs to the initial formation of the militant—but is only one of the elements of this education, for many other competencies besides "faith in Christ" are indispensable. These include, first, knowledge of the terrain: only analysis of the "milieu," intimate familiarity with its modes of thought and production, a belonging (if possible from birth) to its elite and participation in its decision-making organs would allow the militant to operate "like a fish in water." "Class solidarity" is as important as "faith in Christ." For militants are not satisfied with their own conversion, which

nevertheless depends solely on themselves (except for grace). Instead, they intend to add the conversion of their "milieu" to it—which arises from a laudable sentiment. They take their means from this milieu or rather give them to it—and that's the drama. For what is most dangerous in such an attitude is less the obnoxious triumphalism that claims to dominate a world than the blasphemy of a utilitarianism that knows how to make use of the conversion to Jesus Christ (among other things) for a different goal—influence within the "milieu." Whether this goal is realized or, as most often happens, it reduces its pretensions to dialogue, or even to a simply tolerated presence, and even if this goal presents itself as spiritual, the blasphemy remains, the goal identified as a kind of simony—using spiritual means to acquire power (cultural, political, etc.) over one's neighbor. This was one of the temptations Christ endured. And because it comes from the Evil One, once the price (of blasphemy) is paid, the defeat can follow all the better.

One might object, why immediately speak of blasphemy? Is that not going too quickly and too far, by turning one's nose up at people? Yet, it is not here a matter of people, whom no one may judge, but of the concept of the layperson as militant. The means that militant laypeople use explicitly contradict the normative (because Christlike) practice of evangelization, that is to say, the apostolate. "Apostolate" first of all does not indicate a pious activity (attempting to convince the other of the validity of one's own discourse), but a manner of relating to God: Like Christ, the apostle, that is to say, anyone who is baptized, can only speak with authority inasmuch as his word does not come from himself but from He who sends him (cf. John 14:24). Only the apostle speaks differently because he comes from elsewhere. His word has no autonomous power and can expect its confirmation only from another, the Father. Strictly speaking, it is only in this weakness that power can appear. And that is why this power really appears as other, in order to confirm not only the word of the apostle, but its other origin. In this game, the apostle must admit the delay of the confirmation, and the (maybe provisional) reality of defeat. "Not that we are competent of ourselves to claim anything as coming from us; our competence is from God, who has made us competent to be ministers of a new covenant" (2 Cor. 3:5–6).

By contrast, militants cannot allow for any delay in the confirmation. If the event begins to disappoint their expectation, they must immediately analyze the reason for the failure in order to transform it into merely apparent defeat (false application of the right words, false use of correct principles) and take up their effort again. The militant must be able to count on the immediate truth of his or her word; he cannot and must not depend on any outside confirmation, even a divine one. Or rather, for him, it is not doubtful that God will not stop confirming the soundness of his analyses and the validity of his initiatives immediately and abundantly. Any well-trained militant must thoroughly control this indispensable hermeneutic: It alone exempts him from the dangerous uncertainty in which the apostle finds himself and from which he will not be raised until after having endured death (maybe that's where the judgment lies). In short, in contrast to the apostle, the militant must reassure himself: his personal conversion is acquired by right, because without it the conversion of others would become impossible. The conscious and organized militant speaks and acts as an adult, as one puts it so well, and not as a child of God, hence starting from himself. And acting "in the service of his brethren" confirms it: he can all the more give himself, forget himself, bury himself, and so forth, as he possesses himself, masters himself, and has already settled his own case. A good militant, even a Christian one, has no qualms [*états d'âme*]. And if he has a soul [*âme*] left, he dulls its shooting pains with "spiritual resources."

Consequently, one understands that militancy remains unattainable to the majority of the baptized: It imposes an intense asceticism, implies a mobilization without restriction. But, above all, in its pure state, it openly contradicts the baptized mode of life by challenging its apostolic dependence and by claiming to be finished with conversion. One used to regret that so few of the baptized became good Christian militants—thank goodness. Today one corrects this: while there are few, they are enough to "permeate the human dough"—unfortunately. For the baptized can and should proclaim the Gospel of Christ only as if they were forced to it, with difficulty and almost in spite of themselves. This word that sends them not only does not come from them but contradicts and disqualifies them in the eyes of the world by highlighting their deficiencies. Far from conquering the world and unfolding their "adult" self-importance in it, the baptized proclaim a word that no confirmation can assure. Caught in their own sin, they proclaim Christ first through repudiations, then via procrastinating delays, finally via dangers and efforts, never via the self-satisfaction of a conscious, organized and blasphemous militancy.

2. But then, if such a sketch hits home, despite or because of its caricatural excess, how shall we understand the fact that the model of the militant was able to make the layperson preferred over the baptized? In order to understand this, one has to call on a second characteristic of the layperson; *the ideological doubling of reality*.

Very few laypeople are found among the people of God. They form an elite both by their limited number and by virtue of other very specific characteristics. First, professionalism. Or at least, when we are not talking about the highest leaders of the system, the only ones who are (badly) paid, one finds salaried workers who exercise a professional, remunerated activity toward an end other than itself (that is, maintaining the commitment and/or offering a field for militancy). This professionalism has a consequence: laypeople devote themselves totally to their responsibility in such a way that the daily reality is confused (at least for the best of them) with militant intervention and becomes a field of application for Christian conquest. And, as this "evangelization" does not work without the hermeneutic omnipotence of "the signs of the times," it is necessary that all of daily reality unceasingly confirm, directly or indirectly, the validity of the militant word and of its certain knowledge. As such, a reality that cannot be analyzed becomes unthinkable: it would constitute an unendurable refutation of the militant intention. Between reality and its interpretation no difference remains.

A second distinctive trait of militant elitism adds to the picture: exclusive devotion. Precisely because he devotes himself totally to what becomes *his* cause and *his* ideal, the militant does not maintain any existence outside of the commitment. The assurance that the action requires of him or her is limited to action alone. Outside of it, he renounces any verification, any knowledge, any supposedly neutral references. He "cuts all ties," as one says, with those who, even among the other baptized, do not "share his commitment." Paradoxically, the devotion to certain "others" permits him, at least in the beginning, to exclude multiple other "others" and, if worst comes to worst, to devote himself to others like himself—thus, to himself via the insertion of others. On this narrow basis that exclusive commitment handles for him, militancy thus produces a new reality, the only one it recognizes. A common history shapes a group and allows it, in retrospect and via a suitable reading, to "recognize Christ working in it" (according to the schema of Exodus). In this way a different salvation history emerges, more real than that of reality, just as the chosen community is taken to be more real than the Church.

Together with professionalism and exclusive devotion, a third factor necessarily institutes the ideological doubling of reality: the milieu. We should not dismiss the decisive importance for Catholic Action of its choice in favor of a definition of movements by "milieu" rather than by some other criterion (as an example, not a model, think of the Social Teams). Apart from the fact that one can dispute the privilege thus granted to a sociological criterion (itself at times very hazy—for example, one should examine the diversity of "independent" milieus) within a spiritual undertaking, the primary issue to underscore is the loss of reality that follows from it. Reality is first reduced to what sociology can grasp of it (and is only individualized in this way), and then to a single region of the sociological area. This double impoverishment immediately facilitates the recourse to a privileged ideology. For if the reduction of reality to an object by a method constitutes a science (by limiting it and just as much by validating it), ideology begins when this science finds itself used outside of its limits and conditions of possibility and is at the same time substituted for all the other regional sciences. For reasons directly connected to the model of militancy, as soon as some Christians substituted a counter-reality for reality and, at the same time, in order to act as real militants, needed to ensure their action through an infallible and confirmative knowledge, they had to produce or adopt an ideology. One really must underline that, if certain moments of specialized Catholic Action were and are under the hold of Marxist ideology, this is essentially not because they chose it deliberately. Rather, it is first of all because they understand themselves in accordance with the model of militancy, which inevitably implies the use of an ideology. The sympathy for Marxism results from the choice of militancy, hence from the adoption of a Leninist model, with the imitation of the Bolshevik party. Certainly not all the movements of Catholic Action have adopted a Marxist-influenced ideology. But the most "bourgeois" among them had to produce or adopt an ideology. Even when very weak or inconsistent by dint of "humanism," ideology can be developed with "liberal" themes. For if liberalism does not constitute, as an economic doctrine, an ideology, it becomes one when specialized Catholic Action salvages and improves on it, in the numerous analyses of reality that it is constantly producing. As for the most fanatical anti-Marxism, it has itself borrowed an ideology from the "extreme right" and taken refuge in it: fundamentalist militancy is no less fearsome and deadly than the other, its symmetrical opposite.

A double ideological function for the laity results from this. First, the perversion of the apostolate by militancy comes from an unconscious refusal of the delay of confirmation. The laity becomes the place where an ideology will be able to play its role: assuring an action, reassuring a minority. Indeed, ideology offers to the militant Christian the assurance that he knows the rationality of things, that he can act efficiently on their course, without it being forbidden to him—at least he can believe this—to extract a "Christian meaning" from events. Thus, when the Christian militant feels himself a minority and deprived of assurance at the very moment when his intention to "evangelize" seems most to require it, he appeals to the ideology most apt to furnish him with a borrowed assurance for his discourse and a comforting belonging to the majority of his "milieu." Majority membership probably remains at base inversely proportional to the assurance of a specific discourse. But a compromise is better than the double trial of a total loss of assurance and an absolute marginalization. Ideology reassures the Christian—in this way, the apostle becomes a militant. Here the laity is the place where the Church risks giving in to ideology, that is to say, to what is most mundane within the world: the absolute assurance of man by himself, with no regard for reality.

This contempt for reality indicates the second ideological function of the laity: it permits the clerics to reassure themselves. The cleric, in fact, whether bishop or priest, undergoes an even greater trial than the baptized: economic and social marginalization are added to the strangeness of being Christian (the cleric does not produce and thus is close to nonexistent for modern society). He is therefore subject to the doubled temptation of ensuring the success of his word by himself, in order thus to avoid the test of the delay of the confirmation. If the cleric gives in to this great temptation, he goes in search of an assurance for his pastoral ministry. Where can he find it almost without fail? Precisely there where the Christian's discipleship has disappeared to the benefit of ideological assurance: with the lay militant. We must not tone down the strange seduction that the layperson can exert on the cleric, whether voluntarily or not. For there is a link of mimetic rivalry between them. The panic-stricken cleric recognizes in the militant layperson the least good of what he is and the best of what he believes he must be. The least good: the sought-for marginality (professionalism, exclusive devotion, etc.), in short, a marginalization almost as great as his own; but also the best: assurance of a knowledge that authorizes the tactics and justifies the results, without delay in the confirmation. The credit so easily given to those who claim to be lay, militant, engaged, adult people, and so on comes from this. Obviously, it is a matter here of a bizarre cult of raw effectiveness, supposedly self-justifying by virtue of this fact alone. "Scientific" competence, youth (or its relative semblance), and femininity become acceptable means for reassuring oneself: "What I have doubts about is true after all, because those successful people believe it." The militant layperson thus becomes something like a living lie, or at least runs the risk of becoming one, in a doubled fashion. First, because he unfolds an ideological certainty, in the name of his practice or knowledge, which forbids him from playing the apostolic role of the baptized person. Then, because he lends himself to the game of enabling the clerics to imitate his own lie, he makes them believe, or worse, allows them to persuade themselves that "faith has a future" because he (and others like him) proves this triumphantly through his fragile but decisive "presence in the world."

Of course no one, neither the layperson sure of his or her militancy nor the somewhat reassured cleric, raises the real question, which, to be specific, is not the cynical (and in fact naïve) query: Are you representative? Are you numerous in your certainty? For such questions always aim at reassuring oneself about the assurance offered, and hence at reinforcing the prestige of assurance and thereby the danger of militancy and the denial of discipleship. The truly formidable question would ask whether one should substitute any sort of assurance for discipleship. Even more, does not this imported assurance (of practice or of knowledge) conceal the properly Christian reality of conversion and of testimony, equally linked in the logic of the Cross? For ideology, when it introduces the appearance of a reality and of a rationality, perhaps satisfies the need for assurance but closes off, maybe just as definitively, access to the ultimate level of reality: death and resurrection, in the trinitarian play of filiation. Wouldn't the militant layperson's job be to hide from himself as well as from the cleric whom he seduces the fact that no one becomes Christian except through the imitation of Christ?

3. It now becomes easier to understand why the laity arises from an excess of *clericalism*: the layperson first of all serves the cleric. Besides, who most often disputes the decisive role that the ecclesiastical apparatus is inclined to acknowledge for him? The baptized who are not amenable to the model of militancy. Who usually takes on the defense of the militant layperson challenged in this way? Some cleric. There is no paradox here: militant laity assure for many clerics an assured and reassuring relation to the world, the only one they have and desire. That this elite only represents a small minority of baptized people matters little to the clerics who regard them as a prophetic avant-garde—in short, the reality of the future, which grants exemption from grappling with today's reality. Certain clerics do not place themselves outside of the world (like monks, those nonclerical baptized), but surround themselves with an extended, albeit tear-resistant, film of militant laypeople who take their place as substitute for the real world, as an individual and portable world, we might say, the only one that conforms to their vows. The cleric is anyway often tempted to choose laypeople in his own image. He fashions them into a privileged community and will put his trust in its exemplary authority as soon as some bishop, some colleague, or some assembly of "other" baptized people contests him, or even as soon as the profane world disappoints his assurances. Thus it is that there are clerics who serve militant laypeople: the latter assure them a grasp of a (false) reality, and in turn receive the assurance that they constitute the (true) people of God, while together they

invoke the witness of the future when the pressure of the real becomes too heavy.

What has come to be called the "promotion of the laity" confirms this mimetic dependence. To the militant, the cleric offers what he himself considers to be his authority and his power, but by adapting it to the model of the layperson, which he, as cleric, imposes on the baptized. Curiously, he nevertheless does not acknowledge a complete equality between himself and the layperson, and does not consider other means of bestowing it on the layperson except by assimilating him to himself, that is to say, by imposing clericalism in its highest degree as a universal model. But simultaneously, the cleric judges his own role to be insufficient and only transmits it to the layperson via this insufficiency, as if to abandon the responsibility for it to him. From this comes the pretension of transmitting the presbyteral priesthood to any layperson, but in the devalued form of a simple function, without the [sacramental] character or celibacy. From this stems the delegating of presiding over the Eucharist, but a Eucharist that is entirely relational, one of intention, symbolic, and so forth. From this comes also the admission of laypeople to a theological "science," official but without dogmatic authority or precise outlet, and so on. In short, the "promotion of the laity" presupposes that the laity must be promoted somewhere in order finally to become fully Christian, as if baptism were not sufficient for this. Clericalism triumphs at the very moment that it abolishes itself. And it does so in three ways:

(a) If the baptized person is still lacking some dignity in order to become truly Christian, it is because the cleric has a factual superiority over the baptized, even if only in the form of powers to share and functions to redistribute. The interpretation of the Church on the basis of power and its exercise hence becomes strongly confirmed by the very people who presuppose it so as to combat it and in this way exercise a (counter-)power. The dispute over clerical power is, since Ockham, a clerical specialty. The laity (the emperor, the proletariat, or what have you) only form a mass operation, a militant rank and file.

(b) The "promotion of the laity" envisions redistributing what is explicitly considered a privilege (presbyteral priesthood) only by devaluing it. This indicates that, besides the heaviness of the political model that rules this ecclesiology, the layperson actually only finds himself "promoted" by appearing like the cleric: he remains powerless to administer the sacraments fully (the Eucharist debased to a brotherly feast and penance on the wane, to mention just the two most frequent sacraments in the life of the baptized). Perhaps a harsh word is not entirely out of place here: this "promotion" can be understood in a basely commercial sense, comparable to a fire sale on luxury goods.

(c) Above all, by broadening the ever less numerous staff, the "promotion of the laity" allows the cleric to pass on his model, by transferring it to a new population. The clerical state outlives the clerics by means of the laity. And clericalism can, in fact, outlive the Church. In a sense, it can only grow if the Church diminishes; for clericalism lives on marginalization, and the Church on evangelization.

The Communion of Priesthoods

The militant thus appears when the baptized no longer understands himself. But because the baptized listens to his pastor of his own accord, his perversion into a militant comes to him from elsewhere, namely from the cleric. But from where does the cleric come? Probably from a lack of understanding of the priest. If clericalism remains the enemy—the enemy of the Church, of course—it is because it gives rise to a double perversion: the priesthood of the baptized turns into the militancy of the laity, and the presbyteral priesthood turns into clerical power. The restoration of the specific dignity of the baptized without a doubt must proceed via the theological determination of the organic connection between the two kinds of priesthood. Let us attempt an outline of them. But first, let us examine two objections, incidentally grounded in the same confusion, which forbid any but an antagonistic approach to the link between the two kinds of priesthood.

1. The first obstacle consists in thinking the baptismal priesthood an inferior imitation of the presbyteral priesthood, and/or as the simple point of departure for an initiation. In fact, imitation and initiation (with their antagonistic or "promotional" variants) both assume that the baptismal priesthood keeps expecting a greater dignity—when in fact it would be enough that its eminent dignity be recognized. The baptismal priesthood truly has no need for a supplementary trait of which the presbyteral priesthood would rob it (or would eventually grant it). In the face of such demagogical trivialities, two theses are necessary, paradoxical in appearance, but also in reality:

(a) The baptismal priesthood is founded on Christ. Its perfection, like that of Christ, has no lack and requires no "promotion."

(b) The presbyteral priesthood is irreducible to and distinct from the baptismal priesthood only by essence not by degree (*Lumen gentium*, §10), only as a service that enables the baptized to exercise their royal priesthood. The functional distinction of the presbyteral priesthood is required by the absolute perfection of the baptismal priesthood itself.

In fact, priesthood results for the Christian from his baptism, which bestows it on him in absolute fashion. The Christian becomes priest because he is chosen (1 Pet. 2:9). For baptism incorporates us, carnally because spiritually, into Him in whom the divinity took a body, Christ. Yet, ever since Christ, all priestly functions have become null and void before the sole possible and real priest. The only priest that God allows between Himself and humans is the God made man (Heb. 8:1–2). The priestly game (election, alliance, sacrifice) is played forever between the two wills of Christ, the human will abandoned to the divine will, and the divine will returning the human will to itself by giving it an infinite freedom. Everything plays out corporeally (that is to say, also in "reality," according to the play on words in Col. 2:17) in the body of Christ, who alone can speak Psalm 40:7 and 9: "You have wanted neither sacrifice nor oblation, but you have made for me a body. . . . Hence I say: 'See, I come, for it is me who is in question in the scroll of the book, in order to do your will, oh God'" (cited according to the Septuagint in Heb. 10:5–8). Since Christ, the only priesthood that remains is the one he was able to offer as a "rational worship" (Rom. 12:1: *logikēn latreian*), that is to say, an offering and a reverence conforming to the *logos*, the one that forms us into the image and likeness of the *Logos* himself, "come to pitch his tent among us" (John 1:14). This sacrifice puts into play what in the human is most intimately close to God, his decision-making power. Christ's priesthood consists in only a single act: to accomplish the will of the Father. In short, to be converted. Thus, if we are incorporated into the reality of Christ by baptism (Gal. 3:27) and if Christ, "whom we have loved, washed in his blood our sins and has made us a royalty and priests for God, his Father" (Rev. 1:6, 5:10 and 20:6), then our sole and unique priesthood can be summarized in a single word: to be converted ourselves. The baptismal priesthood begins, reaches its peak, and is completed in the conversion of the baptized to the Father, in the figure of Christ as archetype, and thanks to the "Spirit of holiness" (Rom. 1:1). The baptized exercise their full priesthood by making sense of their baptism in themselves—by being converted (Acts 2:37–38).

Converting ourselves means to convert everything to God, our will as much as the entire world. That is the only thing we have to do, and any other requirement would merely be its consequence or be taken as a useless precept: What could be added to the fullness of conversion? Any addition would risk emptying it of any substance by specializing it cheaply. If one says in advance that converting oneself means first of all doing or saying something or other, one implicitly limits conversion to being only something or other. Yet what is proper to conversion is that it does not have any limit, unless one wants to impose some precise pharisaical norm that would substitute a "human precept" (Matt. 15:1–9) for the divine demand: The apparent requirements of this precept would allow one to provide oneself with a good conscience by condemning the other believers. But conversion is characterized by the universality of its insistence: the conversion of everything—in me, in us, and in the world—to the Father, in the Son, through the Spirit. The baptismal priesthood displays its royalty in this single task, which merges with that of Christ and is confirmed in it: recapitulating all things in Him (Eph. 1:10; 1 Cor. 15:28). It is a matter of making the liturgy cosmic by being converted to the point of also converting the world. As the Church only constitutes the progress of this conversion across ages and cultures, nothing surpasses the eminent and royal dignity of the baptismal priesthood within the Church they form, a priesthood that owes nothing to anyone except to Christ.

2. Here, according to the false oppositions that raise inevitably endless debates (because they are without real theological stakes), a second objection yields its misinterpretation without fail: Does not the acknowledged primacy of the baptismal priesthood, as its immediate consequence, make the presbyteral priesthood useless? Does not its humiliating and imperialist function as an obligatory intermediary, far from opening the baptized Christian to Christ, block any direct access to his human and divine Brother, and in short annul the filial adoption through a hierarchical subjection and deny the "freedom of the children of God" through a cultural constraint?

Exactly the opposite is true, as becomes obvious as soon as one stops giving a clerical interpretation to the presbyteral priesthood—a translation into clerical terms, that is to say, into power (which is to be abolished, probably in order better to maintain its model). For if the baptismal priesthood constitutes the first and foremost task of the Church, it is only valid in Christ, only as an infinite incorporation of individual (hence also communal) conversions into the initial and unique conversion of Christ himself to the Father in the Spirit. The baptismal priesthood can only be royally unfolded on one condition: that Christ would be present among those gathered in his name, that they would really gather *in* his Name. That is what one must understand as concretely, as humanly, as little "spiritually" as possible (for heresy, even disguised under the term of incarnation, always remains docetic). It is necessary for someone to call together the priestly people in the Name of Christ because it is precisely this summoning that elects it as priestly. But this man would lie and deceive the community as much about himself (self-idolatry) as about itself (corrupted into a cult), if he were to call it together in his own name. As it happens his name is radically inappropriate. Examples abound all around us of the kind of corruption that destroys a whole community called together only by a man: it is ruined by the two usual tools of the power relation, namely, violence and sexuality. In order for the royal priesthood of the baptized to become possible, it would accordingly be absolutely required that a man (Rom. 10:17) call together the community, but a man who does not speak in his own inappropriate name but who speaks instead in the name of the Name, in order to "proclaim in the Name (of Christ) the conversion in order to release us from our sins" (Luke 24:47)—an individual and concrete man, who speaks in the name of another, in the Name of the Other: *in persona Christi*, who holds the place of Christ and incarnates it anew, in order to allow all to become priests in a royal fashion. This man is called the priest. He is such only so that the community can exercise the baptismal priesthood in its unparalleled splendor.

To repeat that the priest is at the service of the community says one thing and one thing only: by presenting himself *in persona Christi*, as "servant of the servants of God," he renders the community the eminent service of making it priestly inasmuch as it is baptismal. The more the priest gives himself, the less he exercises any "power." The more he agrees to being only his function and being completely summed up within it, the more he abolishes his personality *in persona Christi* and the more he stresses the royal splendor of the baptismal priesthood—by making it real and therefore possible. The rest is only chatter, that is to say, a smokescreen that (badly) hides the lie of the collapse and kills the baptized by depriving them of their unique dignity as brothers of Christ. What is left is just the masses without baptismal priesthood, to whom the clerics and the "promoted" laypeople will devote themselves in order to assure their *leadership*,[3] no longer knowing them as friends but as inferiors, condemned to a passive subservience.

Baptism is an inalienable mark, which transforms those who receive it—it is a *character*, an indelible and structuring stamp, to the point of forming a royal priesthood. The brilliant, fixed and definitive doctrine of the Council of Trent established that the presbyteral priesthood, in order to fill its unique and exclusive role of serving as the condition of possibility for the baptismal priesthood, must be a stamp that is indelible and structuring (*character*) of the man who, by receiving it, would henceforth live *in persona Christi*.[4] By disputing that the presbyteral priesthood is valid as *character*, one certainly puts into question that the baptismal priesthood in whose service it finds itself and without which it is not possible, is likewise valid as a *character*. The priest who fails to recognize what he is despises in himself not only the sacrament of holy orders but also and above all the sacrament of baptism in all the faithful. Not only does he kill himself (which is, after all, his right) but he kills (which is not his right) those he thus deprives of their priesthood. Not only does he grieve the Spirit in himself but he also suffocates those whom he no longer allows to receive the Spirit necessary for conversion.

Without a doubt, the identity crisis of the presbyteral priesthood must not call for any condemnation of specific persons, for the baptized person recognizes neither its rigor, nor its stakes, nor its difficulty. But the mortal danger involved must also be recognized. With the identity of the presbyteral priesthood, much more is at stake than the human equilibrium of some individual or other; the same is true for the baptismal priesthood. Must this be stressed? Far beyond the symptoms, such as liturgical deficiency, intellectual weakness, prevailing unbelief, and so forth, the prodigiously fast disaffection of the baptized for religious practice has no deeper reason than the suspicion (whether justified or not, it is certainly not my place to judge) that the presbyteral priesthood has impugned its *character*, and thus its service, and thus the baptismal priesthood. This shrinking of the presbyteral priesthood (or what has been able to appear as such) would constitute, moreover, a masterwork of clericalism: it forbids the baptized to exercise their royal priesthood and subjugates them by scorning them, as simple militants, employed to ensure a faltering power, at the risk of losing themselves. There are lost believers, who are much more dangerous, humiliated, deceived, and wounded than lost soldiers. The Church in France was able to notice it with fuss and (most probably) loss.[5] Maybe it still needs to understand why it must suffer from it and where the real responsibility is to be found.

3. Henceforth the two arguments put forward can be assembled into a single paradox: The more the baptized exercise their priesthood in a royal manner, the more the presbyteral priesthood, which makes the priesthood of the baptized possible, must be affirmed. Far from the growth of one implying the degeneration of the other, the two grow together. Conversely, if the royal priesthood claims to put itself into action alone, it collapses into the "promotion of the laity" and becomes supremely clericalized. And if the presbyteral priesthood asserts its role unilaterally, it immediately turns into a clericalism that is not even ashamed. That both grow together means that their respective identities are reinforced by their communion: distinction alone unites them; union alone authorizes recognition.

Distance appears here also, as it does everywhere where the Trinity functions as hermeneutic model. Concretely the paradox requires definitively renouncing the mimetic pair cleric and laity, in order to reach the communion of the bishop with the baptized. It is not only true that "where the bishop is, there is the Church," but the Church resides *in* its bishop. Any mediating body (even the presbytery, certainly the elite of the laity, a fortiori the screen of national secretariats) must continuously and, if possible of itself, be refined, become invisible (and not "transparent," which instead in clerical or lay language means a self-satisfaction at becoming immediately "the face of Christ for others"). If the communion of the two priesthoods must appear explicitly as the communion of the baptized in Christ, it is first necessary that the bishop fully take on his Christlike role and hence begin by understanding and accepting it. Then it is necessary that the hierarchy be understood in its sole theologically correct sense (such as Dionysius the mystic defined it) as immediate mediation. Finally, it is necessary that the baptized demand unceasingly from the Church the only thing that it committed itself on the day of their baptism to give them: faith and eternal life. And that means that the baptized have to understand that no role has more dignity than the royal priesthood, whose whole office consists solely in complete conversion, for oneself and thus for the world.

The Bishop and the Baptized

Now that the theological link between the bishop and the baptized begins to filter through as the concrete figure of communion of service between the two kinds of priesthood, we must still (as positively as possible) go back to the initial question: the proper role of baptized Christians who are not ordained to the presbyteral priesthood. The Second Vatican Council gave a response that is worth taking seriously: "But the laity, by their very vocation, seek the kingdom of God by engaging in temporal affairs and by ordering them according to the plan of God" (*Lumen gentium*, §31). And then, "*as those everywhere who adore in holy activity, the laity consecrate the world itself to God*" (*Lumen gentium*, §34). Two arguments appear clearly here. On the one hand, the consecration of temporal realities, that is to say, the reality of the world itself with its weightiness. The proper office of the baptismal priesthood is the full conversion of the self and the world. And on the other hand, the chronological rule is applied here that nothing is redeemed that had not already been assumed. The baptized cannot convert anything to the Father, in Christ, through the Spirit that they have not known, taken responsibility for, and modified. That is the management of temporal things.

    1. One must clear up a misunderstanding here: The world where the baptized person lives has nothing to do with a unique and homogenous "milieu." A Christian finds himself at the intersection of several "milieus,"

indeed of several cultures that are contemporaneous within him, like parallel or successive lives. In short, he is always in the midst [*au milieu*] of several "milieus." Certainly he always fits into a situation that is determined, contingent, limited, in a word, unique. But the set of determinations that weigh on him (such and such a culture, such and such a history, such and such a character, such and such a profession, such and such a political option, and on top of everything, such and such a wife, such and such a husband, such and such children) impose his identity in the world on him in a manner that is as heterogeneous as it is restrictive. What's more, the conflict in him is permanent and visible not only in the complex identity that the world imposes on him, but also and especially between this identity and the identity of the baptized that Christ's election gives him. In order to remain, that is, to become a Christian, the baptized must be converted. Yet as he comprehends in himself indissolubly everything that is not identical with him but conditions him such that, precisely, even what is not him is as profoundly him as he is, he can only be converted by converting also and just as much what makes him. Being converted becomes only vaguely possible by converting if not the world, then at least the most narrow circle of this world (the cultural *Umwelt* [environment]).

This remark first has the consequence of rendering useless the dilemma between evangelization and human promotion. But more profoundly, it implies that the baptized person only lives limit-cases—or even better, that he lives at the limit, at what separates the world from Christ. In living "at the limit" the baptized person is not necessarily marginalized, for the limit offers precisely the encounter of two realities, their overlap, their confrontation, their orientation. Inasmuch as the baptized person dwells in uncertainty, he lives at the boundary of the Church and occupies its borderlands [*en occupe les marches*]. Thus in some sense he commits only himself. Without doubt, in investing his faith, he also involves the entire Church. But, his situation being decidedly unique, limited, and representative of itself only (anyway, this is more than enough for him), he knows that he neither can nor should commit the Church as such. He knows himself irretrievably responsible for his share of reality and for his Christian election, but he does not recognize himself charged with any "mandate." The only mandate that motivates the baptized person is given by his baptism. The decree of Vatican II on the apostolate of the laity (*Apostolicam actuositatem*, §24) says it well: the mandate only sanctions "*certain* forms of the apostolate of the laity," namely, those that are collective or representative in an exceptional way. If the authority of a bishop turns to asking a baptized person to intensify the commitment of his baptism by a responsibility in the name of the Church, he will obviously accept. But he will experience this dignity as a burden and, far from adapting to it, will hope for its end. As for laying claim to such a representativeness on his own or from his fellow baptized, he will only be able to see in it an incongruous adaptation of a political or management model to the Church and a complete lack of understanding of the theological concept of the apostolate.

The absence of any mandate and the renunciation of representativeness follow from the constitutive particularity of the baptized that alone allows him to convert the world in himself. In contrast, the specificity of the apostolate of the bishop (and hence of the presbyteral priesthood) begins from itself. Where the bishop is, acts, and speaks, there the Church as such is present, acts, and speaks. For the bishop realizes the only necessary and sufficient condition for the Church to be born, by calling it together *in persona Christi* in the Name. A surprising consequence ensues from this: The bishop (and hence the priest whom he takes on) can evangelize with infinitely more authority than the baptized. To the contrary of what the model of militancy would suggest, it is the bishop (and his presbytery) who can make a decisive breakthrough in one go, open up a territory that the rank and file of the baptized, patient infantry, and queen of conversions, will slowly and heavily (because loaded down with *impedimenta*) come to occupy. Under our very eyes, the bishop of Rome exerts himself in this way, putting himself on the line. And the baptized will not fail him.

2. The baptized only converts the world in himself inasmuch as he assumes it in all its risks and perils. From this results the terrible slowness of his conversion, precisely because it converts a reality. Thus an essential function of the baptismal priesthood emerges: the reality, on which he can only work by incorporating it, imposes on him the passage of time, teaches him patience, accustoms him to failure. When he endures it, he is removed from ideology and from what the ravings of interpretation attempt to mask: that the confirmation always arrives with a properly eschatological delay, that conversion never ends, in short, that the event comes to us like the "day and the hour" of the Father and only of the Father. The baptized always walks too slowly, dragging his feet in the mud. But the mud is reality. And he can only walk toward Christ by bringing reality to him on the soles of his shoes. The baptized has no plan of evangelization except the daily effort and his uncertain asceticism, no goal or time limit other than his very life (which will only last the time that he will need to convert the part of the world that is in him). Encamped without cease at the front of conversion, he has long understood that all the analyses, methods, tactics, and other teaching skills will only be able to modify reality by passing through the ordeal of the confession of faith, the putting into

operation of charity and the patience of hope, that is to say, through the conversion of individuals. The baptized knows only one effective tool for the conversion of the world: his soul and that of his brothers—souls, flesh for conversion. For him, who only has one soul, the primary urgency consists in converting it, while knowing very well that he will not manage this himself neither while he is alive nor on his own, but by grace and through a common (taking) charge. Besides, what would an appeal to conversion of the other mean, when one knows well that one's own is barely sketched?

Thus the baptized hardly appreciates the bitter reproach of not having taken upon himself responsibilities, as remote as they are general (wars, crises, earthquakes, etc.), before which he is helpless most of the time. He also does not appreciate the refusal of urgent, efficacious, and free help for which, in order to persevere in conversion, he feels and knows the need for what is his due in the world: the Word and the Bread. From the presbyteral priesthood he expects neither "promotion," mandate, nor excuse, but the spiritual means for his work on reality (which he knows to be spiritual through experience). If the baptized in fact hardly enjoy hearing the world discussed from the pulpit, that is not first of all because the discourse is incompetent or partial (as is bound to happen), but because they constantly suffer everywhere else from the din of the world and because they die if they do not hear the Word. The baptized expect from the presbyteral priesthood one single but considerable thing: to be continually re-incorporated into the body of Christ so that they can then tangentially incorporate the world into him.

3. The conversion of the world through the conversion of self requires assuming the absolute contingency and the weightiness of reality. It also implies, together with responsibility (which is happily acknowledged for the laity), its obligatory correlate: the right to error (which is not often granted to the baptized). It seems strange that the praises of pluralism, the calls to audacity, and the encouragement to initiative are offset by the often pitiless indictment in front of scandals and (undeniable) injustices in which all Christians without exception bear their share of culpability. This is in fact only an apparent contradiction, because often the cleric, by delegating (formally or not) his responsibility to the militant layperson, makes him take (or encourages him to take) the risks that are really those of the priestly office. Yet as we have seen, the Church only takes a stand in reality as such through the bishop who, in this act, cannot and should not delegate what he alone, by his *character*, is in a position to do. The baptized person also cannot and should not act except according to his priesthood, that is to say, in order to convert the world in himself. His word and his action are only worth as much as this conversion, of which they also mark

the curve. That curve can sometimes drop to the point of betrayal. But, besides the fact that no failure is ever irreparable, neither does this error of the baptized ever affect the truth of Christ. It only reveals the (provisional) limits of an initiative of conversion. Error marks the Christian as inevitably as sin, but no more than it. The baptized, because he converts a part of reality in himself, is subject to error. He should not to be blamed with self-satisfaction by those who, whether voluntarily or not, do not maintain the same connection with reality. For reality, contingency, implies error.

The baptized who makes mistakes has the strict right to instruction, and to not be hastily found guilty of sin. This is different for the bishop, who as such must speak only with authority because he expresses himself *in persona Christi* and has in this condition no right to error. Or rather, while for the baptized error is not always a sin, for the bishop error is always a sin, and not the least. For the truth concerned here has as its property the power to give life. Thus, if it is corrupted, it has the power of letting die, even of killing directly. That has been seen. A final consequence results from this, which also seems quite surprising: if the baptized demand acknowledgment of a quasi-institutional right to error, any "theological" discoursing [*prise de parole "théologique"*] by clericalized laity (in the name of what is supposedly obvious in a pastoral, scientific, or other sense) can only give rise to distrust. In exchange, if one might thus present a new demand, the baptized wishes (without daring to lay claim to it) that the revealed Word be said and repeated to him in such a way that he would be able to live by it and exercise his priesthood in a royal manner. That means that the words of the bishop are almost infallibly modeled on the true Word [*Parole*] who is the Word [*Verbe*], the only exegete of the Father (John 1:18) and only hermeneut of what is said of him in the Scriptures (Luke 24:27). Without doubt the task allocated in this way to the presbyteral priesthood surpasses human strength. But is that not also true for the conversion of the world entrusted to the baptized as their royal priesthood?

For if the role of the baptized must increase in the Church, it will always be due only to the growth of the dignity of the bishop. But, in truth, who does not know this?

5

The Service of Rationality in the Church

I

To wonder about the role and history of the Catholic intellectual today—this undertaking seems to go without saying, it even seems trite. Yet instead, it should appear highly problematic because it presupposes at least two terms that have become highly questionable and fragile, if not obsolete.

First, the very term "intellectual": its reputed fading away keeps the newspapers and the essayists fairly busy. For once they are not wrong to note this as an established fact. But they are wrong to be in despair over it. For the "intellectual" as the one whose model strictly speaking extends from Voltaire to Sartre, reaching its peak in Hugo, rested on two principles, which are as simple as they are questionable today. First the principle that a noted competence in a specific field of knowledge or of the arts confers authority to make decisions in lots of others, indeed in all the realms of thought. The Cartesian doctrine of the unity of the sciences in the single "human wisdom" taken as "universal" thus found its continuation in a supposed right to speak, in the name of a science one has (at least partially) mastered, about other realms of knowledge about which one knows (almost) nothing. The principal victims of this drift in Cartesianism are ethics and philosophy, even religion, with which a great many respected physicists, astrophysicists, or biologists believe themselves authorized to deal authoritatively, whether for relaxation or for pleasure. The principal authority invoked is any exact science whatsoever, provided it enjoys the prestige of the moment. One could here speak of a principle of universalization of the right of competence.

After this there follows the principle that the supposedly universal competence in the realm of knowledge would suffice for (or even force) decisions in the realm of politics. This is a matter of one order being transgressed by another, to take Pascal's thematic up again: the authority in the order of minds, far from being satisfied with confining itself to this second order, therefore assumes the right to intervene in the order of bodies, of politics, and of the regulation of morals. The transgression is thus doubled: first from a particular knowing to a universal knowing, then from knowing as such to political decision making. This model can easily be distorted—it would be enough to know almost nothing in a realm sufficiently inaccessible to the unsuspecting public, in order to make them admit a real political and moral authority for someone who, under the ambiguous title of "intellectual" actually drops to the rank of a simple enthusiast. Without going to the point of caricature, one sees well that here the petitioner inherits (with what devaluation!) the Platonic model of a philosopher-king, or, by default, of a king-philosopher. The intermediary figures were the Christian king, then the enlightened despot, resulting either in the "scientific" revolutionary militant or the protesting militant (who, as in the case of the ecologist, always lays claim to a scientific backing). In the two cases, knowledge must decide.

These two principles, which legitimate the figure of the "intellectual," result directly from the history of metaphysics (universality of knowledge, therefore unity of sciences, transgression of the orders by the philosopher-king). They hence also follow its destiny: for inasmuch as metaphysics is fulfilled in nihilism, so these principles are also disclosed as such, are devalued, and, for that very reason, become obsolete. The model of the "intellectual" can only last in a strictly metaphysical scheme. As soon as suspicion falls on the unity of reason and on the rationality of politics, the "intellectual" is eclipsed. This is the case today. Sartre was first of all not only the last of the "intellectuals," but also the first to trace their decline, slowly and with clarity. Without doubt one must abandon the model of the "intellectual," on which other, more modest and less noxious attitudes already follow: a specialist competent in a particular field, who does not claim any authority beyond it, but in the other realms yields to the universal ethic, to which he or she at times tries to be connected via the mediation of a regional ethics, of a theory of decision, and so forth. Besides, if the return of ethics has been able to lay itself out (or make itself heard) with this much force, it was probably because it was opposed in this way to the figure of the "intellectual" and took over from it. Henceforth, the ethics proper to those who follow after the "intellectuals" could well be summarized in this way: only to speak of what one really knows, thus to speak little, and, for what remains, simply to follow morality—in short, a kind of "provisional moral code." Let us thus no longer concern ourselves with "intellectuals."

II

Yet when a term like "intellectual" is joined to the adjective "Catholic," the resulting term becomes even more problematic. Several primarily historical reasons explain this fragility of the very notion of the "Catholic intellectual." The first goes without saying: in France, the Catholic Church having witnessed the party of "intellectuals" (e.g., Jansenism and the Enlightenment thinkers, etc.) arrayed against it had no immediate reason for admitting their legitimacy or utility. But there is more: the Catholic Church not only mistrusted "intellectuals" who attacked it from the outside, but almost more so those who defended it from the interior. In most cases, the Church either did not understand, support, or even recognize them; or it preferred shallow journalists, limited hacks, or apologists without imagination. In short, better Louis Veuillot or Augustin Bonnety than Chateaubriand, Verlaine, Bloy, or Bernanos. A study of these quasi-official lay thinkers active in the French Catholic press during the last hundred years could be made—and the results would be cruel. In other cases, explicit condemnation took over from misunderstanding and indifference. It can never be stressed enough how the modernist crisis (that other "Dreyfus Affair," but specific to the Church) and the response that was given to it—both growing together in a shared blindness—played no small part in strengthening a mimetic antagonism between "faith" and "reason." This cold war, where each gained a certain tranquility at the prize of a certain isolation, has profoundly marked the "Catholic intellectual" with the suspicion of a weak faith, already worn down by doubt, marked by the fraud of insufficient prayer or commitment, and so forth. These factors underlined a fundamental conviction: Faith manages easily enough without theology and philosophy, which the pastoral replaces very well with words of a simple nature. Traditionalism and "progressivism" equally admire these presuppositions, either by celebrating "the perennial faith" or by glorifying the Catholic Action militant. In any case, one cannot deny that, even today, intellectual research and the apostolate of intelligence by intelligence remain, by far, the poor parents of the French Catholic Church: Neither encouraged nor developed, they are almost never even mentioned in the declarations of the Conference of Bishops. Thus it goes without saying that intelligence and "intellectuals" at best indicate problems to confront but never offer any solutions, any chances, or any forces of evangelization. The "intellectuals" do not even enjoy, within the Church, the lot, albeit limited, available to them within the PCF [French Communist Party]—that of "intellectual workers," indispensable albeit marginal. From this there follows the quite appalling reign of these products of substitution for a pastoral initiative of intelligence by intelligence, namely, "statements" and press campaigns. In short, if the Church has lacked or still lacks "intellectuals," or what I would rather call authorities in the order of knowledge, it is because it has never looked for them nor desired them. Let us thus no longer concern ourselves with the "Catholic intellectual."

III

Even so, we must concern ourselves with "Catholic intellectuals" because they exist, even if there is no rigorous concept for them. How shall we define what stands out generally and without concept as a "Catholic intellectual"? What action permits us to enter for sure into this narrow sociological population? For the case of the "intellectual" in general, we have suggested that it had to do with taking a political stance on the functioning of society (often but not always critical) by virtue of a limited (at least presumed) intellectual competence. By analogy, one will define as a "Catholic intellectual" someone who, by virtue of a limited (or at least presumed) intellectual competence takes a stand on the functioning of the Church. This taking a stand is in the immense majority of cases and for structural reasons overwhelmingly critical. Nevertheless, let me underline strongly that this criticism can come with equal violence from "traditionalists" and "progressives." What matters is not the orientation of the critique toward the Church—and first of all toward the episcopate or the papacy—but its sharpness, indeed its intransigence. Without doubt, most often one claims to intervene in the name of the "people of God" or of the "tradition" or the "poor" or the "eternal Mass." Likewise, one most often pretends to intervene in spite of oneself, in spite of one's great modesty, in spite of one's status as a private person, by exposing oneself obviously unwillingly and courageously to a great risk of scandal and disapproval, even of censure, by assuming nothing less than the role of "prophet," and so forth. By what right does one self-proclaim oneself a "prophet"? By the right given by the "Spirit," the "truth," "dialogue," and so on. Thus the need to have available one of the many vague theologies of the Holy Spirit that free the charisms from any obedience and guarantee a sedevacantism generalized to all the levels of the apostolic structure of the Church. In short, one would become a Catholic intellectual on the necessary and sufficient condition of publicly denigrating the Catholic Church and of claiming to do so for its own good.

Doubtless, this description of the "Catholic intellectual" by analogy with the definition of the "intellectual" in general is something of a caricature. But, perhaps one would grant that it is a quite recognizable caricature. And at least the author of these lines recognizes himself there first of all. Anyway, what is surprising about the aptness of such a definition? The intellectual can speak and knows how to argue; why would he not criticize the Church, either because it deserves it (*semper reformanda*), or, at least as often, because it does not deserve it while we do deserve it, so that we blame the Church for *this* very thing—that *we* ought to reform ourselves, and that *above all* we do not want to do so? There is certainly nothing scandalous about criticizing the Church and every Christian can denounce the Church's sin. All the more so because in many cases for a Catholic to attack the Church amounts to practicing self-critique. But—and this is the whole question—in order to act as a Christian or especially as a Catholic intellectual, it is not enough to denounce the sins of the Church: one must also confess one's own sins, so as to reform the Church already through one's personal conversion. For what reforms the Church are neither posted theses, nor pamphlets, nor petitions, nor "critical" or "faithful" movements, but the holiness of each Christian, who asks the Spirit each day to reform the part of the Church that abides in him, that is to say, to ask for the conversion of his heart. Thus what the Catholic intellectual ignores is that the Church only lives from holiness. In analogy to the lay intellectual, he plays only in the first two orders, that of the mind (intelligence) and of the flesh (politics), knowing next to nothing of the third order (charity), which should, however, offer him the proper realm. Only saints reform the Church, because they love it, while the Catholic intellectual does not love it, at times even hates it. But in order to love the Church, *mater et magistra*, one also must love, period. Yet only life in Christ that is, for us baptized, life in the Church teaches us to love. Therefore to love the Church one must remain in it, and in order to remain in it one must love it: this hermeneutic circle forbids the leap out of the Church, a leap that, by allowing for criticizing it like a stranger or an enemy, alone establishes the Catholic intellectual.

IV

Have we then in this way finished with the "Catholic intellectual"? Most probably, but only in a negative mode. We would still have to define in a positive way the function that this ambiguous phrase conceals or corrupts. How shall we proceed? By ceasing to think of this still anonymous function on the basis of an originally sociological model, alien to any theology: precisely that of the "intellectual." One would have to start from an indisputable ecclesiological situation so as to reach a correct theological concept of what would have to replace "Catholic intellectual." The point of departure remains the baptized (inasmuch as he is opposed to the ambiguous and imprecise concept of the "lay" person). The baptized live, or at least can live, the fullness of the imitation of Christ through the sacraments; they receive them in the Church within which they are integrated, without any reservation other than their sins. To accomplish such a sanctification, the baptized hence have no need for new institutional or sacramental powers in the Church, for the simple reason that the Church, through Baptism (filiation of the Father), the Spirit, and the Eucharist (body and blood of the Son), gives them the totality of Christ's trinitarian life. Accordingly, the baptized deeply love the Church (as one fundamentally loves the air one breathes and without which one dies), are defined by that very love, and potentially criticize its faults only by recognizing in it first of all the trace of their own sins; or they criticize it out of disappointed love. From this results the paradox that the baptized are not fundamentally interested in the Church, and even forget it or ignore it, because they never consider it from the outside, so much do they remain within it. In fact, focusing attention on the Church, its laws, its organization, or its apparatus always betrays a double weakening of Christian life. First, because one thus assimilates the Church implicitly or explicitly to an institution, which it indisputably is only as a result of its original mystery (ecclesiology results from christology, not the reverse). Then, because one stops taking it as a means (dispensing Christ's trinitarian grace) at the risk of idolizing it as an end; yet it does not offer an earthly city and not even an ideal earthly city, but simply the community of the baptized incorporated into Christ. The Church gives us a body, but Christ remains the head. What we see and live in it is precisely not the Church but Christ. What we should and can criticize in it would be only its possible opaqueness, masking the access to Christ; but then it is no longer a matter of institutions but instead of the sinful functioning of the institution, and thus of real, specific, individual sins; it is a matter of contrition, of reconciliation, and of holiness rather than of the reorganization and the redistribution of powers. Thus I would maintain this paradox; the baptized do not think of the Church, because they live in it and, in this setting, see Christ.

Consequently how do we get from the baptized in general to the figure that should replace the Catholic intellectual? We just saw that a (possibly critical) attitude toward the Church as institution does not fundamentally define the baptized in general, nor therefore the particular figure for which we are looking. We must then admit a different characteristic. Let us go back to the "intellectual," the "intellectual worker." How should one define him, once one has abandoned his two metaphysical presuppositions? It is not a matter of an intellectual worker in opposition to a manual worker because, from the Industrial Revolution on to the technological revolution of today, almost all workers work intellectually, and almost none manually. The intellectual will be defined, rather, as the one who not only works according to pieces of information given to him (machine, computer, networks, etc.), or the one who actually produces the merchandise of new information (teaching, media, administration, banking systems, etc.), but the one who invents and produces information, concepts, images, and so forth, which without him would have remained unknown, and thus become useable by others through him. In this precise sense, we can maintain, for lack of a better term, that of "intellectual," without the critical reservation of the quotation marks. One immediately encounters here a formidable question, even if only to deny it: what validity other than economic, what truth other than instrumental, and what reality other than technical do these kinds of information attain? This manifold question is raised, albeit in very different terms, in scientific discourse, in painting and in music, in the humanities and social sciences, and, obviously, in philosophy. In the majority of cases, whether by theory or by negligence, even out of contempt, it remains unanswered, and the production of information swells up all the more as it gives up on knowing what it really produces, and thus only produces what does not need to be in order to act: pure abstraction, money.

It is here that we meet up with the characteristic function of the intellectual baptized person. It consists in understanding the question about the validity, the truth and the reality of information that he produces, by considering the actually incredible hypothesis that he does not so much produce them as transparent, alienated, fully known objects, but incites, discovers, and makes them appear as what springs up new, rational in itself, and endowed with a proper meaning. Most of the time this hypothesis cannot be confirmed. But it must always be considered. To attempt to think the information one produces without necessarily thinking it would come down to recovering the requirements of the dear and already a bit old-fashioned "theology of earthly realities" with one close difference: it would no longer be a matter of finding the theological meaning already immanent in the realities of the created world, but, more modestly, of wondering about a general sense of these realities and also, more ambitiously, of distinguishing in them what offers a meaning from what does not offer any. It is not, then, first of all a matter of a directly theological hermeneutic of "earthly realities" but of the simple project of maintaining toward them the possibility of a hermeneutics in general. The rationality of the world no longer goes without saying: it must be built as we produce the world—a world that we produce going forward, namely, without comprehending it before having produced it. In this sense, the intellectual baptized person has as primordial function to contribute, in a specific domain, not only to the invention of information but even to making it sensible. He shares this function with scientific communities (or ones supposed to be such), while nevertheless for the most part remaining a minority. His singularity does not depend on this function but on the fact that *he*, at least and first of all, cannot evade it.

V

Such a function of the intellectual baptized person nevertheless raises a classic problem—if his "state duty" consists in looking after the rationality of "earthly realities," does he not risk entering into contradiction with theological reason, indeed with the logic of the faith? This conflict, as perfunctory as it may seem, controls modernity so fully that no one should underestimate its intensity, which often reaches tragic dimensions. The list of believers, and often the best, who have succumbed to it corresponds largely with that of the highest figures of intelligence. The best of the "atheists" comes from among ardent baptized people, intellectually exceptional and—to crown it all, at times perfectly honest. Anti-Christian philosophy especially is fed by Christians (and Jews) who have entered into contradiction with what they assumed about their faith of origin. What kind of responsibility the institutional Church bears in this exodus—historians will need much intellectual and spiritual honesty to establish that. If the Church has to a large extent lost the battle of intelligence in the last two centuries, this is obviously first of all due to itself because it wanted to wage an intellectual battle without using intellectual means. In fact, faced with such a conflict only a single attitude works: the unwavering respect for the principle that the truth never contradicts itself, that one truth never contradicts any other truth. Between two truths, the conflict remains only apparent, for (i) either a difference of degree, of order, or of status separates the two authentic truths (for example, between the redaction history of a text and its theological inspiration, between the eternity of the world and its created status, etc.); (ii) or the declaration of worldly rationality is in no way indisputable, contrary to what seems obvious at the moment (the "death of God," the concept of matter, absolute determinism, logical empiricism, etc.); (iii) or finally the theological declaration has only a limited and null relevance (the assumed geocentrism of the Scriptures). Revelation controls its own formulations, which it explains only partially and at times provisionally, just like the rationality of the human realities controls its own declarations, which do not stop criticizing themselves, according to the very definition of scientific progress. This double relativity is admittedly accomplished for contrary reasons: in the sciences because absolute truth is never and will never be attained, in theology because absolute revelation will never be summarized in human formulations. The historicity of truth comes in one case from its lack, in the other from its excess. But at least one certainty results from it: any contradiction remains provisional or turns into fraud. The intellectual baptized person who adheres to these two different exercises of rationality can and must know this. For it comes down to him taking on the outlined role of challenging the dilemmas into which the religious and scientific authorities have such a great propensity to trap themselves, in the name of a perverted use of the opposition between faith and knowledge. Faith and knowledge are not opposed to each other in a sound theology (as maybe in scientific inventiveness), but engage each other dialectically and generate each other mutually. Fideism and positivism do not express the correct connection between faith and reason but distort it, thereby missing both. Guardian of two truths, of their difference and their dignities, the baptized Catholic must be suspicious of the doubled ease of both fideism (a simple flight outside of the badly mastered rational) and positivism (a simple refusal of the complexity of the given) in order, by sheer work, to challenge the usurped truth or truths and think the distance that could possibly unite them.

An essential consequence emerges from this attitude: the duty to argue. But in the Church this responsibility does not first fall to the magisterium, which has as its irreplaceable function the proclamation of the faith, the kerygma. What has been received must be transmitted as it has been received, so that anyone can gain access to the Word. The magisterium announces the Word as such, uniformly because universally. And this magisterium is a charism as much as a mission. "Woe is me, if I do not preach the Gospel!" (1 Cor. 9:16). But the kerygma cannot, as such, immediately play the role of an argument or of a doctrine within the debate in the public square. Not by lack of truth or of force, but to the contrary because it gives almost directly an event outside of the norm, indescribable due to the excess of evidence and which takes away our word [*parole*] when it gives it back to the Word [*Verbe*]. It is, moreover, at least partly for this reason that the ordinary teaching of the Church, above all when it remains as close as possible to the Gospel, stirs up irritation, frustration, or disinterest among unbelievers (that is to say, also among all the unbelief that dwells in the majority of believers). The magisterium has as its proper task to spread the kerygma, even and above all when it cannot anymore, as such, convince argumentatively. Its own suffering is to know and endure this.

To transform the kerygma into arguments, weaker than it, amendable, even falsifiable, hence always provisional, but for that very reason usable in public debate, would be, it seems, the proper function of the baptized. They would have to transform the uncontrollable energy of the Christic event into a domesticated force, utilizable by the networks of finite rationality, refine the raw gold, or rather break it down into more common alloys; in short, negotiate revelation (like one negotiates a good, a treasure, or a business deal) so that it would infuse the systems of common rationality, intervene in public debates, and so that the potential decisions are situated (positively or not, it matters little) in relation to it. Declining revelation into negotiable arguments implies two different tasks, which one must not confuse or separate. First, that of arguing in favor of the Gospel, in order to make its relevance visible (the "apologies" of the first Fathers); the lack in this domain is obvious today. On the contrary, arguing on the basis of the Gospel so that its logical rigor can illuminate the debates of general interest open to all voices (formulating what Christians can say about morality, peace and war, death, etc.). For if there is a Christian truth, it must be able to interact rationally within the play of arguments; to withdraw to the sole repetition of the kerygma would amount to thinking it powerless, hence finally to betray the "efficient word" (Heb. 4:12). Here it is not first of all a matter of "defending" Christian truth; the truth does not have to be defended because, to the contrary, it defends itself and us with it. It is a matter of unfolding the kerygma into the arguments with which it can nourish a public debate on common problems, not at all a matter of destroying the opposing position but of contributing to a truth acceptable to all—and to Christians first of all. Acceptable to all, just because it is true. The line of conduct goes without saying here: "For we cannot do anything against the truth, but only for the truth" (2 Cor. 13:8).

And if there must be "new evangelization," we see that it first consists in such a work of reasoning on the basis of revelation. It will be a matter of a new effort for Christian rationality to intervene in common rationality, and the intellectuals among the baptized will be defined by the contribution they make.

6

The Future of Catholicism

The future of Catholicism can be thought on the basis of strictly theological concepts. Yet it can and must also be established according to the consideration of its relations with the world, if only because the world's future will change depending on whether Catholicism has a real future or not. What, in other words, is the future of Catholicism from the point of view of the world—and not from the point of view of Revelation?

This way of putting the question should not surprise or shock, if one considers the situation in which Catholicism finds itself in Europe today, especially in France. On the one hand, it appears on the way to a widespread and lasting sociological marginalization—on this point the situation is no longer any different for the countries in the south than for those in the north. On the other hand, Catholicism retains a capability for cultural intervention, for moral mobilization and for spiritual authority without equal in regard to the whole of civil society. Catholicism is not in the majority as regards average convictions and behaviors, but it still exercises a primordial function in the discernment of norms. From the exterior point of view, that of the world, wondering about the future of Catholicism comes down to asking what the supposedly normative discourse of Catholicism can give to civil society as a whole. In other words, can Catholicism contribute in the future to the good of civil society in general—even and above all when it finds itself forced to condemn the majority leanings of society? Even more clearly, will Catholicism be good for anything, if it has no other role than impugning the arguments on which the *quasi-consensus* of civil society becomes settled?

Before pursuing this further in order to give a response to this question, let us note a prerequisite: the often antagonistic relation between what the Catholic Church says and the majority opinions of our civil societies does not imply that Catholicism no longer plays any positive role; to the contrary, its contribution lies precisely in the capability it demonstrates of saying the very word that contradicts the predominant opinion head-on and openly, and at the very least renders society the invaluable service of showing that this opinion is not self-evident, that it involves infinitely serious presuppositions and runs the risk of falsification. Even when the world contradicts Catholicism, it still needs it in order to avoid merely proclaiming platitudes. The world might not even become conscious of its innovations and its declines if Catholicism had not been there with enough courage to awaken its bad conscience—for a bad conscience remains still and first of all a conscience. Catholicism can lay claim to such a role, one that is already as remarkable and respectable as many others.

But one can also hope for another role, if God gives it and thus if the Church asks him for the strength for it: that of replying directly within the pursuit of its own aims, as if the Church alone and by an undeserved grace held the key to the diagnosis of the crisis or even the word [*parole*] that frees us from it. In this encounter, the Church would no longer speak at the wrong moment, but, still proclaiming the same paradox of Christ crucified, would speak at the right time, so as to be heard. The Church has been granted the task of giving a single and unchanging Word [*Verbe*] to the world without adapting or lessening it, because He does not belong to the Church—instead it is his. At issue is not a modification of orientation, which would depend on the Church but, rather, a gift of God. A gift of God cannot be foreseen any more than a future can; but both are foreseen in the manner of a gift happening to our far too limited expectation, which is always surprised—when it finally even sees them!—by the superabundance of the promises kept. Today, perhaps, it is necessary to catch a glimpse of such a situation. The right to confess the faith, which we laid claim to in times when doubt bore it away with confusion and derision, neither disappears nor becomes blurred.[1] But grace might happen, which would permit confessing it to be able to make the reasonable discourse of its original logic heard, which is all the more admissible as other kinds of logic have become bankrupt.

What does the world say of itself? The world such as it functions and is understood is still chiefly defined by the traits of modernity. Modernity is characterized by a fundamental equivalence: *I* comes down to *I*, in accordance with the instantaneous mediator of self-consciousness. Descartes radicalizes the Delphic motto "Know Thyself" by knowing himself as knowing, in such a way that in all other kinds of knowing, the knowledge of the *I* by itself will be known first. Heidegger was thus right to develop Descartes's *Cogito, ergo sum* [I think, therefore I am] into a *Cogito me cogitare* [I know myself knowing]. I never think anything without first thinking that I think (myself), I think the self that thinks, *I* think *I*. A different equivalence follows from this—actually the same Fichte unfolded: $I = I$ just as $A = A$. And Hegel will enrich it with enough mediations for it to resume the whole of reality in its equality via knowing, the concept, and absolute spirit. The absolute recapitulates all things inside, henceforth without exterior, of the dialectically mediated equality of the mind or spirit with itself.[2] Mind or spirit *reverts* to itself, as much in the sense of a strict equivalence, as in the sense of a complete appropriation. It is not a matter here of a recklessly exploited metaphor but of the founding figure of modernity's knowing. The principle of identity (non-contradiction—Aristotle) of previous metaphysics is realized concretely and primordially with the identity of consciousness with itself. The principle of sufficient reason (Leibniz) is limited to generalizing the search for equivalences, above all in realms where logical equivalence cannot function. The modern emergence of the sciences could probably also be read as a generalization of equivalences—all derived from the primordial equivalence of consciousness with itself. The constants of the natural sciences were added in unlimited number to the tautologies of formal logic and to the equations, the systems of equation, and the striking identities of mathematics. In analogical fashion, other domains bear the same mark of equivalence: the "great equilibrium" in economy; more equilibrium in psychology and psychiatry; the equilibrium of terror in strategy, and so forth. It even applies to the logic of desire, which only aims at equality between partners, potentially by homosexuality as the ultimate refusal of dissimilarity. Man reverts to man, and the world reverts to man only by reproducing this fundamental equivalence in it. It is then only logical that history itself would have to return to equivalence: the eternal return of the same in Nietzsche does not contradict the (Cartesian) essence of modernity, but brings it rigorously to a close, much better than the simplistic eschatologies of progress; for progress itself aims at pushing the equivalence between the world and man to its end, so that man would here progress only toward his equivalence with himself.

Finally, one must underline that such a generalized tautology is not a philosopher's ravings because it instead receives its most exact formulation in the most restrained practical philosophy there is, that of Kant, who, better than anyone else, defined man as absolute end of himself, as final goal: "A final purpose is that purpose which needs no other as condition of its possibility. . . . The existence of man has its purpose [or end] in himself." It follows that "man (and with him every rational being) is to be thought of as being *an end in himself*; that is to say, he is never to be used by anyone, not even by God himself, as a mere means."[3] By a paradoxical but inevitable reversal this means today that everything that can claim to serve man as a final goal immediately justifies itself; man himself can become a means for man, understood as end—state violence, biological manipulation, attacks on life *in utero*, and so on, maintain their supposed legitimacy of claiming to serve Man, end-in-himself,[4] at the risk of reducing very concrete men to the rank of simple means. The fact that the in principle absolute and transparent equality of man with himself is turned against itself is not what is least odd about modernity. Man can certainly think of himself as his own final and nearest goal, but one must still decide *who* is such a man. Or instead one will impugn this equality by revoking its other extreme: what does man mean, to whom we are all as atomic individuals supposed to return and to match ourselves as our end?

The aporia pinpointed here, which is actually that of modernity, inaugurates what one could not fail to call postmodernity (although it is a formula as vague as what it goes beyond): man does not *revert* to man, man does not equal man, neither as consciousness, nor as end. Nietzsche saw this and said it: Each human goal results from an evaluation, each evaluation accomplishes one of the states of the will to power; accordingly the goals, even and above all the most transcendent ones, depend directly on man as overman, final authority on any evaluation; every goal takes place among the "thousand and one goals," of which none is hence the final goal, but the sole effect of the will to power at work in the evaluator. All goals are possible; hence none is final or absolute. The overman does not say to man who he is or should be, but only tells him that "man is something that shall be overcome."[5] In this way the transparent equivalence of man with himself is broken; only the immeasurable gap between the overman's will to power and his thousand and one goals remains.

Linked to the Cartesian origin of equivalence, this break would be formulated in this way: the equality $I = I$ presupposes that one of the two "I"s named in the equation not only exactly reverts to the other, but also knows this equality. Yet the fact alone of seeing the other, even if the other is apparently equal and similar to me, provokes a fundamental inequality between him and me: for it is to me that recognizing oneself as me [*soi-même comme moi*] reverts; I am not only one of the members of the equivalence,

I also measure and master it. Even if no real inequality were to distinguish the known I (the end, what is seen) from the knowing I (in some way the one who sees), the polarization of the aim by this I that I am, which decides it and practices it on an I holding the place of the ideal, inflicts on this latter a functional and transcendental inequality that no excellence will be able to curb. It is the same with man in his essence as with the empirical individual: he will never be able to see himself, although he sees everything else, except maybe by an inverted symmetry. Not only death and the sun cannot be looked in the face: this is also true of the I (and of God). From the simple fact that I (man) posit and decide on an identity for myself, by becoming mine that identity falls under my influence and paradoxically can thus no longer offer me an image of myself. Any image of myself, if it is myself that puts it up, immediately forfeits its standing; the image cannot be more than me, if it is by me. What I know of myself by myself definitely regresses to what it tries to make known—the I, inasmuch as it precedes all the kinds of knowledge that come forth from it. If, transgressing this strange rule, man claims to revert to himself—by the equivalence of knowledge or of finality—he actually reverts to less than himself, and, confusing himself with what is demeaned in him, he misunderstands himself [*se méprend*] or, in some way, despises himself [*se méprise*]. When the crisis of this mistake [*méprise*], in the proper sense, can no longer be concealed, as is the case today, then self-affirmation becomes homicide, the "know thyself!" is fulfilled in suicide. Not everyone is swallowed up by a volcano, like Empedocles, but the majority lose themselves in less than nothing—in any case in less and for less than what was human in them. In modernity, one often dies in order to know oneself, actually in order to know only the latest truth—and this latest "value" is worth less than man precisely because it results from an evaluation derived from him. In modernity, man does not stop praying to idols of himself as the original whose inaccessibility to the pure spectacle of self by self he does not know. If man does not go back to himself, he therefore goes back to much less than himself. How then does he attain himself? Only by going back to more than himself.

For man to be finally equal to himself, it is necessary for him to go back to more than himself—meaning more than the image that he can see of himself, where he misunderstands and deceives himself. For man to know himself, he must acknowledge that man goes beyond man. What does knowing more than man mean here? Obviously not knowing a different object substituted for man—for the "new man," except in its Pauline meaning, gives license to barbarities. But maybe it points to a kind of knowing in a mode different from objectification, so as to reach something better than an object, which is by definition controlled by the subjection of the mind that knows it. Knowing without demoting into an object would imply knowing what no mind masters, organizes or produces; cognizing without mistaking could be called recognizing.[6] Recognizing a human feature [*une figure de l'homme*] that would not straightaway be subject to us and hence unworthy, because we did not produce it, but instead received it as a gift. If man can only be known in matching his infinite dignity by going beyond any object knowable in the mode of objectification, then he will reach this surplus only by exceeding objective knowledge itself, which is in turn only possible if man exceeds himself. Exceeding oneself does not mean pushing back the limits of one's finitude (which would thus be reinforced and concealed at the same time), but, precisely, ceasing to extend the empirical and objective realm of knowledge, in order to await recognition. Recognition of an image of man, "not made by human hands,"[7] in the gift that God makes to man. Pascal points to what is essential here: "Man transcends man . . . Let us then conceive that man infinitely transcends man and that without the aid of faith he would remain inconceivable to himself . . . but for this mystery, the most incomprehensible of all, we remain incomprehensible to ourselves."[8] What can grant man recognition of a face of man finally worthy of him because removed from his mastery? Pascal says faith. Indeed, faith knows what it does not master, because it is given to know without certainty, and hence knows in the mode of grace.

Today, the function of the Catholic Church could consist in this: to let it show that God alone can give man the freedom to go back—first—to man himself, by giving him the freedom to resemble nothing less than God himself. That man would recognize himself as created "in the image and likeness of God" does not imply his submission to some strictly defined essence (which would limit his freedom, according to Sartre's shallow misinterpretation), but instead releases and exempts him from the duty of being conformed to any known norm. Resembling God releases from having to be conformed to the ideological models that dismantle the humanity of man. In fact, if man resembles God, he does not resemble anything known, because God is precisely defined by unknowability: "Therefore, since one of the attributes we contemplate in the divine nature is incomprehensibility of essence, it is clearly necessary that in this point the image should be able to show its imitation of the archetype . . . since the nature of our mind, which is the likeness of the Creator, evades our knowledge, it has an accurate resemblance to the superior nature, figuring by its own unknowableness the incomprehensible nature."[9]

God does not give a fixed and closed essence to man as things and animals have it; God gives him unknowability itself, which frees him from any definition; bearing the image of the likeness of God means—according to Gregory of Nyssa—to be exempted from any reductive knowledge, hence to be liberated from any idol that man could produce for God and, in the same move, for himself. Unknowability marks the inalienable freedom of God and also of man as a result of this gift that accomplishes creation. Consequently, a great many theologians hold correctly (with Saint Bernard) that the freedom (*libertas arbitrii*) given to the original image can never be lost by the creature. Man does not bear the image of God like a slave bears a branding, a product to be marketed, the sign of its manufacturer, a piece of data, a code; he bears this image like a painting bears the style, the touch, and the talent of the painter on its entire surface, which makes it immediately identifiable as such by an expert: "This is a . . . !"—In this sense, one must say of man that "this is a God!" so thoroughly does he bear the indisputable mark. The image that he thus bears of God is not one with his own image, no more than a portrait by Cézanne would stop being first of all of a portrait of his wife, of Vollard, or of a peasant. The image and the resemblance are vouched for by what man most irreducibly himself sends back, by the perfection particular to his face, to a glory that honors him and overwhelms him, without his even knowing it, provoking it, or noting it. In this way, man exercises a rationally incomprehensible freedom, which, precisely because it does not go back to anything of what man knows, effectively puts to work the incomprehensible and witnesses, quite naturally, to the glory of the Incomprehensible in person. God renders this service (not to say this grace) to postmodern man in order to give him, not so much a new definition of himself, which would become one of the innumerable ideological ideas with which the vague, gloomy battle floods the world with ridiculous horror, than the revelation of his essential unknowability, mark of his freedom, seal of his creation. In this way God grants man to go beyond all that he will never be able to have the least idea of—for the greatest idea will always be less than the recognition of what escapes our capability of producing ideas. Man only reverts or comes down to himself by coming to the Unknowable.

We asked how Catholicism, that is to say, the Christians assembled by the Catholic Church, can today help civil society to survive, even to be reinforced? One response seems established, at least in outline: they should ensure the vigil of the unknowable. Neither advocate of one party among others, nor trustee of a science in competition with others, the Catholic says that man, myself, my neighbor, cannot be known in the manner of an object, of an ideal or of an idol, but that he is received, definitively unknowable, as a gift of the God who remains forever unknowable.

Nevertheless this response attracts an inevitable objection: To express that man cannot be known, in the best of cases becomes a matter of an exhortation, but it does not contribute to clarifying or enriching real conceptual debate. And just as agnosticism concerning God ends up favoring atheism under a pious cover, in the same way, applied to man, it could authorize worse desertions. There really would be difficulty if we thought we were putting forward a new thesis—"man, this unknown" or "unknowable man"—among other possible ones—"neural man," "libidinal man," "structural man," and so on. That does not seem to be the function of Catholics as guardians of the unknowable. They do not propose a new slogan in the market of ideas, even a scientific one; rather, they impose a norm on all the discourses that, today and tomorrow, claim to be anthropological. A discourse can demonstrate that such an organ of the human body complies with such and such a model, itself borrowed from some material science or other (regardless of how strange and "spiritual" this matter might be): that's one point. Yet it is an entirely different matter, different *toto caelo*, to claim that this analysis concerns, even in the most minimal fashion, something like man; the only transition from one to the other depends, the majority of the time, on a negative statement: If one contradicts the discovered material model involuntarily (via sickness) or voluntarily (via murder), what really dies is or was a man. This negative proof confirms what we have known for a long time: Knowledge, when it is applied to man as to an object, almost inevitably is sure to kill him. But the reverse is not established so simply. Doubtless, the soul does not appear under any scalpel, scanner or analysis; but this is not something to rejoice about; for the soul exists, before it is put to death; and the more we know what it abandons or what it was managing, the less we know it itself. When a doctor, a biologist, a psychologist, an ethnologist, and so forth speaks, one should assume a double attitude: first to listen to them in order to learn, then to understand to what extent what they say *does not* concern man. Anthropological problems are not decided in terms of positive knowledge, but in terms of the law (juridically, philosophically): In the future we will have to *decide* regarding which among possible technologies should not be applied to humans. This fearsome challenge can only be met if we have first understood that man cannot be known and that one only respects him to the extent to which one does not allow any techno-science to treat him as if he were not glorified by unknowability. The unknowability of man is a fact—a theoretical fact observed by postmodernity in spite of itself—but it is a fact that requires a law for defending it because we do not make this fact effective, but we receive it as a gift. To know that he is nothing but what he has received is the defining characteristic of man; he has received being so radically that being comes down, without any remainder for him and for him alone in the world, to receiving himself. Man is uniquely in debt to himself.[10] This debt should neither be paid back nor weigh like a curse; it only demands to be recognized. Not known but acknowledged—accepted as a gift. That is why we must—that is a commandment of Christ—love ourselves; otherwise we will never forgive, will not forgive ourselves anything, and will become suicidal as much as homicidal. Learning to recognize themselves as being in the mode of the gift, Christians gathered in the Catholic Church possess by right the duty to devote themselves to this according to the *imitatio Christi*, which makes them *accomplish* in themselves the likeness of the unknowable. But it is also possible that this same and unique duty would define, as such, their most precious and most indispensable contribution to the destiny of our common civil society. For the time is coming when, in order to remain human, one must have a will for it, and in order to want it truly, one must have the capacity for it. And in this urgent situation all means are justified, for each and everyone—even the gift of God.

PART III

What Is Possible and What Shows Itself

7

Nothing Is Impossible for God

I. Possibility

Discussing miracles can seem old-fashioned, today as formerly. We know quite well—it has even become a proverb—that "there are no miracles." Everyone has always known this, those opposing Christians (from Celsus to Voltaire and Renan) and even a number of Christians (from Father Malebranche and Leibniz to Bultmann and any number of contemporary theologians). And, besides, it is obvious: potential miracles, when they are not reduced to more or less voluntary illusions, are merely facts waiting for explanation. And we have firmly decided to wait the time it will take for figuring this out and for dispassionately crossing one more miracle off the annoying list of phenomena that refuse to state their identity. "There are no miracles": we say this very often. And even so, that does not prevent us from sometimes saying, "it's a real miracle."

We thus have a different relationship with the miracle than the one that calm reasoning provides to us. Sometimes in a tough situation—in sports, when the tying goal is a long time coming and defeat seems unavoidable, in money-related matters, in the progression of an illness, in the splitting up of a loving relationship—we experience a very strange paradox. If I adopt the reasonable and supposedly rational point of view of an observer dispassionately analyzing the causes and objectively weighing the probabilities, then there is no longer any doubt that no miracle will take place; I know perfectly well and am completely persuaded that the other team will win, that I will have to sell, that death will ensue, that divorce is necessary. Even if another onlooker or a friend tries to tell me, with more or less sincerity, that all is not lost, I myself know very well, as by a certain and conclusive science, that it's all over. To say "there are no miracles" in this case shows that I have abandoned all hope because I accept that "it's all over." Yet even so, nothing is over—there are still two minutes to play, I could still borrow or attempt a final arbitration, I am still alive—why then get ahead of the end, which although it is foreseeable is not yet in any way effectively there? Obviously because "I no longer believe it." But this moment when I no longer believe precisely gets ahead of the one when everything will eventually be over. Thus when I accept that there are no miracles, I do not conclude this from any kind of knowledge but decide it by my will. Nothing is actually finished yet, but I myself am quite finished. What precludes the miracle here is not any knowing, but *the renunciation of possibility*: I agree to accept that an impossibility has in advance overwhelmed any possibility, however slender, that time still leaves open to me. "There are no miracles" means, within the real exercise of my thought, that I give up on the least possibility.

Consequently, should we in reverse fashion recognize in the formula "It's a real miracle" the acknowledgment of a possibility? When the tying goal is shot in the final minute, when the heart starts again contrary to all expectation or the deep coma lifts, when, against all odds, the ashes allow an ember to rekindle a kiss, what does my cry then hail? It does not pay tribute only or primarily to the saving event, but to the amazement over its realization at the very moment when I took it to be definitively impossible. What I call a miracle refers not to its effective occurrence but rather to the possibility within it of the very thing I know certainly to be impossible. I call "miracle" the possibility of what was formerly and certainly impossible, hence the real possibility—the possibility of the impossible. This paradox is illustrated by a messenger, who proclaims a victory that was beforehand denied by everyone:

- O
Triumph!
What glory! What human heart would be strong enough to support
This?

And in response the hearer stammers the definition of the miracle:

—Speak! what? what are you saying . . . [. . .]
That the kingdom is saved? That we still live? [. . .]
I hear you in trembling! How is this possible?[1]

In sovereign fashion, the possible has overwhelmed the impossibility that despair, but also reason, had already accepted. The possible appears miraculously because it makes actually possible what should never have been able to emerge from impossibility. As long as what really occurs sticks to the possible, it stirs up no glance; but when it violates what is forbidden or, rather, establishes impossibility, then there is reason for the gaze to be stunned by its wonder. Without leaving the everyday, we hence encounter situations that deserve to be called miracles and provide us with a first definition: we call miracle any event that by really happening[2] proves the possibility of what I held beforehand to be definitively impossible. This way of expressing it calls for several remarks.

Oddly enough here, reality [*effectivité*] does not come after possibility but precedes it. Logically speaking, a thing or an event should first comply with possibility (non-contradiction, representation, plan, etc.) in order eventually to move to reality [*effectivité*]. In the case of the miracle, the terms are arranged differently: because impossibility appears as established, the possibility of the event is canceled out; thus it is only possible for it effectively to materialize without preparation from any possibility and in formal contradiction to canonical impossibility. What's more, this paradox is illustrated by any number of formulations in military and sports prowess ("It was impossible, but I did it." "He did it because he didn't know it was impossible." "We do the impossible every day." [lit., "The impossible is not French."], etc.). From now on, effectiveness no longer has its goal in itself, but becomes the symptom of a possibility that is out of the ordinary, unforeseeable, and, strictly speaking, unbelievable: It testifies, afterwards and in fact, that the possibility scorned by common sense and reasonable reason has from the outset gone beyond canonized impossibility. In reality, possibility not only becomes emancipated right away from the supposed impossibility, but from that point on it overhangs reality [*effectivité*] itself; from now on "nothing is impossible" because at least once the impossible itself has been made [*fait*] real—by an event [*par un fait*]—thus it is (im-)possible.

Even so the miracle does not inevitably abolish any boundary between the possible and the impossible. It proves only that one time at least the boundary that I had set up between them has been shown to be false by the event. In short the possible that has effectively come to pass has at least once gone beyond the possible anticipated by me, by adding to it a part of what I held to be impossible. Thus the question of new possibility arises after the fact, although one must still understand how this impossible really happens and proves itself possible. Two standpoints are then opposed to each other: either admit the fact and its possibility, even if I do not understand it provisionally or definitively; or instead deny the effective itself (by whatever means, including absurdity), in order not to have to revise the primary boundary established between the possible (for me) and the impossible (for me). The difference between these standpoints does not run between rationality and credulity, but between the recognition of occurrences [*faits*], even at the cost of their explanation, and the censoring of events [*faits*], even at the cost of real evidence, thus between empirical acceptance of an "impossible" possibility and the banning on principle of the possibility of "impossible" events.

Accordingly, as it operates in the everyday, the miracle does not present anything absolutely exceptional. Or rather it is only an exception to the boundary I demarcated between possibility and impossibility at a given moment. Before challenging the "laws of Nature" (if "Nature," moreover, ever includes any laws different from those provisionally assigned by each stage of techno-science), the miracle puts into question the fullness of what I can recognize as possible and the portion that I sacrifice to the impossible—in short, the miracle brings to light the limits of what I build as my world. But according to everydayness, the miracle is a matter of faith: of the faith that "everything is still possible" amid the greatest despair, and above all of the faith that acknowledges the event occurring before my amazed eyes. The greatest difficulty does not, in fact, consist in hoping against all hope (for in a sense, brute animals do this much better than humans, glued as they are to their will to live), but in recognizing that what I no longer hoped for, indeed what I excluded straightaway from being able to happen to me, has happened to me. Joy often appears too beautiful to the one who does not want to believe in it. The miracle, in fact, pushes us toward a very difficult attitude, namely *to believe our eyes*.

II. The Miracle of Revelation

The concept of the miracle does not belong to the strictly religious realm but comes out of the conceptual if not specifically philosophical analysis of everydayness. Although the miracle really puts faith into operation (the mind's faculty of believing), it does not presuppose faith (in the sense of religious adhesion), for every individual life encounters events that come out of the concept of the miracle; the very refusal of calling them by that name incidentally testifies still more that the concept of the miracle is at stake. The analysis that leads to releasing the category of the miracle within everydayness in general has no need to consider the Revelation of

Christ in order to achieve this. Instead, the analysis must attempt to establish the connections that such a concept of the miracle in general maintains with the Revelation of Christ. This immense task cannot even be sketched here; at the very least one would have to privilege some fundamental indications. Christ "does miracles"; but that is not what distinguishes him from others because miracle workers were in no way exceptional during his time: thaumaturgists were at work in the majority of sanctuaries in the Mediterranean basin. Sages practiced as much as priests, in some cases in the name of a god, in others in their own name. In the Jewish tradition healings and marvels also occurred regularly. But Christ was distinguished by the manner in which he accomplished them, by radicalizing two traits already clearly characteristic of the prophets' behavior and setting the norm for the apostles.

Christ did not accomplish miracles in his own name, but in the name of the Father; therefore, he did not so much accomplish specific miracles as he did one single and whole miracle. Without doubt he healed this specific woman, gave life to this man, fed that crowd, saved those individuals from a storm and delivered this soul from its demons; however, these particular acts only took place with a single goal: to show that the power of God surpasses human powerlessness, or that it surpasses what humans in their present condition take to be radically impossible (and in a sense quite rightly so). In each specified miracle one must show the tremendous shift to which God subjects the boundary that humans draw and impose between the possible and the impossible: "Who then can be saved?" they said. Fixing his gaze on them, Jesus said to them, "For humans, that is impossible, but not for God, for all 'things' are possible with God." (Matt. 19:26; Mark 10:27).[3] And also: "Those who heard him said, 'Then who can be saved?' He said to them, 'Everything that is impossible with humans is possible with God'" (Luke 18:27). From Genesis (18:14) onward, the divine word [*parole*] overcomes the impossible—for example, by giving a son to the aged Sara—but only the Word [*le Verbe*] unfolds absolutely a "living and efficient (*energēs*) word" (Heb. 4:12). The miracle hence has value not for itself, but as a "sign"; it is the indication if not the proof that God makes the impossible possible because he makes it real [*effectif*]. As a "sign" and not a spectacle, the miracle manifests its proper phenomenon as the indication of the possibility opened by God and of its excessiveness. The disciples speak in every language, but this miracle, which is sensed (for it is one, Acts 2:7), only has value for pointing to the event of Revelation, which cannot be sensed although it is certain (Acts 2:36). In this way the miracle witnesses to Revelation, far from exhausting it or substituting for it.

What does the miracle reveal? It is enough to consider Christ's greatest miracle, the only one that he does not do himself, but that he receives from the Father by the Spirit: his own resurrection. The resurrection reveals definitively the paradox of the possibility of impossibility. In fact, by accepting death Jesus accepts the end of any possibility for himself; in the eyes of his disciples, of the politicians, even of himself in his human consciousness, "everything is finished" with his death; everything reaches its end (John 19:30)—his own life, the liberation of Israel, the glorification of his Father. With this death, more than with any other death, death triumphs, as the end of all possibilities, because with the death of the Holy One it is a matter of putting to death the possibility of everything and for everyone. It is precisely this mundane impossibility that God's omnipotence strikes with impossibility: "This man . . . you crucified and killed by the hands of those outside the law. But God raised him up, having freed him from death, because it was impossible for him to be held in its power" (Acts 2:23–24). During the paschal night it has become impossible that impossibility (death) would triumph over Christ. Thus the resurrection marks innovation par excellence, so that it inverts, for the first time and "once and for all" the entropy of sin by subjecting death to life and no longer life to death. Accordingly, as "the first to rise from the dead" (Acts 26:23), Christ also becomes the "firstborn among many brothers" (Rom. 8:29), to whom he opens possibility: being the "newness of life" (Rom. 6:4) in person, he can "make all things new" (Rev. 21:5). Thus all the biblical miracles point to the miracle of the resurrection; but this final and first miracle has nothing else to indicate: It perfectly shows and reveals that the love of the Father is given to us as it is given to the Son, namely, in the "power of the Holy Spirit" (Rom. 15:13). In what does such a power of the Spirit consist? It lies in the fact that for love nothing remains impossible, for no powerlessness—even that of the Cross—can forbid it to give itself.

Consequently, how is the question of the reception of miracles raised? We have acknowledged from daily experience that the miracle puts a kind of faith into play; first the faith of leaving even the tiniest possibility open when impossibility seems guaranteed; then, and above all, the faith of allowing that the real happening [*l'effectivité*]—which at times overwhelms the impossibility that so far was thought to be guaranteed—well and truly shows a miraculous surplus of possibility. It requires a kind of faith to recognize that our expectation with its certainties and its despairs must allow itself to be fulfilled by an occurrence that it took to be impossible. Besides, this self-critique can lead to discovering pieces of information and laws that have remained unknown to my expectation, or were censored by it. This kind of critical work will discover that possibility was richer and larger than previously thought. In this sense, the miracle will not disappear as long as it is not displaced: it will no longer bear on a physical event but on my consciousness itself, provided that it accepts being self-critical in order to reach a more comprehensive rationality. Admitting for this case such a surplus of effective possibility over our expectation already requires a standpoint of faith the majority of the time: even in rational inquiry one must know how to recognize the unknown.

Of course, faced with the miracle of Christ's resurrection by the Father, a different meaning of faith is at stake. The paschal event does not only or first of all require believing in something effective that exceeds any expectation of possibility; for it does not concern an impossibility that has become effectively possible—which we could investigate, reflect on, discuss, possibly reserve our judgment about while awaiting additional information, or even dismiss as unfounded. We must decide immediately to admit or to refuse the effective possibility of this impossibility, for at least two restrictive reasons.

First because we will inevitably and very soon die; yet the resurrection of Christ is offered as the death of death. Thus our decision on the subject comes down to a decision about our own subject: Do I accept or not that my death decides my end? I can certainly accept it, even with very noble motives (stoicism, etc.), but I must say, at least to myself: impugning Christ's resurrection equals resigning oneself to one's end. Second, because Christ's resurrection does not propose one case among others in the surplus of possibility over impossibility in such a way that I could ask for additional information, as for the miracles of everydayness. Additional information (for in two thousand years of reflection there has been some) could never fill in the gap between the event and its entire intelligibility, for one fundamental reason: Christ's resurrection constitutes the single and radical archetype of any real surplus of possibility over impossibility, because it concerns the only fleshly resurrection ever seriously and constantly claimed, because it concerns the highest impossibility (sin as a whole, death in its double depth), and because it concerns the highest possibility (God's very power, the deification of all people). We hence do not have to make up our minds faced with a specific event of possibility but, rather, before possibility itself, becoming an event at the heart of impossibility—which receives him not. All the other miracles, which are only understood or decided within this frame, can wait for additional information, for that matter always conceivable; but this one, by way of paradigm and of a priori, silently requires a decision without any other time limit than my death—because deciding on it is precisely what is at stake.

III. The Miracle in Metaphysics

The double determination of the miracle by everydayness and according to Revelation depends on a shared argument: Possibility can effectively surpass impossibility, and an event can effectively happen that consciousness held to be impossible and thus demand of consciousness to admit an incomprehensible possibility (definitively or not, little matter). Does this thesis have a legitimate meaning for the philosopher? The sketch of the response that I will attempt will presuppose a precise meaning of philosophy: Metaphysics, such as it develops according to an onto-theological constitution and, on this basis, agrees (following Aristotle) that "it is clear that actuality (*actualité/energeia*), is prior to potency (*possibilité/dynamis*)";[4] in other words, for our subject, possibility is subjected to actuality [*effectivité*].

This conceptual decision submits possibility to actuality [*effectivité*]; but actuality in turn only appears on the basis of the knowledge that anticipates it. Not only is nothing possible but that which will become real [*effectif*], but becoming real itself must first be made intelligible via the concept. Possibility is standardized by actuality [*effectivité*]; hence it is also regulated like it, namely, by what the concept can intelligibly anticipate about it. It matters little for our purposes whether the provisional concept is practiced according to categories of being (Aristotle), of simple natures (Descartes), of the understanding (Kant), or the concept in person (Hegel), because in all these cases possibility finds itself predetermined by conditions that settle its intelligibility. The Kantian formula of "conditions of possibility" must serve here as the guideline; possibility allows for conditions; being first of all goes back to being possible (Suárez); but being possible is expressed in advance according to the requirements of the concept. That possibility allows for conditions also means that it does not impose itself as possibility starting from itself, but lets itself be defined: possibility, also and above all, obeys the conditions of its own possibility. Metaphysically, one must distinguish two of them, in accordance with the two metaphysical principles formulated by Leibniz in exemplary fashion. The principle of non-contradiction assures the truth of the necessary terms in the sciences of reasoning and guarantees the possibility of the terms in the sciences of fact.[5] The principle of sufficient reason, which justifies by a cause or a reason "why something is so and not otherwise," assures truth in the sciences from the fact and the effectiveness of the possible.[6]

Let us convert these two principles in order to explicate them: nothing contradictory is possible (or true); nothing that occurs without cause is true (or hence truly possible). Consequences ensue almost necessarily: the miracle becomes illusory or excluded, first because it is defined according to a contradiction (what was dead lives, what was lost is found). If this contradiction is definitive, it loses any right to truth; if it is only apparent or provisional (death was not really death, etc.), there simply was no miracle. It also becomes illusory or excluded because it cannot produce any other sufficient reason for its effectiveness than a totally undetermined "power of God" or a pure absence of cause, which comes down to the same thing for intelligibility. If by chance a cause known as secondary or discovered later were to intervene, there simply would not have been any miracle. In either case, these classical theories of the miracle, even and above all in Christian authors (Malebranche, Leibniz, Locke, Hume, etc.) all attempt to reduce its importance and utility so that the two principles of non-contradiction and of sufficient reason universally extend their empire. In consequence therefore of the marginalization or critique of the miracle, it is Revelation itself that passes under the control of the rational moral law (Rousseau, Kant, Fichte, etc.) or, in order to benefit from an ambiguous sanctioning, must be identified by force with the concept (Hegel, Schelling). As for God, if he remains still acceptable, he must on the one hand manage "possibilities" that are logically independent from his creation (Suárez, Leibniz), or, on the other hand, only intervene as "the final reason of things,"[7] "bearing Reason in his existence with himself."[8] The exclusion of possibility as such goes together with the limitation of divine initiative. Possibility becomes impossible and the miracle is turned upside down. The field is opened to all the positivist criticisms, without any difficulties or surprises.

The aporia of the miracle according to classical metaphysics marks, conversely, the impasse where it is trapped when, upon encountering a miracle, it is confronted with possibility in its most radical sense. Yet classical metaphysics does not equal all of philosophy or exhaust all of its resources. In particular, its fundamental decision—"It is obvious that actuality precedes possibility"—was subject to a strict inversion in the decision Heidegger made in the name of phenomenology: "Higher than actuality [*effectivité*] stands possibility."[9] In fact, phenomenology strives to return to the things themselves; this summary formula would nevertheless very quickly have turned into a slogan if one had not developed it in the direction of what Husserl established in 1913 as the "principle of all principles," which he defines in this way: "Each intuition given in an originary way is a legitimate source of knowledge; whatever presents itself to us in Intuition in an originary way (in its fleshly reality so to speak) is to be taken simply as it gives itself, but only within the limitations in which it gives itself there."[10] This principle enacts a revolutionary advance because the answer to the question of right—of the right of phenomena to truth, thus of the right of deciding about the possibility of accepting a phenomenon as certain or not—will henceforth no longer come from an authority or a principle anterior to the phenomena themselves or different from them, but will depend solely on the fact of their real givenness (in the flesh) to intuition or not. The question of right allows for a response of fact: phenomena no longer need to be justified before a tribunal of reason, but are given as such. Givenness finds itself erected as the self-justification of the phenomenon as such: everything that is given to intuition and only what is given to intuition is real as a phenomenon. Moreover, because Husserl widens the intuition of the sensible (Kant) to the categories, the givenness of intuition can take on a magnitude without known metaphysical precedent (except maybe the Cartesian *intuitus*). From then on, possibility is liberated from any preliminary authorization in the face of any principle whatsoever: everything is admissible as a phenomenon, and hence as a being, that is given [*se donne*] and to the extent that it gives itself [*se donne*]. Without a doubt, everything that is given does not give itself equally: illusions remain illusions, but henceforth they remain precisely as illusions, givens that deserve (or, rather, require) examination. Actuality or effectiveness, acknowledged rightfully for any possible givenness, must then be adjusted, according to all the possibilities of givenness, in an infinity of degrees to be subtly distinguished, instead of splitting into only two extremes (univocal existence and nonexistence). In other words, all the lived experiences of consciousness, even those that make no claim to objectivity (the intentionalities of praise, demand, veneration, repenting, etc.), thus all the volitions (charity, benevolence, etc.), all the beliefs (nonscientific "holdings as true," etc.) appear as phenomena by full right, precisely because they appear inasmuch as they are given. Without a doubt, certain intentions are given without intuitive fulfillment, and certain intuitions do not fit into any eidetic intentionality; however, even these extreme cases cannot put into question the principle of principles because, to the contrary, they are the ones that demand the most authentic phenomenological work—that of determining the degrees and the types of givenness. Henceforth the phenomenon ensures its possibility in terms of autonomous givenness, no longer from heteronomous sufficient reason.

How does the miracle fit into the phenomenological advance? First by the fact that phenomenology liberates possibility by giving up deducing it from some preliminary condition or other and by deciding about it according to givenness: what gives itself effectively is possible, what is given in the flesh gives itself effectively. If the fact decides the right, then the miracle only raises a problem of fact and not at all one of right. The question amounts to asking whether this phenomenon *is given* in the flesh or not. Second, if givenness can be realized without foresight, cause, or reason; if the possible can happen without being presupposed by genealogy, even by contradicting any expectation, then the miracle offers the purest example of phenomenological givenness. In its case, more than in any other, the phenomenon must and can be understood starting only from its autonomous givenness. Finally, phenomenology admits among the number of phenomena (at least with Heidegger in *Being and Time* §7) even what does not manifest itself at first glance, but must be indirectly put into visibility with the help, for example, of indication and of difference. This arrangement probably does not concern only Being (*l'être*; to be read starting from being [*l'étant*]), which Heidegger privileges, but also Revelation, to be read starting from the "signs" and the parables that announce it. By freeing the possibility of the phenomenon as given, phenomenology thus makes possible the possibility par excellence—the miracle.

IV. The Paradox

Even so, this advance still does not free the miracle entirely—assuming that it frees the phenomenon completely. In order to perceive this difficulty, let us recall what miracle we are discussing. After having recognized the miracle from everydayness, we have deepened the concept with Christ's miracles; but far from ending in the wonder they provoke, these always point back as "signs" (symptoms) to the God of all power and all possibility, and they explode once and for all in the resurrection of Christ, where the heart and sum of Revelation is manifested. The miracle that we must here determine thus leads back to Revelation like a "sign" via the resurrection as paradigm of any miracle. In front of this requirement, even the progress of phenomenology marks off its limits. These limits do not ensue either from a blindness or from a refusal, but from the two most essential characteristics of any phenomenon: the constituting I and the horizon. But the miracle (understood on the basis of Revelation in the resurrection) has a duty to contradict these two characteristics.

The horizon precedes the phenomenon. Not because it would prejudge its possibility by making it first appear before a tribunal of reason, but because the freest possibility of the phenomenon itself coincides with the horizon. The phenomenon can only stage itself on a stage, before a background, in a frame, where it stands out in order to appear as the thing itself. This horizon can vary in accordance with the respective phenomenologies: objectivity (Husserl), time (Heidegger), flesh (Merleau-Ponty, Henry), ethics (Levinas); but the phenomenon always gives itself as such only by being outlined against a horizon—carving the contours and the traces of its appearance into the fabric of this horizon. Therefore, any phenomenon must admit that its possibility is decided in advance within the dimensions of its horizon of appearance. This limit coincides with possibility because it is always a matter of the possibility of *appearance*. This precedence suits any phenomenon, provided that it appears within the possible world—a world of possible phenomena. The frame of a horizon hence suits any miracle that belongs entirely to the world. Conversely, if a miracle passes outside the world, because it points to what precedes the world, then this miracle must evade the common condition of phenomena—the inscription within the frame of a horizon. But in contrast to other miracles, the resurrection of Christ happens by transgressing the limits of the world. It does so first because in it Christ crosses, transgresses, and abolishes the insuperable limit of any world: the limit between life and death, thus the difference between being and not being. It does so secondly because it is the Father, who does not belong to the world but creates it, who accomplishes the resurrection, where "the power of the Spirit" glorifies the Father as much as the Son. Finally, it does so because Christ, as Word [*Verbe*], hence as principle of creation, contains the world within Him and from all eternity, more than he belongs to it; so that even and above all in the Incarnation, Jesus, by his full *exousia* [power], escapes from the world. Revelation, which manifests the miracle par excellence of the resurrection, certainly happens within the world, but starting from and within sight of an absolute outside-the-world [*hors-monde*]. In this sense alone, it actually fulfills the perfect possibility of what the world by the limits of its horizon takes to be definitively impossible: for example, passing through death. For as far as any horizon foresees possibility, the Revelation that the resurrection manifests, as the single miracle outside the world, challenges in advance any horizon.

Nevertheless, every phenomenon appears within a horizon. If the resurrection claims to appear, how will it still be able do so without the least horizon? We have said that the resurrection, as miracle par excellence, appears—but by challenging the limits of any horizon. The formulation of the difficulty actually already points to the terms of the solution. Obviously, the resurrection enters into a horizon, because it appears in a world, a time and a space, and is exposed to being, like the flesh, like the mundane object, like another ethics, and so forth. But all the same it challenges this horizon by evading objectivity (entry into the upper room), alterity ("Do not touch me"), the flesh (which Thomas would not have had to touch if he had believed), space and time (Matt. 28:19–20), and, radically, the difference between being and not being. How then can a phenomenon that challenges any horizon appear in the horizon of a world? By saturating it. The resurrection, as miracle par excellence and by confirming in this way a trait outlined by other miracles each time to a lesser extent, saturates any horizon. By *saturating phenomenon*[11] I mean that which the manifest given surpasses—not only what a human gaze can bear without being blinded and dying, but what the world in its essential finitude can receive and contain. In the common regime of phenomenality, our intentional aim most often reaches significations that no intuition will be able to fill adequately, so that we are accustomed to a relative shortage of visible givenness. Here instead, in an entirely reversed fashion, intuitive givenness infinitely surpasses what our intentional gaze can hope of significations and of essences, as well as what our intuition can bear of fulfillment. The most common and crudest error in regard to Christ's miracles—and especially of the resurrection—consists in characterizing them by a shortage of intuition, of givenness and of manifestation, for which faith would have to compensate, at the risk of illusion, by a so-called "wager." Yet the connection between the two Testaments indicates formally that the obstacle to the recognition of Christ before and after the resurrection consists in the refusal to acknowledge the evidence; hence, more essentially, in the powerlessness to bear its glory. The resurrection gives rise first to terror before the infinite excessiveness of the possible that it carries out: "*ephobounto gar*—they were in terror" (Mark 16:8). This short ending of the Gospel of Mark already counts as a perfect recognition of the resurrection. The resurrection, as saturating phenomenon, can only be detected by the interference of its horizon, like the luminous rays that, by being reflected in the frame of a mirror, interfere with and hinder each other or, in contrast, gather their lights in an unbearable bedazzlement. Thus the significations, the intuitions, and the infinite indications that are gathered for giving the figure of the Resurrected, saturate not only the capability of any human gaze, but first of all the opening of any possible mundane horizon. This phenomenon—for it is given as such and par excellence—only appears by contradicting by excess the conditions of any appearance: its glory (*doxa*) is always exercised as a paradox, where evidence shows itself through bedazzlement.

The *I* constitutes its phenomenon: this second phenomenological characteristic of the thing itself becomes henceforth questionable. The constitution of the phenomenon follows directly from two constants. First, the total object never totally gives itself in the same instant, even in the series of all instants; thus one must (re-)constitute it starting from the limited appearances, where it outlines its face each time, which remains invisible as such (for we have never been able to *see* even the most banal object from all its sides). Then, only the *I* can operate this constitution because, on the one hand, it receives givenness and, on the other, it ensures its constitutive synthesis; it thus controls givenness so as to constitute it into an object. In principle, the object depends on an *I*, even if the *I* does not produce it. How does the constituting *I* play in reference to the resurrection, the highest phenomenon and miracle? Before responding directly to this question, it is necessary to specify that, from Husserl himself onward (in particular with the doctrines of time and of passive synthesis), but especially with Merleau-Ponty and Levinas, phenomenology has not stopped relativizing the constituting primacy of the *I*—to relativize it means to make it dependent on a relationship to someone other than itself. In the exceptional case of the resurrection, the relativization is radicalized exceptionally. This saturating phenomenon could not permit itself to be constituted: by definition, the possibility that it sets free overwhelms the constituting gaze and scrambles the horizon of constitution. The disproportion between the gaze of the *I* and the scope of the phenomenon forbids not only the repetition of the constitution here, as if it were nothing ("constituting Christ resurrected"—the phrase itself sounds like blasphemy), but it inverts it: the phenomenon *here* constitutes the *I*, precisely because the Resurrected alone can say, in truth and before the world, "I am"—for "I testify on my own behalf, and the Father who sent me testifies on my behalf" (John 8:18). Only Christ can still say *I* on Easter morning, so that any transcendental *I* must recognize itself before him as constituted—a self [*moi*] called out [*interpellé*] because stunned [*interloqué*]. The Revelation that is fulfilled in the privileged miracle of the resurrection divests the *I* of any a priori character. This is commonly said as: Revelation reveals the *I* to itself, in the sense where a man can erotically reveal a woman to herself (as Maurice Clavel said).

The resurrection as a phenomenon constituting its interlocutor as stunned [*interloqué*] and not as a phenomenon constituted by an *I*, takes up again a common phenomenological character, but here also by inverting it. It indicates the position of the *I* that has become a *me* [*moi*]: responding to a givenness rather than objectifying it. From now on it becomes more comprehensible what faith Christ demands in order to allow others to perceive his paschal appearance. It is not a matter of compensating the poverty of facts via fideism, but of admitting that a saturating phenomenon, by definition, cannot be constituted by an *I*; in order nevertheless to receive it, the *I* must allow itself to be constituted, "revealed," and stunned [*interloqué*] by this paradoxical phenomenon. Faith in the resurrection does not reconstitute a badly given phenomenon, but gives itself, by converting itself from the *I* to the *me*, to givenness come from outside the world.

The final miracle is that I would believe in the miracle par excellence—the resurrection where any and all Revelation is accomplished. And no one can receive this miraculous faith without entering already into the unique resurrection with his flesh and blood.

8

The Phenomenality of the Sacrament

I. At the Limit of Phenomenality

The question of the sacrament, or more precisely that of the sacramentality of the sacrament, undoubtedly belongs first of all to theology. If—at least as a formal point of departure—we admit one of its normative definitions, we might say with the Council of Trent's "Decree on the Eucharist": "Indeed the holy Eucharist shares in common with the other sacraments that it is a sign of a holy thing and the visible form of an invisible grace (*Commune hoc quidem est sanctissimae Eucharistiae cum caeteris sacramentis symbolum esse rei sacrae et invisibilis gratiae formam visibilem*)."[1] It is on the basis of the Eucharist that we must pose and try to formulate the link between the sacramental symbol and that to which it gives access, the "sacramental thing" (*res sacramenti*)—the grace of Christ, such as it governs all the other sacraments, beginning with baptism. According to this link between the senses and grace in a single symbol that brings them both together, everything goes back to the original linking of the extremes that the Incarnation of the Word accomplishes in our humanity. Henceforth, the flesh (the physical body and the soul that senses) becomes hypostatically united at this point to divinity in Christ, such that it can unfold this unique communion in certain gestures and acts, which also are linked together according to the symbol of the thing and of grace.

Yet, as radically theological as it may be, the question of the sacrament nevertheless calls upon some of the terms philosophy has claimed for itself. This has been the case in at least one of philosophy's major movements for more than a century—ever since Husserl's *Logical Investigations*, which inaugurated in 1900 what has subsequently developed unceasingly under the name of phenomenology. Indeed, by way of the doctrine of the phenomenality of phenomena, phenomenology inquired into a basic and therefore, in a sense, very simple question: How can sensory or even intellectual appearance give rise to the manifestation of the thing itself, whether in the mode of the true or in the equally determining mode of the false? In other words, how does appearance find itself taking responsibility not for a mere misleading illusion, but for a full and complete appearance whose integrity in the end would offer the sole and final framework to manifestation—of the true as much as the false? For in the end, certain knowledge is always determined according to clarity and evidence, and therefore in accordance with a manifestation. And the formal methodical and discursive criteria, which will then possibly come to discern it, will only ever confirm its indisputable and primordial authority. In either case, what is or pretends to be, in the end, will have to appear. And no appearance could possibly disappoint as long as it remains the unique attribute of the manifestation, and therefore the unique agent of truth. The question, then, of the sacrament (and first of all of the Incarnation itself, which gives the paradox its currency) undoubtedly implements two terms arising from the phenomenological debate because it combines very precisely the visible and the invisible, as the two inseparable faces of a single phenomenon: "The sacrament is a symbol of a sacred thing and is a visible form of an invisible grace (*sacramentis symbolum esse rei sacrae et invisibilis gratiae formam visibilem*)." We can therefore ask: Must the sacrament be received as a phenomenon? And what particular phenomenality does it concern?

The tradition indeed speaks here with a single voice, defining the sacrament in terms of phenomenality. Saint Augustine defines it in these words: "The sacrifice, therefore, is the *visible* sacrament of an *invisible* sacrifice (*Sacrificium ergo visibile invisibilis sacrificii sacramentum*)."[2] Saint Thomas takes up the same duality: "sacraments are *sensible* signs of *invisible* things by which man is sanctified (*sacramenta . . . sunt quaedam sensibilia signa invisibilium rerum, quibus homo sanctificatur*)."[3] The pair *sensible/invisible* is equivalent to the Augustinian pair *visible/invisible* because "the divine power operates invisibly in them under visible signs (*virtus divina invisibiliter [operatur] sub visibilibus signis*)."[4] A double consequence follows from this audacious assumption of a visibility of the invisible. First a positive one: Because in any sacrament it is a matter of rendering visible the invisible grace of God granted to the Church in Christ, theological reflection cannot get by without a strictly phenomenological analysis.

In particular it will be necessary to wonder about the double phenomenality that is implemented here: a visible thing that is one and the same (the thing called a *sacramentum*) appears on the one hand as an already constituted phenomenon (the mundane thing—bread, wine, water, oil, etc.), visible among the other visible things of the world. On the other hand, it appears also as the not yet constituted intermediary toward another term, still invisible (the "thing" accomplished by the sacrament, *res sacramenti*, the sanctifying grace of Christ) and yet supposed to be constituted in a final phenomenon. We will first have to ask how the same phenomenality may be doubled in the visible "thing" in order to turn it, beyond its own worldly visibility (the appearance of itself), into the visibility of something else, albeit something that is supposed to remain invisible (grace). From this comes the first question: how may the same visibility serve two phenomena?

Then on this basis we will not be able to escape a second, negative or at least aporetic, consequence: How can we conceive the visible (and moreover the *sensible* visible, not simply the intelligible) as being able "to act on" (and even "sanctify") the invisible, whatever it may be? How can one conceive that the same phenomenality—by definition visible—extends itself univocally to the invisible? And the difficulty here does not result from the in this case theological origin of this invisibility (the grace of Christ), but purely and simply from the status of the invisible in general. For in phenomenology the fundamental correlation between appearance and what appears—such that it opens all possibility of phenomenality—always plays out in principle between two terms that are rightly visible. On the one hand, a first visible, or at least a first perceived one, the experiences of consciousness (the *data*, the *Erlebnisse*) that are not yet constituted in a phenomenon with full rights (the simple appearance). On the other hand, a second visible, the intentional object constituted around its noematic kernel, which is fully phenomenalized (namely, what appears). Yet in the very particular case of the sacrament, it would be a matter of an absolutely new correlation, because it is between a perceived visible and an "intentional object" (most probably an already inadequate term that we will only use here with some reservation) that is destined to remain definitively invisible. The two faces of the sacrament therefore do not remain within the phenomenality of the visible, because only the first implements it, while the second decidedly and definitively avoids it. In fact, the noematic kernel does not stop standing out identically at the very core of variations of fulfillment, which always illuminate it differently, but determine it all the more visibly. On the contrary, the *res sacramenti*, the grace of Christ, will never appear as such in the light of this world. It will never be counted among worldly phenomena, even if sacramental acts are performed at each moment of our lives from our baptism onward—for their visibility will never extend beyond the intra-worldly things toward "what no eye has seen" (1 Cor. 2:9).

Therefore if one had to approach the sacrament according to the common requirements of phenomenology, it would be necessary to conclude that it belongs only partly to phenomenality, but that in the last analysis it transgresses phenomenality in order to aim—at its own risk and peril—at an authority definitively resistant to the visible. According to this aporia, the sacrament would be a matter of phenomenality precisely only in order to set up its limits and to remove itself from it—unless it is in this way admitting the limits of its own rational coherence.

II. Models of the Gap

Obviously theology did not wait for this phenomenological aporia before it attempted to join the visible with the invisible in the same and paradoxical manifestation. By schematically recalling several attempts made in this direction, we will delineate their limits, without criticizing them—indeed, one could not reproach them for not having overcome an aporia that they knew to be insurmountable. When it is a matter of the sacrament, the point is never to reduce its terms to univocity or to integrate what is invisible in the *res sacramenti* into the visibility of the *sacramentum*, but to comprehend as precisely as possible which models of intelligibility can clarify the paradox and what exceptions it imposes upon them in turn.

The first model that theology can use to attempt to reduce the gap between visibility and invisibility in the sacrament comes from the metaphysics of substance, or more exactly from the relation of inherence between a substance and its accidents: accidents appear directly, substance appears only through their mediation. A theological possibility can be surmised from this gap: the same visibility of the accidents (aspects such as the whiteness of the bread, the redness of the wine, the translucence of the water) could turn from an account of a worldly substance (bread, wine, water) into that of a nonworldly substance (body and blood of Christ, grace of filiation). As natural aspects of a substance, the same accidents become the non-natural species of a different substance. This model is characterized by two difficulties.

(a) A philosophical difficulty emerges only after its theological employment by Saint Thomas (unless this difficulty alone makes this employment possible, by weakening it): One can much more legitimately consider the (theological) possibility of a transfer of the accidents of one substance to another, since no substance itself can (philosophically speaking) be directly manifested as such but must always go back indirectly to the visibility of its accidents. As such, no substance affects us immediately; in short, none appears to us first and foremost as a phenomenon.[5] Consequently, the theological argument ensures less a phenomenality particular to the sacrament than it replays the metaphysical non-phenomenality of any substance in general in its own favor. The sacrament does not find any way toward manifestation, but recovers in a particular way the universal shortage of manifestation of the substance, already reduced to the level of the thing in itself.[6]

(b) The other difficulty, properly theological this time, can be formulated as follows: by what right can the body of Christ enter in person and irretrievably into the accidents of a substance that is not only finite, sensible, and material but without relation to the individual human substance that he assumes in his Incarnation? Especially because, according to strict philosophy, substance does not enter into its accidents but, rather, withdraws from them at the risk of no longer affecting us and hence not appearing to us. Theology thus could not legitimately assume that the (quasi) substance of the sacrament really appears as such in the species of the accidents, except by presupposing a real engagement of the *res sacramenti* in the visible. It would be necessary that what the sacrament claims to take responsibility for is truly given to see, gives itself [*se donne*] visibly as invisible. In short, it *gives itself without withdrawal* to the point of abandon.

In order to try to fill the same gap in the sacrament, theology can borrow a second model from metaphysics: that of the invisible cause of a visible effect. For in philosophy one can perfectly admit that, in certain (even physical) cases only the effect reaches phenomenality, while the cause that "explains" it (gives it reason) remains itself invisible—only "proven" in its existence by the effectiveness of the effect.[7] Yet even assuming that this schema, which was initially formalized to explain the natural world, could legitimately be applied to the phenomenality of the sacrament (which is debatable), the distribution of the roles is not self-evident. No doubt, the matter of the sacrament concerns the visible, but one could not take it as an effect because the sanctification of the faithful receiving the grace created in them follows from *ex opere operato* itself; the effect of the sacrament remains thus perfectly invisible. As for what must be understood as its originating cause, it concerns the invisible par excellence because "the principal efficient cause of grace is God himself, and the humanity of Christ stands to him in the relation of a conjoined instrument (*Principalis autem causa efficiens gratiae est ipse Deus, ad quem comparatur humanitas Christi sicut instrumentum conjunctum*)."[8] The materiality of the sacrament remains an accidental instrument, caught between a principal cause and a spiritual effect, which are both equally invisible. How can theology nevertheless legitimately employ the causal schema? By assuming that God enters without reservation into the humanity of Christ as into his "joint instrument" and that Christ enters irrevocably into the materiality of the sacrament, to the point of qualifying its visibility as the very visibility of his fleshly body. Only on this condition can the sacrament cross the gap between visibility (its matter) and invisibility (of the cause and effect). But to satisfy this condition, it would be necessary once again that what invests the sacrament really is given to be seen, gives itself visibly as invisible—in short, *gives itself without withdrawal* to the point of abandon.

To ensure a phenomenality of the invisibility of the sacrament, theology finally has at its disposal a third, semiotic model: to interpret the sacrament as a "sacred sign (*sacrum signum*)."[9] Here the gap between the visible and the invisible should be able to be crossed by putting trust in the arbitrary but inseparable unity of the two sides of the sign. The duality of the sign itself can most probably be understood here in two senses. (a) On the one hand, by dividing the sign itself, in which case the matter of the sacrament *ex opere operato* would be like the signifier and grace like the signified.[10] Yet in this configuration there is strictly speaking no sign, because the sacrament does not unite a signifier with a signified, but a sensible being that is already real in the world (bread, wine, water, etc.) with a being that is insensible and invisible within the world (sanctifying grace). To understand the sacrament as a sign, it is thus necessary to widen this concept to a semiotic relation between two beings. In short it is necessary to move to the consideration of the referent. (b) On the other hand, then, [the duality can be understood as] the distinction between the sign (taken as a whole) and its referent. In this case, the sacramental act applies to the sign and Christ to the referent, inasmuch as a sacrament memorializes him, manifests his grace, and announces his coming glory.[11] And of course this semiotic model of the sacrament functions exactly in proportion to the link between the sign and the referent within it. Yet with what right can one assign an invisible referent with a necessary connection to a sign, or even only an invisible (unrepresentable) signified to a (visible, representable) signifier? Who would have the authority to do so? Certainly not the speaker or the one who benefits from the sacrament. Then would it be the referent? Would it have to be requested that a referent come in person to validate a sign while acting as its guarantor—by guaranteeing that, if the sign is used, then the invisible referent will be visibly accomplished in it? Does it make theoretical sense to speak of such an engagement of the referent, and is it probable that this would have occurred? No doubt only theology itself would have the means for backing it up. Yet, in any case, in order to validate this model, it would once again be necessary that what invests the sacrament as its sign truly gives itself to be said and effectively done in person, hence visibly gives itself in the sacrament as invisible, or in short *gives itself without withdrawal* to the point of abandon.

Three models (among others) are thus available to theology for thinking rigorously a continuity between the visible and the invisible in the sacrament: the relation of substance to accidents, of cause to effect, and of sign to referent. None of them can as such ensure the phenomenal coherence of the sacrament, apart from satisfying a condition that cannot be demonstrated or shown—the condition that the invisible (substance, cause, referent) delivers itself up without withdrawal to the visible, that is to say, that it not only starts in the visible but gives itself there to the point of abandon. To define the phenomenality of the sacrament, one must see that within it the invisible is translated, delivers itself up, and abandons itself to the visible to the point of appearing in it as the invisible that it remains. To conceive this condition requires considering two questions. (a) The phenomenological one will ask whether the possibility of [something] giving itself without withdrawal or return concerns the possibility of [something] manifesting itself, whether self-giving [*se donner*] allows self-showing [*se manifester*] (section III).[12] (b) The theological question will ask whether the kenotic abandon of the Word to its humanity and of Christ to death achieves—among other gifts—that of the phenomenality of the invisible, therefore of the sacrament (section IV).

III. Self-Giving, Self-Showing

The difficulties, which have just emerged in the enterprise of defining the phenomenality of the sacrament, certainly concern to a large extent the difficult and undetermined relation within it of the visible with the invisible, but undoubtedly also the fact that the notion of the phenomenon in general seems so deceptively obvious. Clarifying it as succinctly as possible would therefore assist in removing unjustified obstacles and allowing the authentic difficulties to emerge.

The establishment of the "phenomenon" in metaphysics indisputably goes back to Kant, who accords it the role of a central concept, in relation to which the thing-in-itself remains a marginal authority (a margin or, more exactly, a limit). It is all the more remarkable that by being acknowledged in this way the phenomenon is immediately misunderstood by being equated with the object—within the universal framework of the division of objects into noumena and phenomena, under the aegis of the "supreme" concept of the transcendental object = X.[13] Is it self-evident that every phenomenon results in an object and falls under objectness? The question is essential primarily because it belongs to the objectness of the object to allow itself to be synthesized (thus produced) starting from another pole than itself, in this case starting from the originally synthetic unity of apperception, i.e., of the "I think," in short, of the *ego cogito* raised to the rank of the transcendental *I*. This structural alienation of the object from the ego removes the initiative of its appearing from the phenomenon. More detrimental still than the "subjectivism" thus imposed on the phenomenon, this decision above all sanctions the solipsism of the ego in the field of theoretical reason: it only knows what it produces by synthesis; it experiences no exteriority beyond what it could truly know. Husserl inherits this restriction of phenomenality from Kant and does not fundamentally dispute it. Neither the widening of intuition to the categorial and to essences, nor the recognition of passive syntheses, nor the nonobjective intentionalities (the other, time, my own flesh, etc.) will lead him to call into question "the privilege of the primordial objectness (*Urgegenständlichkeit*)"[14] as the ultimate horizon of phenomenality. The same privilege of the transcendental *I* inevitably follows from this, exercising control over all phenomena by the constitution that it secures for them. There also results the same difficulty of acknowledging phenomena that could not be constituted by the *I*—the phenomenon of the other stands out as first among these. The phenomenon cannot occur to the *I* as an event that would move it from the center in order to accomplish or transform it, except as a marginal exception, which calls into question the ordinary mode of phenomenality.

These aporias are sufficiently well known that I need not develop them. It is better to insist on their origin: the phenomenon, lowered to the level of the object, is alienated from the transcendental subject and, more radically, loses its initiative to appear. It no longer depends on the phenomenon to set in motion the process of its arrival at the visible. It must leave it up to synthesis (Kant) or to constitution (Husserl), in any case to the now uncontested transcendentality of the *I*. Heidegger became the first to have dared to question this subjection of the phenomenon to the *I* by challenging its interpretation as simple object. This decisive revolution is achieved with the imposition of an unprecedented definition of the phenomenon, which is henceforth understood as "what shows itself in itself." What shows *itself* in itself does not receive its visibility from somewhere else, for example, from the transcendental *I*, but properly from itself. It can also, at least formally, show itself *in* and *as* itself because it comes *from* itself and only *by* it. Phenomenology no longer aims at constituting (even less at synthesizing) the lived experiences of consciousness in an alienated object, starting from the apperceptive activity of a transcendental subject, but aims at "showing from *itself* what shows *itself* in such a way that it shows *itself* from *itself*."[15] And in fact, *Dasein* phenomenalizes itself from itself, no longer under the yoke of a transcendental subject: either because fundamental emotional tonalities (boredom, anxiety, care) happen to it at their own initiative, or because it achieves its own anticipatory resoluteness without deciding the moment or the modalities of its initiative. And if—as is open to debate—a "being phenomenon"[16] could ever phenomenalize itself, it would obviously not do so by starting from a being (even the *I*), but under its own light, appearing only from itself. Appearance no longer imposes itself on the phenomenon with the status of an object coming from a transcendental authority but, rather, erupts at its own initiative. The phenomenon appears in and by itself. It owes the crossing of the gap between the invisible and the visible only to itself.

Would it be necessary to accord a *self* to the phenomenon, to recognize for it an ipseity equal to that of the ego, in short, to separate ipseity from *egoity*? We doubtlessly must do so, thus running counter to the entire trend of metaphysics. At the least, the greatness of phenomenology in its Heideggerian moment lies in its having attempted this. Yet can one conceive such an ipseity of the phenomenon and grant to it a *self*, other than metaphorically? Can one define such a *self* of the phenomenon, of which Heidegger says nothing? The response to this question will take shape—perhaps—if another difficulty is considered, one that Husserl identifies with the "essential correlation between *the appearing and that which appears*."[17] In fact, phenomenality assumes that appearance does not deceive us and does not amount to a simple appearance, which would itself apply only to the visible and would hide any thing when it itself disappears. It thus assumes that the appearing takes charge of an appearance, which receives a visibility from this appearing but, in turn, fills it up with its still invisible reality. In order for appearance to yield to phenomenality, there must thus be a primordial correlation between appearing and appearance, an engagement of appearance in appearing. How should we qualify this engagement? It refers to the characteristic of appearing to give to appearance to the same extent as appearance enters into the appearing. On this model, phenomenality accomplishes itself in the full phenomenon insofar as the appearing gives the appearance and the appearance gives itself by entering into appearing. It is a question of "two absolute givennesses,"[18] the givenness of the appearing and the givenness of what appears by and as this appearing. By givenness, one must here understand the ultimate accomplishment of phenomenality, indubitable because it is perfectly reduced to immanence, such that it makes it possible to calibrate and accommodate all the degrees of presence, evidence, reality, and actuality, yet without itself being returned to them. The phenomenon thus recovers the sovereignty of its appearance only while being phenomenalized of and by *itself*, in showing *itself* from *itself*. Yet it attests this *self* only when the appearance enters into its appearing. And it enters into the appearing and commits to appear only if it gives *itself*. Nothing shows *itself* that does not first *give itself*. This rule of phenomenality in general measures the legitimacy and the possibility for any phenomenon to show itself according to the measure of givenness.

IV. The Phenomenality of the Sacrament as Phenomenality of Abandon

From such a redefinition of phenomenality, can we reconsider the preceding aporia—that of a visibility of the invisible in the sacrament, "*rei sacrae et* invisibilis *gratiae* formam visibilem"? Undoubtedly the specificity of a theological and in this instance inevitably christological theme must inspire us with great methodological prudence. And again undoubtedly, phenomenology, even when pushed toward new resources, cannot, any more than metaphysics can, unlock complete intelligibility for the Christian mystery. Even so, starting from the principle that nothing shows *itself* that does not first *give itself*, reasoning by analogy becomes possible and legitimate, provided that it helps us better to conceive what we would nevertheless never be able to comprehend. I will thus briefly but clearly try to outline here an approach to the phenomenality of the sacrament by analogy with the phenomenology of givenness.

In fact, as we have seen in section I, a certain mode of phenomenality is at stake in the sacrament. For by rights it is a matter of Christ's manifestation—not of a manifestation that Christ would fulfill only like an extrinsic act in the economy, at a point in the drama of salvation, but of a manifestation intrinsic to theology, which defines the very person of the Son, who is thoroughly directed toward the manifestation of the eternal mystery of God in the Spirit. Christ is manifested as the Son under the title of "icon of the invisible God, the firstborn of all creation" (Col. 1:15). Icon, thus visibility—of God, thus of the invisible. It is the eternal linking of the visible to the invisible as such, which remains invisible even in its manifestation. In this way the transition from the invisible to the visible—precisely what phenomenology knows how to think as such—determines the very person of the Word assuming flesh in Christ. The Son's mediation joins Christ's mediation in the same rendering visible of the invisible. Certainly, the analogy with the question of the phenomenon rightly concerns the sacrament—it manifests an invisible effect, grace, because "an instrumental cause, provided it is manifest, can be called the sign of a hidden effect (*causa instrumentalis, si sit manifesta, potest dici signum effectus occulti*)."[19] But first of all it concerns the origin of the sacrament and its only source of legitimacy, namely, the eternal involvement of the God of Jesus Christ in the process of *self*-manifestation and *self*-showing. God's self-dispensation is at stake in the sacrament, not as merely one of its effects or even one of its gifts, but as Himself. When God gives, he never gives less than himself. God causes in person: "It is God alone who works actively to produce the interior effect of the sacrament (*Solus Deus opereratur interiorem effectum sacramenti*)."[20]

We are thus on solid ground: the sacrament accomplishes and increases the intrinsic manifestation of the Son, the transition in him from the Father's invisibility to Christ's visibility, spread by the Spirit in its Church. In fact the Church consists only in allowing the trinitarian mystery to show *itself*—to phenomenalize itself according to all the figures of grace: the rhythms of the liturgy and prayer (*lex orandi, lex credendi*), the duty to the letter of Scripture and thus to its infinite hermeneutics, the sacraments beginning with baptism and the Eucharist, charisms directed at the good of the community, and all the fruits of holiness that result from it in countless and endless forms. More than a society, even the society of the children of the Spirit, the Church is defined in the world as the only stage where the manifestation of God's invisible can be accomplished, in accordance with the simultaneously visible and invisible work of the Spirit. God's holiness is able to show *itself* in this manifestation, against all likelihood, even through finitude and sin. It thus exercises an analogously phenomenological function: "I give you a new commandment, that you love one another. Just as I have loved you, you also should love one another. By this everyone will know that you are my disciples, if you have love for one another" (John 13:34–35). In the (obviously sacramental) communion of the faithful, a unique charity shows *itself*, the charity they share, because it unites them with Christ and connects them even to the union between Christ and the Father. In this union God thus shows *himself*—theologically speaking, manifests his glory—to the eyes of the world: "that they may all be one; even as you, Father, are in me and I am in you, may they also be in us, so that the world may believe that you have sent me" (John 17:21). The sign and accomplishment of salvation are actually indicated by a universal showing forth, therefore by the phenomenalization of the entire glory of God, according to the radical apocalyptic principle that "nothing is covered up that will not uncover *itself*, and nothing secret that will not *make itself* known" (Luke 12:2). One can and must obviously speak here of phenomenalization. Yet one can only do so with the reservation of an analogy: not because the phenomena of revelation show *themselves* less than those of the common realm of experience but, on the contrary, because they show *themselves* infinitely more. It is not a question here only of the constitution of objects starting from a transcendental subjectivity, which controls them by the initiative of intentionality and guarantees them via the assurance of intuitive fulfillment. Instead it is about receiving phenomena that show *themselves* from God's intentionality, such as he reveals himself in and from Himself, contrary to our expectations, projections, and purposes, according to the unfolding of an intuition that is "too much" (Mark 9:3), too strong for our capacity— the very glory of God. Before such phenomena—saturated phenomena of the mode of revelation—the usual problems of constitution give way to far more formidable difficulties of reception and its limits. At stake is admitting phenomena for which the excess of the intuition given goes beyond the range of concepts that we would have at our disposal to constitute them as objects. Because one must always aim at knowledge, it cannot remain confined to the processes of objectivation, but must always be accomplished by going beyond itself, that is, by being assimilated to faith. Faith is the mode of knowledge suitable for the saturated phenomena of the mode of Revelation. Thus, it is advisable to situate the sacrament within the horizon of God's Revelation in his icon, Christ, and to apprehend it, by analogy with the phenomenality of the world, as a phenomenon that shows *itself* par excellence and in excess.

Yet can one maintain this analogy? By what phenomenological right could one admit that the sacrament shows *itself* to the point of manifesting the invisible in God? It certainly shows, but simply what it gives to see as a phenomenon at face value—this bread, this wine, this water, this oil. By what right should one see here more than these simple things of the world, which anyway are perfectly sufficient to fill a gaze, a hand, and a human desire, or even that of an artist? By claiming that the invisibility of the kindness, the glory, and the grace of God shows *itself* here, do we not yield in the best case to a symbolic overvaluation or in the worst case to a magic delusion? This "enlightened" objection has its force, but also its weaknesses. Two decisive points must be considered.

First, any thing of the world, when it truly shows *itself*, that is, when it appears in its fullness and as such, instead of traversing our visual field during the short moment when we employ it for a purpose that remains foreign to it (everyday tools or technological implements), makes manifest much more than its materiality or its immediate utility. Water appears first of all as what saves my life (alleviates thirst, washes a wound) or threatens it (drowns me, sweeps me away); bread, as what maintains my strength, even poorly; wine, as what rejoices my spirit, even if it also troubles it; oil, as what comforts my flesh, embellishes it or embalms it. This means that the thing of the world *already* brings more than simply matter to the visible; therefore, it always renders manifest an invisibility (a sense, a promise). Any thing already shows infinitely more than its materiality. One does not require the gaze of a painter to be sure of this—one just needs an eye open to more than economic interest. And these moral and spiritual tonalities already appear at the outset, intrinsically, with the materiality of the sacrament, which thus implements a determination of phenomena in general in a mode that is simply more radical. Here, as in all cases, what the thing shows, at least when one allows it the freedom to show *itself*, depends on the extent of our welcome and the meaning it carries with it. But who or what gives it to the thing? He who gives it to us or we ourselves who accept it as given? What does "to give" mean here?

The second point follows from this. If we wonder about what (or who) gives what we will see, in order to decide what we actually see there, or rather what we are to see there (expecting to see there), this question refers us to strict phenomenology before any analogy. For as I established earlier (section III), nothing shows *itself*, which does not *first* give *itself* and to the extent to which it gives *itself*, because after all a phenomenon can manifest *itself* only inasmuch as it is *itself* given in real-life experience, as it enters in the flesh and in person into the field of consciousness. If water and bread, oil and wine already manifest more than their materiality, it is because from the outset they present more than matter to human consciousness, always already a total experience of itself. And this excess already authorizes them to phenomenalize the invisible in their appearing. By analogy, could one not envision a case where what is given would give *itself* in fact so radically that it guarantees, by this very engagement with our consciousness, that all it claims to give to see really shows *itself*—every invisible that it promises to see, because it gives it? Should one not consider the hypothesis that what gives *itself* would give *itself* so definitively that everything it promises to show really shows *itself*? In this context, the sacrament would show *itself* (would manifest the invisible within it) by virtue of the authority of what (or who) gives *itself* (or *himself*) within it: nothing less than the Spirit, such as Christ gives the Spirit by delivering *himself* up on the Cross to beloved humans, in their desert of love: "He said, 'It is finished.' Then he bowed his head and gave up his spirit" (John 19:30). Only this self-givenness—*kenosis* as abandon that enters irrevocably—immediately captures the authority that considers water and blood as more than daily tools but as the matter of the sacraments of the Spirit: "One of the soldiers pierced his side with a spear, and at once blood and water came out. (He who saw this has testified so that you also may believe. His testimony is true, and he knows that he tells the truth)" (John 19:34–35, see 1 John 5:5–8). The phenomenality of what gives *itself* extends to the givenness of the invisible; in short, it describes the sacrament as a phenomenon by full right, although by analogy, because what gives *itself* is given to the point of death and of the death on the Cross, because he who gives it gives *himself* absolutely. Christ gives *himself* to the point that even the invisible face of the Father can show *itself* among us.

That is enough to consider the sacrament in a perfect and whole phenomenality.

Originally translated by Bruce Ellis Benson

Transcendence par Excellence

The declaration that "God is love" (1 John 4:16) does not go without saying. Or, rather, it goes too well and too often without saying, having become a worn-out banality ("How would God not be *good*?") or a politically correct platitude ("At least this God does not drive people to war"), or even a placid piece of relativism masking discreet apostasy ("God is wherever people love each other"—and nowhere else). In short, to name God as love would more than any other naming mark off the offensive and consensual "humanism" into which Christians would once and for all like to dissolve the vertical and violent rupture that Revelation imposes on the world and its thoughts.

Even so, several hints should make us more cautious about this apparent harmlessness of the declaration that "God is love." First, the fact that philosophy, in the shape of metaphysics, has never (to my knowledge) picked up this name for referring to what it understands by the name of "God." It has sometimes thought of him as the One or the Good (Plato, Plotinus, Proclus). More often it speaks of him as the highest being [*l'étant*] or substance (Spinoza, Leibniz, Hegel) or even as Being [*l'être*] itself (Aristotle, Thomas Aquinas, Heidegger, etc.). Or as the infinite (Duns Scotus, Suárez, Descartes) or an idea of reason (Kant, Nietzsche, Husserl). Yet, in all these cases, these determinations lead in the end to the attribute of omnipotence, in the shape of efficient causality, final reason, or prime mover, and so forth. In all these cases, metaphysics degrades love to the derivative rank of one attribute among others, or it keeps a deafening silence on love altogether.

There are good reasons for this silence: basically it indicates a clear refusal of love as a possible determination of "God." First because metaphysics, at least modern metaphysics, in the end sees in love only a "passion" of the finite mind, completely unworthy of the first being (explicitly in Spinoza and Malebranche). Or it actually interprets love as mere "edification," whose subjective kindness would be unaware of all the "gravity, pain, patience, and negative work" that only the concept could put to work in the dialectic of reason, which alone would reach the absolute (Hegel). In short, in contrast to omnipotence, being, and the concept, love absolutely does not have the means for reaching the absolute, and thus for reaching what metaphysics understands by "God." One must abandon it among the anthropomorphic metaphors that thought can use in its infancy but which must disappear at the age of reason.

Yet there is more. Religious thought itself most often does not privilege love. Without speaking of Eastern kinds of wisdom, where the very notion of a "God" remains questionable, one must point out that neither Islam (which extols omnipotence, without which mercy would not have any legitimacy and which demands submission) nor even modern Judaism (where holiness leads to justice, which enacts omnipotence) do not privilege love, at least not as such and as the primordial determination of God's divinity.

But in the Christian Bible itself, this expression seems to come to the foreground only with difficulty and belatedly: Neither the Torah, nor the prophets, nor the wisdom writings, nor the Synoptic Gospels chance it; one must wait for the First Letter of John for it to become established literally.[1] It is as if the event of the Cross and of the resurrection and their apostolic hermeneutic had been necessary in order finally to end up seeing the core and the meaning of what they express. Obviously, we can from that point reread all the preceding texts as so many announcements, verifications, or explanations of the privilege henceforth accorded to love. But this retrospection itself confirms the wait for and the slowness of this acknowledgment. One might even venture to suggest that the revelation of love as the final Name of God represented precisely what Christ's contemporaries could not (and did not want to) hear—and especially so when the announcement stared them in the face and rang in their ears. Not because they did not want to see or hear anything at all, but because what they expected of God and what they hoped for from the Messiah coming to them did not really line up with the revelation of such a love. They did not ask for God to love them but for him to deliver and restore Israel, through a liberation as much political as religious—indeed a religious liberation, but one that would also confirm their election and privilege as God's people before all others. And in order to accomplish this, God first had to reveal himself as the God of armies or at least as the lord of universal history and the master of the created world. Consequently, as long as the event had not required the stamp of the kenosis of God himself as his highest revelation, as long as the resurrection had not taken root in the depth of the death on the Cross, as long as God himself had not publicly and irrevocably challenged what people imagined about "God"; in short, as long as one was still able to proclaim something other than "Christ and Christ crucified" (2 Cor. 2:2), it remained inconceivable that God himself would be named in accordance with and as love.

Naming God in Jesus Christ as "love" hence still involves quite a "scandal" and a kind of "madness." Yet from where exactly do they arise? Without doubt first from the fact that love should describe man more than God. For we know from experience that no man can avoid the test of love, at least its possibility. If we did not desire it so much, we would not suffer so much from failing at it, nor would we protect ourselves so much against it. Man as such is also love, even before being rational or thinking, political or laughing. It is enough for each man in his simple humanity to be able to love, even if on only one occasion and only a single time, and to know that it unfolds a rigorous, restrictive, univocal, almost merciless logic, which does not leave any doubt about its rationality, so different from calculating reason. The privilege of love is the only thing, in fact, at least among the things of the world, without which man cannot be understood. It seems to follow from this that love should be able to be understood by and starting from man, even exclusively within his scope: outside of man, there is no love. The "scandal" and the "madness" instead would consist in imagining love outside of man, for example, in God.

In a word, it would consist in imagining that love, with all its violence and its passivity, its apparent absurdity and its implicit mortality, its contingency and its temporality—in short, love such as humans experience it—could in any way be appropriate for God. And, vice versa, it would consist in fantasizing that God would in this sense (and there is no other) be able to teach us anything where love is concerned, even though he is completely clueless about it—as the Greek gods were clueless about our pains and serenely laughed at our sorrows. On the other hand, coming to terms with the "scandal" and the "madness" would come down to allowing for the possibility that God is more legitimately defined by love than we are. That would also mean that God himself would define love more exactly than we would. For God to be understood through love (better than us), it would first be necessary that he understand love (better than us). But in either case, it would above all be necessary that he practice this love better than we do. That, in turn, assumes two requirements. First, it would be necessary that God would love with the same love as we do, if one can say it like that, for otherwise it would no longer concern love *for us*, practicable by us, because it would no longer concern us. But it would also be necessary that God, practicing the same love that we do, nevertheless would exercise it in a radically different mode, one that would be unbelievable and unthinkable for us, that would, strictly speaking, be *divine*. The "scandal" and the "madness" are due to this conjunction, within the same gesture of God among humans, of the univocity concerning the practice of love with the equivocity concerning its mode of being exercised. The difficulty comes certainly from the concept of "love" (assumed to be common to God and us), but above all from the mode in which God exercises it (without any common measure with ours). For, to reiterate, God precedes us and transcends us, but first and above all in that he loves infinitely better than we love. God outdoes us as the best lover.

And the Scriptures say nothing different. If "God is love," it is because he loves "first" (1 John 4:19) and "to the end" (John 13:1). This perfection of "love (*agape*) is revealed in this way . . . not that we loved God but that he loved us first" (1 John 4:9–10). By sending his Son, God is ahead of us [*prend de l'avance*] in the act of love because he makes overtures [*fait des avances*] to us—thus acting like a lover. For the lover makes overtures and provokes love where none is found as of yet; he takes the risk of loving first and alone, without return on the investment. For better and, above all, for worse. For worse, when we are dealing with a human lover, such as the wretched Don Juan who does not maintain his lead [*son avance*] for very long, precisely for want of love, for want of force and of courage. For better, when we are dealing with Christ: for he not only commits [*s'avance à*] to loving those who do not love him yet (and who, as one sees right away, will love him only very little, very late, very badly, even never), but he commits to loving those whom nothing renders loveable, to the point of dying from loving them.

Why to the point of dying? Because "no one has greater love than this, to lay down one's life [one's soul] for one's friends" (John 15:13)—in other words, love can go to the point of loving the life of the beloved more than one's own (unconditionality). Actually, God's way of loving goes further; it doubles its first perfection by a second one—not only to prefer to one's own life that of the friend but even that of the enemy: "Love your enemies . . . For if you love those who love you, what reward do you have? Do not even the tax collectors do the same?" (Matt. 5:44, 46; that is to say, going beyond reciprocity). But a third degree of perfection still applies to love according to God: Giving one's life not only to someone who will not give anything back, but even and above all to someone who in no way deserves it, because he remains a sinner, that is to say, does not love love. "Indeed, rarely will anyone die for a righteous person—though perhaps for a good person someone might actually dare to die. But God proves his love for us in that while we were still sinners Christ died for us" (Rom. 5:7–8) (substitution). God loves according to the meaning of love as we know it, but he practices it in a way that is absolutely different from and opposed to ours. And in Christ's gesture we see these degrees of perfection performed in action: he dies, so that those who do not love him and who "do not know what they are doing" (Luke 23:34) can live the divine life. Instead of expecting someone to love him in order to decide to love in return, he loves in advance [*par avance*]. Instead of loving a loveable other, he loves someone who does not love (the sinner, the enemy), who does not love him and will never love him in return. Instead of loving someone who deserves it, he loves someone who does not deserve it. In short, instead of loving in order to be loved (like the human lover), he loves at the risk of his life—this means not only that he pays with his life, but that he loves irrevocably, without cease, without condition, and forever.

The saying that love knows no measure applies to man only secondarily; it first and foremost defines the manner in which God, and he alone, loves; besides, who among men has ever claimed to put the saying into practice?

It was Christ's masterwork among us to come into the depths of love, which *for us*, when made (or attempted) *by us*, proves most of the time to be a vague disaster, saturated with violence and lies. But he came in order to accomplish it perfectly and in a divine style, within the very conditions of our world and in the very condition of our humanity (solidarity in sin). And we find it hard not to challenge this masterwork for precisely this reason: we do not know how to love like this and such glory shames us. It shames us all the more given that he asks us to imitate his mode of love, that he even assures us that *in Him* (in the Spirit) we could manage to do so, in a way that leaves us no loophole. We must love now because all the conditions have miraculously come together. One of the ways of understanding the reversibility between love of neighbor and love of God in fact suggests that the former brings experimental proof of the latter into the visible world and into human society: "If someone says 'I love God' and he hates his brother, he lies. The one who does not love his brother whom he sees is not capable of loving God whom he does not see" (1 John 4:20).

Just as Christ makes the invisibility of the Father visible, as the Father guarantees Christ's visibility by his own invisibility, so does love for my brother present to everyone the visibility of my invisible love for God, as my love for God safeguards the invisibility of my visible love for my brother. Consequently, everything can be performed and hence truly decided on this completely open stage of charity.

Yet the truth could really make it obvious that, if we do not love, it is not at all because we cannot do so, but well and truly because we do not *want* to. We therefore hate this love we do not want. Love is not loved. Nor is God. Thus, the refusal itself of God only becomes intelligible inasmuch as "God is love," inasmuch as only love permits one to refuse it. What we call atheism still takes its possibility from God's charity toward us, for I can always "love darkness rather than light" (John 3:19). And in the same way what we call death also takes its possibility from charity, for "whoever does not love abides in death" (1 John 3:14).

One should therefore not be surprised that this naming has continued, throughout the entire history of Christian theology, to appear so much or even especially as a difficulty rather than as evidence. To convince ourselves, it would be enough here to take stock of the contradiction (or not) between the impassibility and the compassion of God, the difficult reconciliation of the names given in Exodus 3:14 and in 1 John 4:8, 16, and the debate on the divine names, the difference (or not) between *eros* and *agape*, the ecclesiological significance (or not) of the erotic paradigm in the Song of Songs, and, of course, the link between the love of God and the love of neighbor. These aporias have spanned Christian theology from its origins to our day and have occupied the greatest minds, at times pitting some of them against others, because the highest determination of God's transcendence is at stake in naming him as love. The highest summons of transcendence—actually the first and last for Christian revelation and for it alone—consists in charity: "comprehend, with all the saints, what is the breadth and length and height and depth, and to know the love of Christ that surpasses all knowledge (*gnōnai te tēn hyperballousan tēs gnōseōs agapēn tou Christou*)" (Eph. 3:18–19). God reveals in Christ's gesture that his divinity is performed and is said according to the "transcendent riches of his grace" (Eph. 2:7) and nothing else. Or more exactly, everything that human thought assigns by way of transcendence to God (as being Being itself, or omnipotence, omniscience, eternity, immortality, etc.), all this either comes from charity and leads back to it, or collapses into pure and simple idolatry. In this sense, love purges our heart of any idol, for it alone is given and said as the name of God, and yet it alone is confirmed in the experience of this world.

The radical nature of this unique transcendence also explains why we cannot completely follow it or form a notion of it. What do the gestures mean of forgiving seventy times seven, turning the other cheek after the first blow, having not even a single stone on which to lay one's head, and so forth? What does it really mean to love one's enemies? Who knows it, who can do it, except he who accomplished it, because he died on the Cross? We do not know it, and the hyperbole of these gestures will continue to remain as inaccessible to us as the transcendence to which they point. What's more, we most probably do not need to force them on ourselves directly since they first of all concern Christ himself, who is the only one to say them because he alone takes them on, perfectly. And most probably we also do not have to do so, for these gestures no more define a moral code drawn from the Scriptures than the paradox of the Beatitudes is transposable into a sociology. The trinitarian model itself does not require its reproduction by us because in the best of cases (I want to say: life in the Church), we can and must allow ourselves to be integrated into the trinitarian space, by adoption in the Son, by our incorporation into Christ. The Trinity no more defines the love of God than this love defines God. The Trinity puts love into operation, through Christ, in us.

PART IV

Recognition

10

The Recognition of the Gift

I. The Aporia of the Gift

Common sense distinguishes faith (like belief) and knowledge by the opposition between things we cannot see and things we can see. Yet, as Saint Augustine magnificently demonstrated, faith in things one does not see nonetheless allows no less for knowledge of them in the strictest sense because it refers to things we know perfectly well, even though these cannot but remain invisible; we can therefore know them only to the extent that they remain invisible. This is the case with a friend's friendship, kindness, will, and, above all, love: "Love in . . . the heart . . . is invisible (*amorem in . . . cordibus . . . est invisibilis*)."[1] Love cannot be seen and yet without doubt we manage to know it—otherwise how would we ever know and know so well that it has disappeared, and even *when* it disappeared?

It is the same for the gift, which most probably comes from love and puts it into operation. For the gift can never be seen. We are not talking here about a gift that would not be truly given or only ambiguously, but about a gift that is clearly and indisputably accomplished. The gift becomes all the *more* invisible the *more* effectively it gives itself. It disappears precisely in direct proportion to its appearing. This is an eidetic law. Therefore one cannot object that the giver would make his or her gift visible by firmly and decisively putting a gift on the table, stressing loudly that he is giving it for good, and that "what's given is given, to take back is to steal." On the contrary, the gift will appear all the *less*, the more that what is given visibly occupies the sight of the witnesses and of the beneficiary with the evidence of a real fact. For what is on the table, establishing its value and its price, its beauty or its utility, already no longer deserves the name of gift but immediately becomes a thing (a present, a tool, a good, etc.), which is useful for something or is worth something, even without being useful to anything other than itself. And the more this thing has been given, truly given, and therefore abandoned without return to the donor, the more it becomes a thing, destined for the naked possession of its user. This thing unfolds itself as such with unlimited ontic properties: material, form, color, purpose of use, beauty, market value, and so forth. All these properties define the thing in terms of real predicates, which make it worth owning, worthwhile for an agent to seize it as his full property and to use as his thing. But who cannot see that the gift, in other words the quality of having been given and the character of the given, are not among these real predicates? The given character of the thing does not define any property of this thing; it is not a real predicate. The given character can no more be described than it could serve for describing the object itself. The thing, which was perhaps formerly given, is already no longer so, because through the very performing of the gift it immediately enters into the *possession* of an owner, who does not count the given character among its properties, precisely because he counts this thing as one of his own properties. The gift has disappeared as such; the only thing that can still be seen is a thing owned.

This paradox should not surprise us because we verify it every day. For instance, when a child receives a present, he often forgets to say thank you; that is, he forgets the giver in order to grab hold of the given gift. By immediately using it and abusing it as a possession, the child also forgets not only the giver but also the gift's character of being given, and the gift disappears, leaving the thing that is owned to appear in its space and place. As a further example, ingratitude consists in nothing other than no longer recognizing the gift's character of being given, of seeing in it nothing more than the fact without its origin, the thing without its source. Ingratitude claims nothing real, but only suppresses what it censures as henceforth unreal—the gift's character of being given—and immediately the gift as such disappears because a non-given gift is no longer a gift at all.

As a final example, when I randomly come across a thing that has emerged from nowhere, lying at my feet or ready to hand, I can see it, that is to say, take it to be a lost object, already having an owner, probably upset and temporarily unknown. In this case I would need to make this object available again and detach myself from it. But I can also see it, that is, interpret it as an abandoned object, without owner, and therefore as a gift given to the first person who comes across it. In this case I could take possession of it. In both cases, the given gift can appear or most often disappear as such for the benefit of an appropriated thing, depending solely on my interpretation and need for possession. Yet this oscillation—sometimes a gift endowed with the character of being given, sometimes a naked possession—is only possible precisely because of the invisibility of the character of the given, and thus of the gift as such.

Therefore, the gift cannot be seen because the character of being given is not a real predicate of the thing. Even so, we live amid gifts and we can distinguish perfectly between gift and possession. How, then, do we gain access to what we do not see? Indeed, do we really gain access?

If seeing the gift that remains in principle invisible is what is at stake, we must resort to a phenomenology of the invisible. This expression will not be rejected too quickly or taken as an absurd contradiction if we keep in mind Heidegger's very sensible comment: "What is it that phenomenology is to 'let us see'? What is it that must be called a 'phenomenon' in a distinctive sense? What is it that by its very essence is *necessarily* the theme whenever we exhibit something *explicitly*? Manifestly, it is something that proximally and for the most part does not *show* itself at all: it is something that lies *hidden*, in contrast to that which proximally and for the most part does show itself."[2] In fact, all phenomenology, understood in its most rigorous sense, is ultimately occupied with making visible what without it would remain invisible, or more precisely unseen. In this sense, the invisibility of the gift is a matter for a radical phenomenology. But even such a radical phenomenology may not be sufficient for rendering manifest the unseen that so particularly constitutes the gift.

II. Knowing the Gift of God

It is actually possible that the case of the invisibility of the gift concerns an unseen with which only theology can deal. At least if by theology we mean Christian theology, understood in its weightiest privilege as arising from a Revelation and focusing only on it. And also at least if by gift one means the gift such that "no one can receive anything except what has been given from heaven" (John 3:27). So I will outline here a theological approach to the philosophical aporia of the gift.

In fact, this particular aporia is straightforwardly identified in Christ's statement to the Samaritan woman: "If you knew the gift of God" (John 4:10). Obviously she knows it no more than we do; so we can try to take what Christ tries to show her regarding the gift of God as an answer to the question of the gift itself. For in theology any gift comes from God and hence the gift of God also gives the gift in general. Let us thus take up the train of the dialogue. Choosing to sit at midday on the edge of Jacob's well in Sychar, Christ puts himself in the situation of being thirsty and having to ask for a drink. Now, this request in itself is already a gift, as the Samaritan woman rightly notices: the Jews never condescend to speak with Samaritans, even less to ask them for anything. Most probably she sees this gift of a request, but even so she does not recognize it *as such*. She sees in it only a request for water, for water that only she can draw because, as she will soon point out (John 4:11), Christ does not have anything to draw it out himself. Thus at first, she does not receive the gift given by Christ (the request itself); then, she puts herself in the position of mastery, not considering the water itself as a gift (of God) and as an opportunity for giving, but as her personal possession. Faced with the aporia of this double misrecognition of the gift, Christ doubles his own gift: "If you knew the *gift* of God, and who it is that is saying to you, '*Give me* a drink,' you would have asked him, and he would have *given* you living water" (John 4:10). This is an extraordinary declaration for several reasons.

The first reason is that God's gift is one with God's identification of himself: knowing what God gives is the same as recognizing the identity of him who asks (for a drink). In what follows, the gift of God is stated in several stages. First of all it consists in what one human *asks* of another; then in the fact that this human is a man asking a woman; next that this man is a Jew asking a Samaritan; then in that this Jew is Christ; and finally that Christ is not only "greater than our ancestor Jacob" (John 4:12) or even "a prophet" (John 4:19), but really the Messiah who says "I am" (*ego eimi*; John 4:26), which only God can say and which he had already said to Moses (Exod. 3:14). In the end, God gives precisely the fact that it is he who gives to humans, and not they who give to God, as they think they do, to the point of only discussing the right place for their supposed gifts.[3] In fact, within the dialogue now only God gives, and as a result he gives what only he can give, namely, eternal life, the very life of God: "Those who drink of the water that I will give them will never be thirsty again. The water that I will give will become in them a spring of water gushing up to eternal life" (John 4:14). God's gift consists in this: that God gives and that he gives nothing less than himself in the person of Christ. The difficulty of the Samaritan woman lies only in being able to recognize Christ as the gift, or rather in recognizing him as God—which comes down to the same thing because it concerns the "gift of God." In any case, she does not have difficulty seeing who comes toward her but recognizing him as a gift.

The crisis that the gift of God inflicts on the world thus lies in a decision: either recognizing Christ *as* a gift of God by referring him back to God and so seeing him *as* God himself, or seeing him *as* a being in the world among others, who gives nothing because he does not refer back to anything, with the result that he can be possessed and perhaps even killed. For in order for a gift to be seen as given, it is not enough that it really appear; it is also necessary that it appear *as* given, hence be recognized *as* such. Yet this very recognition of the gift as gift itself has to happen as a gift. For only those to whom it has been given to see it *as* given will recognize it: "Not everyone can accept this teaching, but only those to whom it is given" (Matt. 19:11). To see the gift, one must double the gift of the gift by the gift of its recognition.

III. Recognition of the Gift, Recognition of Christ

The question of the gift is thus unfolded in exemplary fashion in the question of Christ because Christ appears as the very gift of God: "For God so loved the world that he gave his only Son" (John 3:16). Therefore, won't the aporia of the gift—that it can remain invisible while really being a given gift—extend to Christ himself, who is effectively invisible *as* the Son of the Father, the Christ of God, even though the Samaritan woman sees him with her eyes? In this case, the aporia of the recognition of Christ (as God's gift) would confirm and ratify the aporia of the recognition of the gift in general.

This would indeed be the case if Christ did not transgress the aporia, because he manages to restore in himself the conditions for the visibility of the gift *as* given. For the aporia consists in this: that the gift, as soon as it is given, is imposed on the gaze as an autonomous and independent being, which erases any trace of its source (the giver) and conceals its innate contingency (its character of being given, its givenness). Denying its giver, it frees itself from its givenness in order to be reborn as a subsistent thing, without reference or return to any other authority than itself. In contrast, Christ appears from beginning to end as a gift, even when he is established as a stubborn fact of history and the world. Or rather, he unceasingly demands that his interlocutors not take him as a self-referential fact, but that they recognize him according to his source and his character as given. He appears *as* gift because he does not stop claiming and realizing his return and reference to the one who sent him (John 17:18), from whom he comes (John 5:43), and to whom he turns (John 1:2) and returns (John 17:11), the Father. Christ defines himself as gift in claiming his status as a gift given by the Father and coming only from him: "But now I am going to him who sent me, yet none of you asks me, 'Where are you going?'" (John 16:5).[4]

Indeed, no one asks him this because no one has the habit, the strength, or even the desire to return whatever (whether a thing or ourselves) to whomever in order to turn it into a gift and make it appear *as* such. On the contrary, we maintain the being [*l'étant*] in its autonomy as long as possible in order to reduce it without remainder into the least object of possession. Faced with Jesus, the gaze of the natural attitude does not stop wanting to see him as an autonomous, self-identical being, and without any return to whatever or whomever: "'*Where* did this man get this wisdom and these deeds of power? Is not this the carpenter's son? ... *Where* then did this man get all this?' And they took offense at him" (Matt. 13:54–57). The scandal comes from the fact that Jesus cannot really be summed up in what they would nevertheless like to see, a being equal to nothing more than itself, the son of a carpenter. The wisdom and the miracles—that is, he himself entirely—come to him from somewhere other than him and make him appear *as* the Christ, that is to say, *as* the gift given by God. The hatred against Jesus is about the permanent demand of being recognized as Christ, as the Son of Man, as the Son of the Father—in a word, *as* a gift irreducible to itself. And he was put to death so that one would not have to recognize him *as* this gift of God.

The demand to be recognized *as* God's gift is unfolded according to two references, one ontic, one phenomenal. First, Jesus asks that he be recognized *as* God's gift by referring himself back without reservation to the Father *as* his Son. He does so as much for his acts—"I have come in my Father's name, and you do not accept me; but if another comes in his own name, you will accept him" (John 5:43)—as for his words: "My teaching is not mine but his who sent me" (John 7:16). Obviously, this ontic dependence should not be confused with the gap of creation (the creature depending on its creator), but bears testimony to the trinitarian distance, in which the Son shares equally in the very glory of the Father: "I do not seek my own glory; there is one who seeks it" (John 8:50); "If I glorify myself, my glory is nothing. It is my Father who glorifies me" (John 8:54). This dependence in no way contradicts his glory, but he shares the glory of the Father precisely by allowing himself to be attested *as* the Son. And what is particular to the Son consists in not being by himself, but by another, who gives him, and first of all gives him to himself. To recognize Jesus *as* the gift of God, one must first recognize him *as* the Son of the Father.

How do we understand that at times it falls to the Son to glorify the Father: "so that the Father may be glorified in the Son" (John 14:13)? If glory is shared and exchanged between the Son and the Father ("Father, the hour has come; glorify your Son so that the Son may glorify you," [John 17:1]), that is not only because everything is shared in equal dignity within the Trinity *thanks to* the difference in relations, but also because the ontic reference of the Son to the Father is doubled by a phenomenal reference of the Father to the Son. To Philip's (and our) request that Jesus "show us the Father," there is only one right response: "Whoever has seen me has seen the Father" (John 14:9). In other words, "whoever sees me sees him who sent me" (John 12:45).⁵ Just as seeing Jesus *as* God's gift requires recognizing him according to his absolute ontic dependency *as* Son sent by and returning to the Father, so seeing Jesus *as* God's gift in the same way implies recognizing his face [*visage*] as the form [*face*] of the Father, and, only on this condition, recognizing him *as* the Son. Christ's face [*face*] shows not his own, but that of the Father. Or rather, the face of Christ manifests the only possible visibility of the Father. Saint Irenaeus captured well the paradox of the visibility of the Father in the face of Christ, according to a phenomenality of pure reference: "For the Father is the invisible of the Son, but the Son the visible of the Father (*Invisibile etenim Filii, Pater—Visibile autem Patris, Filius*)."⁶ But there is more. For saying that the Father has no other face [*visage*] than that of the Son, or rather that the face of the Son shows the Father in himself and directly, means in turn that we must see the face of Jesus *as* that of Christ, *as* that of the Son, and hence in the end *as* that of the Father. Or, more precisely, as directly the visibility of the invisible Father. In other words, to recognize Christ *as* God's gift, one has to manage nothing less than recognizing the visible face of Jesus *as* what can be seen of the invisible Father.

The messianic recognition of Jesus *as* Christ, that is to say, *as* the Son, and therefore *as* the visibility of God, brings to perfection the recognition of the gift *as* given. So is it then possible that, in certain cases, the recognition of a gift requires the messianic recognition of Christ *as* the gift come from the Father? Does the practice of the gift *as* such require, at times, the recognition of Christ *as* such?

IV. Bread and Wine as Gift

As we have seen, the aporia of the recognition of the gift lies within the self-positing of the gift, which masks its origin and contingency, that is to say, its giver and givenness. The given gift, insofar as it is precisely perfectly given, becomes established in itself with the authority of its autonomy, so that its constancy conceals its source and so that it ends up being canceled *as* gift. The gift therefore accomplishes itself by going so far as to destroy the trace of its givenness and even of the gift given in it. Heidegger said this clearly: "It [the 'there is' / *es gibt*] withdraws in favor of the gift which it gives."[7] The giver, and especially givenness, are concealed and then shaved off by the resistance of the gift in its insistence. The gift tends to insist within itself to the point of claiming substance by itself and in the end losing the title of gift. By abandoning the given within itself, the gift takes the condition of persistent being, so that it cancels in itself the giver and givenness. Thus if givenness is to appear again, it would be necessary for the giver to become again visible within the persistent being and through it. This obviously implies that this self-persistence becomes blurred, even vanishes and returns as a gift clearly given: then, if the gift becomes sufficiently transparent to the giver, givenness is recovered. Seeing the gift *as* gift requires that it allow itself to be seen transparently as referring to the giver without remainder or disruption. Self-persistence must diminish so that the gift might increase in it. And the gift must diminish so that the giver and above all givenness might increase. "He must increase, but I must decrease" (John 3:30). For the gift to begin again to allow itself to be recognized *as* gift, it therefore has to decrease to the benefit of the donor, thus first to the benefit of givenness, as through a sort of kenosis of phenomenality. The giver, givenness, and the given itself are only illuminated if the insistence of being decreases, that is to say, only if the given gives itself up to givenness and only to the extent of this abandon(ment).[8]

Even in a very quick reading of 1 Corinthians 11:21–26, we can show that such a kenotic gift culminates par excellence in the Eucharist. Indeed, Saint Paul describes the Eucharist in a definitely kenotic manner, because it is accomplished in a triple gift that is pushed each time all the way to abandon. To begin with, there is the gift of the abandoned Christ: "on the night when he was betrayed (*paredideto/tradebatur*)" (1 Cor. 11:23).[9] Christ is *given* up, as one says, namely by and in the betrayal. Given—and given to the point of abandonment—because he really gives up his life willingly (John 10:18)[10] and renounces holding onto his divinity (Phil. 2:6). In this way he paradoxically manifests his condition as Son, as the one who only becomes himself by receiving everything from the Father, thus by abandoning himself to him. The abandonment to death of the perfectly *given* Son in turn perfectly testifies to the giver and to givenness. Second, it concerns a gift so radically abandoned that it can henceforth be endlessly handed on again and again: "For I received (*parelabon/accepi*) from the Lord what I also handed on (*paredōka/tradidi*) to you" (1 Cor. 11:23).[11] The abandonment of the gift, accomplished to the point of the excess of betrayal, now makes the tradition possible. If Paul can hand on what he had received, that depends not so much on pedagogy but on what legitimizes it *here*, namely, the request by Christ himself to repeat this: "Do this in remembrance of me" (1 Cor. 11:24, 25), so that, every day of your present, you both proclaim and request my future: "For as often as (*hosakis/ quotiescumque*) you eat this bread and drink the cup, you proclaim the Lord's death until he comes" (1 Cor. 11:26). Finally, the possibility of tradition in the Church, in other words, of the power to give again the gift that has been given to it, relies on the tradition transmitted to it by the Holy Spirit, that is, the gift of him who "gave up his spirit (*paredōken to pneuma/tradidit spiritum*)" (John 19:30).

The first two instances of abandon(ment) in which the gift is accomplished, betrayal and tradition, point to a third one that brings together the other two as their final intention: the gift of bread and wine. More precisely, the gift of bread "broken for you" (1 Cor. 11:24), or, according to some manuscripts, confirmed by Luke 22:19, "given for you (*hyper humōn didomenon/quod pro vobis datur*)." The gift of bread is confirmed in the expenditure of the wine "shed (*ekhunomenon/funditur*)"[12] for "the new covenant." As simple foods, the broken bread and the spilled wine are already truly given, but given at a loss, consumed without return, in a word, abandoned. But they do not only have this function *here* because a statement overdetermines them: "This is my body" (1 Cor. 11:24). Here, the minimal remnant of a presence that points to the bread and wine must fill, as abandoned gift, the role of the presence of the gift of the Son who has come in the flesh to manifest his dependence within givenness. How could the abandoned gift, almost without any presence or subsistence, give body to the most accomplished gift? How could the minimal persistence appear to us as the body of Him who is, was, and will be? For it is not enough to invoke here the dogmatic definition of Christ's real presence in the bread and the wine—for example, by identifying it as *transubstantiation*; these definitions bring the difficulty of seeing the bread and wine *as* Christ to a head rather than resolving it for us, besides having only this ambition—to establish the impossibility that the sacrament nevertheless requires. The Eucharist thus offers the paradigm of the gap between what experience gives us to see and the gift we are to recognize.

V. The Perfect Gift

The Eucharist is thus recognized precisely as gift. Or rather, as paradigm of any gift of alms, it accomplishes its logic. Consider the gift of the widow in the Temple. Why does her gift give "more than all" the others, even though its amount is the lowest of all, almost negligible? It does so precisely because its material shape disappears to the point where it allows the contingency of givenness and the identity of the giver to appear. By giving so little the widow accomplishes her own kenosis, for she does not give from what she has but, as the text paradoxically says, "out of her loss": this less than nothing is no longer an obstacle to the givenness of the gift, but finally reveals it (Luke 21:4). The more the gift is emptied of itself to the point where it is reduced to a minimal presence, the more the giver appears there in the superabundant light of givenness. The widow involuntarily cancels the reality of her gift and this loss of reality makes it appear as pure gift (nonreal predicate), which no longer presents any obstacle to the manifestation within it of its giver. By giving what she lacks, the widow receives appearing finally *as* a giver no longer hidden by any given. The same is true of the Eucharist: as gift reduced to the most ordinary things whose contingence dooms them to disappearance, its transparency allows the giver to appear: Christ himself who by his kenosis allows the ultimate giver, the Father, to appear. The real presence actually *de-realizes* the matter of the gift, which, paradoxically, in turn phenomenalizes its giver and allows the entire process of givenness to appear.[13]

We can now understand how the gift can be recognized *as* gift, provided that we distinguish at least three situations; for the more the realm of the gift is extended, the more difficult it becomes to recognize it as such. First, the situation of the perfectly recognized but unique gift: the eucharistic gift, in which the bread and wine are recognized *as* body and blood because, more radically, the believer can recognize them *as* Jesus, sometimes without admitting it, *as* the king of the Jews (Pilate, according to John 18:34–35; the Sanhedrin, according to Luke 22:36), sometimes under constraint or force *as* the Son of God (the centurion in Matt. 27:54 and Mark 15:39), and finally sometimes in full awareness, like Peter: "You are the Christ, the Son of the living God" (Matt. 16:16 or 14:33). In whatever form the Spirit works, the gift of the species [of bread and wine] appears *as* the gift of the Resurrected to the precise extent to which Jesus makes himself known *as* Christ. Recognizing the gift *as* such then means no longer seeing the thing in its stubborn opaqueness (this man born in Nazareth, this piece of bread, this cup of wine), but *as* it gives itself (Christ, his body, and his blood), from the point therefore *from which* the gift departs, as it happens, from the Father, because, in the end, in its transparency the eucharistic gift gives the Father to see through the Son and in the Spirit. "Every generous act of giving, with every perfect gift (*pasa dosis agathē kai pan dōrhēma teleion*), is from above (*anōthen*), coming down from the Father of lights" (James 1:17). This does not mean that near God there are, among other possibilities, acts of giving and perfect gifts; but that no gift appears as such if it does not come from elsewhere and that none comes from elsewhere except the one that comes from above, therefore, from God himself. The perfection of its reference to God makes perfect the gift that comes from there.

Now let us take the situation of all the other gifts that are not accomplished, which are the majority. The previous rule applies everywhere: Recognizing the gift *as* such requires seeing it *as* given, that is to say, aiming across its minimalist transparency at the one who gives it. In this way one can, in turn, see the gift from the point of view of its giver, according to the abandon granted by him, all the way to the essential contingency of givenness, and not, as is often the case, from the point of view of its recipient, who is unable not to make himself its owner, cutting it off from its giver, removing any trace of givenness from it, and finally making it an object without reference to anything other than itself. In all these cases, recognizing or not recognizing the gift *as* gift depends on the capacity of the gaze to see, through the transparency of the given thing, the giver from whom it comes forth and the givenness that determines it with contingency (or rather makes it indeterminate). In the end, recognizing the gift *as* gift accordingly depends on the proper hermeneutical decision— on the hermeneutics of givenness.

This mechanism has bearing on all cases in which a thing, a being, or an object could (the conditional matters here) be recognized *as* a gift. But we still need to distinguish two situations. Either the hermeneutics proceeds without an insurmountable aporia and the recognition of the gift *as* gift makes the contingency of givenness so clear that the giver himself can appear transparently. In this case, givenness leads to the alterity of a giver and allows for an intersubjective community, a communion with the other or even an ethics. Or the recognition of the gift *as* gift does not make the contingency born of givenness clear, so that the giver can no longer appear transparently. In this case, hermeneutics still recognizes givenness by the guideline of the gift's contingency, but does not reach the giver. It does indeed recognize the gift *as* given, but without seeing or aiming at the giver. We find ourselves in such an undecided, at times even undecidable situation at first sight and in the majority of cases. Only saturated phenomena allow us to go even further.

Originally translated by Adina Bozga and Cristian Ciocan

11

"They Recognized Him and He Became Invisible to Them"

Why do we believe so badly in God, and so little in Christ? First of all (does it not go without saying?), we are indeed reduced, with regard to God and Christ, to believing, since knowledge of them escapes us. We believe (and believe badly, miscreants that we are) precisely because in this case we cannot reach a scientific certainty, composed of clear and distinct ideas. What exactly, then, do we lack that prevents us from attaining such a scientific knowledge? The answer seems obvious: We believe, or at least we are reduced to having to believe (or not), because, while we have at our disposal many statements and concepts having to do with God (existence, properties, Trinity, creation, etc.) and with Christ (historical reality, death, resurrection, etc.), elaborated to high degrees of subtlety by centuries of tradition and theology, we decidedly lack intuitions that would allow us to validate some and risk rejecting others. Only by recourse to faith can we fill this deficit of intuition with regard to the proliferation of concepts, unless we bury it by refusing such recourse. Faith, according to this way of thinking, would serve, for better or worse, to compensate faulty intuition, (almost) as a means to verify the concepts experimentally. I believe, because, in spite of everything, I want to hold as true what does not offer intuitive criteria sufficient to impose itself by itself. I believe in order to recapture the intuition, which God and Christ cannot or will not give to me of their presence. So argues the majority of the credulous, the men of the world in its normal course—by which I mean experts, scholars, philosophers, and even some theologians.

This argument nevertheless results in a blasphemy. First of all because it makes me, and only me, a "knight of faith"—the singular actor, within the supposed "night" of knowledge, of a faith without reason, who alone decides regarding the existence of God and the truth of Christ, like a god deciding on God. Second, because God and Christ become in this context either impotent (incapable, in fact, of fulfilling the Revelation that they promise), or perverse judges (who, in masking themselves, expose me to unbelief by condemning me to a faith without reason). These consequences alone should suffice to convince us of the inanity of such a definition of faith. It might be that faith does not consist in the compensation of a shortage—or, perhaps, that the shortage is an entirely different one from that of intuition, one that would instead locate deficiency in the conceptual statements. It might be that we should believe not in order to recapture a lack in intuition but, rather, to confront its excess in relation to a deficiency of statements and a dearth of concepts.

An episode from the Gospel of Luke (Luke 24:13–25)[1] illustrates this paradox. Let us attempt a reading. On the road from Jerusalem to Emmaus, two disciples, or rather two former disciples of Jesus, are walking and discussing together (in a word, *hōmiloun* [v. 14]); they chat in a desultory manner, they "exchange" (v. 17) conversation about everything that comes to mind, just to soothe their sadness. In fact, they are talking about a specific, obsessive subject, "about all that has happened—*peri pantōn tōn sumbebēkotōn toutōn*" (v. 14), about incidents that occurred just like that, without any apparent reason, without any foreseeable cause—what we sometimes call "the events" because we cannot or dare not say more. For it is a matter of pure facts, incontestable and confirmed without a doubt, known by all. Won't they, in a moment, express astonishment, with involuntary comedy, given the circumstances, at the fact that one could be ignorant of what everyone (everybody and anybody) knows—"Are you the only pilgrim[2] to Jerusalem who does not know the things that have happened there in these days?" (v. 18). Not know what? "What things (*poia*)?" (v. 19). Their response sounds like a police report: that Jesus of Nazareth, "a prophet mighty in deed and word before God and all the people"[3] was condemned to death, then crucified by the chief priests and leaders. Here is the accident, the incident, the "event," in short, the fact guaranteed by a public intuition offered to all and to which an entire city (and what a city!) can testify. Here is the intuition that they do not understand, that is to say, that they cannot contain, or take back into their concepts—whence the feeling of absurdity due to a deficit of concepts: "O foolish (*anoētoi*, without spirit) [men], slow to understand!" (v. 25).— Let us consider these two men and their obtuseness, for we are their counterparts, their brothers [*leurs semblables, leurs frères*]. We too walk and chat like them, rehashing and reconsidering confirmed facts from every angle (Who today would contest the crucifixion of Jesus, especially if he could draw from it an argument for the end of his Revelation?), arriving, like them, only at absurdities (or bankrupt theologies, which attenuate the absurdities).

Like us, it is thus not the intuition of facts that they lack but, rather, the understanding (the concepts), as is true of us today: well do they know, as do we, with scientific certainty, that Jesus died, and that one does not come back from the dead; we can deplore this fact, especially in this case, but in the end that's how it is; we must stay reasonable and not lose our heads. They stick by this evidence no less than we do, to the point of no longer considering that the question might even be worth discussing. An unlikely paradox follows: Christ overtakes them on the road ("drawing near, he began to travel with them" [v. 15]); probably, he walks faster than do they (he would have been able to continue on when they ask to stop [v. 29]). Soon, we suppose, after some silence, he has them speak of their conversation, of their sad ravings. And, walking along the same path, hearing the sound of his voice, nevertheless "their eyes were kept from recognizing him" (v. 16). By what, exactly? What concrete sign, what sensible perception, what intuition was lacking? Clearly none whatsoever. In fact, they kept *themselves* from recognizing him. Why were they denying the evidence? Not because it was deficient—it wasn't lacking in the slightest—but because it contradicts their whole comprehension (their miscomprehension, or at the least, their pre-comprehension) of a phenomenon that is nevertheless patently before their eyes and in their ears. They do not recognize him because they cannot even imagine that this is really him, He, who has rejoined them, so far do their poor, cobbled-together, honest-to-goodness concepts find themselves outstripped by "events" that leave them petrified within a matrix of irrefutable prejudices. Not that they would not want to believe; they simply do not even imagine any other hypothesis, it never crosses their minds, even for an instant. The dead man is dead, period. Every other possibility finds itself completely excluded, cannot even be considered. They see nothing—in the sense that one sees nothing in a game of chess if one does not know how to play; they hear nothing—in the sense that one hears nothing (except noise) in a conversation if one does not know the language in which it is taking place. They do not see anything happening on the field. Nothing knocks them out (unlike the brutes who come to arrest Christ in Gethsemane, John 18:6), because nothing strikes them—they are duds. Every intuition gives itself to them, but their concepts catch nothing of this.⁴ Indeed, "how true that it is not the eyes alone that are useful for recognizing Jesus Christ" (Claudel).⁵

This situation—a phenomenon intuitively certified, yet missed conceptually—was already known to the disciples. At the time of the Transfiguration on Mount Tabor, where the evidence of Christ's divine glory shone forth so much that his clothes became "intensely white, as no fuller on earth could bleach them," when, that is, the intuition surpassed what the world permits and tolerates, they all "became exceedingly afraid," so much so that Peter could only chatter about three booths, because "he did not know what to say" (Mark 9:3–4, 7). Standing before the crucified, too, the intuition, this time without glory, but sinister and prosaic, nevertheless allowed no one to say anything appropriate—no one understood what they were nevertheless all seeing, to the point that, at the cry, "Elie, why have you abandoned me?" they recognized neither "my God!" nor the words of Psalm 22, but heard only the name of the prophet Elijah (Matt. 27:46–47, Mark 15:34–35, Luke 23:44–45). But this nearly insurmountable difficulty of fixing in an appropriate concept the nevertheless patent intuition of the person of Christ already constituted the entire stake of Peter's confession: "He asked his disciples, 'Who do men say that the Son of Man is?' They said, 'For some, he is John the Baptist, for others Elijah, and for yet others Jeremiah, or one of the prophets'" (Matt. 16:13–14; see Mark 8:27–28, Luke 9:18–19). And, when Peter finally gives him the name (the concept) of Christ, Son of God, Jesus immediately points out to him that such a word, name, and concept could come to him neither by "flesh, nor by blood," but only by "revelation" from the Father himself (Matt. 16:17)—so much do people lack the ability to produce, from themselves, the concept adequate to what the intuition nevertheless unceasingly gives them to see: precisely, Christ. Standing before Christ in glory, in agony, or resurrected, we are always lacking words (and thus concepts) to say what we see, in short to see that with which intuition floods our eyes. When he comes among us—though he comes, or rather precisely *because* he comes—we, who are his own people, cannot "grasp him, understand him" (John 1:11). God does not measure his intuitive manifestation out stingily, as if he wanted to conceal himself at the moment of showing himself. But we do not offer concepts capable of handling a gift without measure and, overwhelmed, dazzled, and submerged by his glory, we no longer see anything. The light plunges us into blackness—with a luminous darkness. What is more, the miscomprehension even appears inevitable—so much does the inadequacy of our concepts to the factual intuition of Christ result directly from the incommensurability of the gift of God to the expectation of men. What is there to say?

So Christ becomes a teacher. Because the two disciples lack concepts, he trains them to a concept. First, he lets them again have their fill of chatting without saying anything: the powerful prophet, who was to restore Israel, but who was scandalously put to death on a Cross by the leaders of the people and the priests, by his people. And all this talk remains, in a sense, true—at least, would remain true if they understood what they were saying. Why do they not understand it? Because they do not reconstruct these significations from the starting point of the passion as revelation of God's charity, hence also of the resurrection as the fulfillment of this very charity. And yet, they had indeed received, even if only verbally, the key to such a hermeneutic. They avow this clearly, making their incomprehension even more obvious: "Yes, and besides all this, it is now the third day since this happened" (v. 21)—without for a moment thinking of the announcement of his resurrection after three days (Luke 9:22)![6] And there is no lack of intuitive symptoms to call to mind this announcement: "Moreover, some women of our company" (v. 22) went to the tomb and did not find the body; they even brought back the message of angels reporting him living; and some men "who were with us" (v. 24) have confirmed it. And nobody "has seen anything" (v. 25). No one sees anything, because no one understands the meaning of the intuitions—"these words seemed to them an idle tale" (v. 11). They cannot, and they decidedly do not want to, understand; thus, while having intuitions, they see nothing.

So Christ, at last, takes his turn to speak. He delivers the proper significations and orders the intuitions according to the concepts missing up to this point. Which ones? Precisely those very concepts that the disciples stammered, stumbled over, and pulled to pieces without hearing anything—"beginning with Moses and all the prophets, he made the hermeneutic for them of everything, *which concerned him*, in the Scriptures (*diermēneusen autois en pasais tais graphais ta peri heautou*)" (v. 27). Not of everything *that* concerned him, but all the Scriptures *as they refer to Him alone*—for everything in the Scriptures, absolutely everything without the exception of a single iota, concerns only him.[7] Some will ask, by what right can he deliver to them such an absolute hermeneutic—the only true, absolute knowledge that we ought to desire, which makes that of our philosophy appear as nothing more than a destitute person's phantasm? By the right that the *Logos*, as sole "exegete of God (*ekeinos exēgēsato*)" (John 1:18), has to interpret the Scriptures that God inspired in order to announce Him to humans as the fulfillment of all his promises. We detect here, in a silence within this unheard-of text (which doubtless protects us from what we would be unable to bear hearing openly), the unsurpassable lesson of any exegesis and of any hermeneutic that wants to constitute itself truly as the science that would treat of the literal incarnation of the Word of life. The text will tell us nothing more of this exegesis, other than that it made the disciples understand that "it was fitting that the Christ should suffer in order to enter into his glory" (v. 26). For this fitness (stronger even than a necessity) appears, in fact, to give by virtue of itself alone a meaning (its concept)—up to that point missing—to the superabundant, but still blind, intuition. And when the concept at last matches the intuition, the phenomenon bursts forth with its superabundant glory: "Did not our hearts [and thus our minds] burn within us while he talked to us on the road in such a way as to open to us the [concepts of the] Scriptures?" (v. 32). This fervor comes neither from the bare texts, nor from the obscured ideas of men, but from the perfect adaptation of the thoughts of God (recorded in the Scriptures) to the acts of God (*gesta Christi* offered to our intuition), which manifest in a perfect phenomenon "the mystery hidden for ages in God . . . the manifold wisdom of God" (Eph. 3:9–10).

From this moment on the teaching can fulfill itself by proposing the requisite significations, no longer only in words, but even in actions. Although they are already approaching their stopping place, the disciples do not yet dare to say anything; Christ waits for them to respond to him or to ask him something of themselves, the truth, for example. To provoke their decision, "he looked to be going further" (v. 28); caught unawares, at the first pretext ("'it is towards evening and the day is now far spent'"),[8] they at last dare to beg: "Stay with us" (v. 28). To stay with him—this is what the Samaritans (John 4:40) and the first future disciples (John 1:38–39) had asked (and obtained) of Christ.[9] This is above all what Christ had asked (and obtained) of Zacchaeus, but also what the disciples had denied Christ at Gethsemane (Matt. 26:38: "Stay here and watch with me"). In fact, the whole question of the coming of Christ and of faith in him comes down to this: "to have his *logos* abiding in us (*en humin menonta*), or not" (John 5:38). For the first time since "the events," the disciples ask Christ, and thus in fact the *Logos* himself and in person, to stay with them and they with him—that is, they ask to receive his *logos*, his interpretation of what has happened in intuition and what they have nevertheless neither seen, nor caught, nor understood. They finally ask him *his* meaning, *his* concept, *his* interpretation of the intuition of Easter, which is public, yet unintelligible to spectators. So "he went in to stay with them" (Luke 24:29), in order to give them, as a sign that cannot be missed, the signification that will at long last give meaning to all the intuitions that up to then had remained scattered and absurd.

What signification? No word, no discourse, no sound—except that of the blessing: "Taking the bread, he said the blessing, broke it and gave it to them." At once "their eyes were opened and they recognized him" (v. 30–31)—because the signification was making visible its phenomenon. In other words, they saw that "this is my body which is given for you" and "in memory of me," and that therefore, as he had promised not to "eat [this Passover], until it is fulfilled in the Kingdom of God" (Luke 22:19 and 15), precisely that very evening, in which he is again eating it, is already part of the Kingdom of God fulfilled in spirit and truth, of the resurrection. At once, "rising (*anastantes*)" (v. 33)—literally: reviving, they acknowledge their burning hearts, go back up to Jerusalem, and again do for the disciples the "exegesis (*exēgounto* [v. 35])" that they had received (v. 27)—the recognition in the sign (in the signification in action) of the breaking of the bread. The disciples accept this as the strict equivalent of their own phenomenal experience: "The Lord has truly come back to life and has shown himself (*ōphthē*) to Simon" (v. 34). The phenomenalization to Simon and the breaking of the bread with the two disciples amount to the same certainty—the resurrection.

What we lack in order to believe is quite simply one with what we lack in order to see. Faith does not compensate, either here or anywhere else, for a defect of visibility: on the contrary, it allows reception of the understanding of the phenomenon and the strength to bear the glare of its brilliance. Faith does not manage the deficit of evidence—it alone renders the gaze apt to see the excess of the preeminent saturated phenomenon, the Revelation. Thus we must not oppose the episode of the two disciples on the way to Emmaus to that of Christ's manifestation to the Apostles, which immediately follows it. For, here again, the difficulty in believing is explicitly equivalent to a difficulty in believing what one sees already but does not admit (and it is not in the least a difficulty in imagining what one does not see). The disciples were "startled and frightened"[10] by what they were seeing or "believed they were seeing (*theōrein*)" (v. 37); was it a "spirit," a demon, an illusion? As to the easiest hypothesis, the most reasonable, indeed, the most evident—that it is Him—it remained the most incredible, the most unthinkable, the only one inaccessible to their state of mind. The obstacle, then, is found here, too, in the deficiency of concepts and significations: they do not have the rational means to think that of which they have sensible intuition. Consequently Christ questions them on their thoughts: "What concepts (*dialogismoi*) rise in your hearts?" (v. 38). Thus he does not undertake to give them a greater intuition of his corporeality, but to have them admit that this body, these hands, these feet, and this pierced side are indeed his ("mine"), that it is indeed "I who am the same"

(v. 39). The very gesture of eating before their eyes aims, certainly, to give them proof of his flesh, but also to repeat the multiplication of the fish: For here, too, "he gave them the remainder" (v. 43, variant), just as previously, "having taken the five loaves and two fish, raising his eyes to heaven, he blessed them, broke them and gave them to the disciples" (Luke 9:16). The goal is simply to have himself recognized as the one who he was among them, first of all through gestures, and then through words: "These are the [same] words (concepts, *logoi*) which I spoke to you while I was still with you" (v. 44). Indeed, they will not truly recognize him until his "words," and thus his own significations and concepts, allow them at last to constitute the intuition, maddening for as long as it remained bare, into a complete phenomenon. And here, as on the road to Emmaus, the point is to replace all the intuitions into the significations of God; for all the intuitions that we receive from the *gesta Christi* can only be understood according to their final intention—"it is fitting to fulfill (*plērōthēnai*, to fill, to saturate) everything that is written in the Law of Moses, in the Prophets and in the Psalms—(all of this having been written solely in view) of me" (v. 44 = v. 27). The opening of the meaning, and thus of the mind (for *noun*, v. 45, expresses both) is decided in and by "the Scriptures," taken not as pure letters but as the recording of significations willed by God in order to constitute the intuitions of his incarnation in a full and wholly complete phenomenon of Revelation.

But if all of this is so, why does this phenomenon disappear at the very instant in which it finally becomes visible—visible because believable? First, because the issue now is not, or is not only, to see him, but to show him "to all the nations, beginning from Jerusalem" (v. 47). In other words, to make it so that all receive the significations that allow them to see what intuition offers, without yet rendering it manifest. Second, because such a phenomenon, preeminently saturated, cannot be touched (John 20:17) nor even contemplated in this world, which, in this time, does not "have the space" to contain the significations that would have to be "written" (John 21:25).

Originally translated by Stephen E. Lewis

The Invisible Saint

I

The saint.¹ What sort of saint? No one has ever seen a saint.² For the saint remains invisible, not through an empirical coincidence, but in principle and by right.

For who could see a saint in person [*en personne*], if no one [*personne*] can recognize the saint as such? In fact, who could say that this person one sees and knows merits being described as holy [*saint*]? (This is even less the case if one does not know the saint well or maybe not at all.) How should one justify sainthood and on what definition of holiness ought it be grounded? To call any ordinary human holy, one must first know what this word "holiness" [*sainteté*] actually means, then one must oneself have direct experience of it, and finally one must be able to assign the quality thus signified to someone legitimately. In other words, one must have access to holiness in its concept; one must oneself have an experience of sanctity and must probe the other's heart. Can one claim to fulfill these conditions for the case of holiness or sainthood in the same way as, for example, for heroism or for intelligence? Indeed, in order to call someone heroic or of brilliant intelligence, one must similarly first know what each of these terms covers, have tested them in person, and finally one must know how to judge the other in one or the other respect. No one doubts that a war hero, accustomed to battle and experienced in war, knows what he or she is talking about and is able to judge whether other people merit the title. Similarly, no one disputes that true scholars or great researchers, as self-aware, know what science and research mean and are able to recognize other minds of comparable intelligence.

Yet it is plain to see that these three conditions cannot be satisfied in the case of holiness, or even in matters of intelligence or heroism. There are three reasons for this. First, no one can claim to define the concept (or the meaning) of holiness without running the risk of the most obvious of idolatries. When a crowd or a faction declares someone a saint, their definition is in fact restricted to what this crowd or that faction (and so their respective ideologies) imagine as holiness, that is to say, their peculiar fantasy of perfection. Regarding such a saint, the idol of the theater (*l'idola theâtri*), one must say what Molière said of Tartuffe: "He is a saint only in your fantasies."[3] Even the highest virtues are debased, when people raise them uncritically to alleged holiness, to the rank of fancies that are more often monstrous than empty. And the most indisputable figures of higher spirituality often risk *being devalued* when they become the often involuntary recipients of homage in assumed and ideologized sanctity.

Then—for all idolatry actually results in self-idolatry—this idolized sanctity right away presupposes that those who assert and define it themselves claim to know what holiness means, and therefore claim to experience it and consequently to incarnate it themselves. Yet by an obvious fact in no need of justification, we know perfectly well that no one can say "I am a saint" without total deception. By a performative contradiction that is intuitively irrefutable, someone who lays claim to sanctity disproves it in himself. Why can holiness not lay claim to itself? Not only because it does not want to yield to the massive pitfall of the pride of its own gratification and the self-affirmation it involves, but above all because holiness is unaware of itself (for reasons that will have to be specified later). In any case, we know that there is no such thing as a self-proclaimed saint. To the contrary, self-proclamation (even through the intermediary of disciples, of the community the saint has founded or tolerated) is the surest criterion of the alleged saint's fraud. The false prophet, like the false saint, always stands out conspicuously by the fact that he or she never allows this affirmation to be questioned.

Finally the last condition for determining holiness remains even more unfeasible, if that were possible; rather, it presents the same unsurpassable difficulty in the case of holiness as in the others (heroism, intelligence): no one can determine another's virtue, regardless of what this virtue or who this other might be, precisely because the other remains inaccessible to any other ego. And especially inaccessible in that it is not only a matter of gaining access to or judging the other's intelligence or any other competence, which is first brought to bear on universal or particular objects that can be shared by any other intelligence. No, what is at stake instead is the other's will, the other's utmost individuality and unsubstitutable selfhood. If I already have the greatest trouble knowing for sure what my neighbor (that is to say my unreachable alter ego) thinks, desires, wants, is capable of, and really is worth, how shall I determine his or her holiness (obviously assuming that I myself would know what that is)? The aporia of intersubjectivity, at least of intersubjectivity understood according to intentionality, applies above all to the judgment regarding the other's holiness or sanctity.

For these three reasons, the project of determining anyone's holiness must be abandoned. In contrast to other qualifications and other virtues, no one can formally attribute holiness to anyone else whatsoever. Anyone's holiness thus remaining *for us* (*quo ad nos*) undecidable, the saint consequently remains *for us* formally invisible. The question of the saint's holiness paradoxically begins to pose itself on the basis of its invisibility.

II

In the case of holiness, the paradox of this invisibility is introduced for initially formal reasons. Yet it is also justified by analogy with other phenomena, which are equally invisible, at least according to the rules of common phenomenality.

The point of departure for the description of this type of invisibility can proceed from a well-known and documented paradox, which arises from witnesses having returned from the death camps.[4] They all underline the limits of their own testimony; they even discredit it by arguing, formally: only those who have returned from extermination after having been sentenced and having come close to death can witness to it. Yet if they have returned from it, it is because they did not remain there, did not die there. They did not remain there because they did not really enter into it, because they did not go all the way to the end—precisely all the way to death and extermination. And it is to this condition alone—to not having disappeared in the extermination—that they owe the power to witness to it, to the extermination. Thus they cannot testify because they have not completely experienced that to which they bear witness. The character of any testimony is at play here, which demands that witnesses do not understand completely that to which they nevertheless firmly testify. Yet it is present with a more distressing acuity: Here, where it is a matter of witnessing precisely to annihilation, the witness, who must still exist in order to bear witness, by his not being nothing cannot but contradict the annihilation to which he testifies. The witness hence remains inevitably a distant, partial, false witness (not in the sense of a fake witness, but an unfounded witness, precariously balanced [*pas un faux témoin, mais un témoin portant à faux, en porte à faux*]). The witness really witnesses, that is, bears witness to what he or she effectively has not lived—the supreme nonreality, death, in the first person, his or her extermination in the first person. And this contradiction cannot be avoided because if the witness had actually known extermination, he would have disappeared and consequently would no longer be able to witness to it.

This first paradox, directly linked to the testimony of extermination, nevertheless does not close in on itself but leads further. In fact, extermination escapes testimony and phenomenal visibility precisely because it brings death into play. Yet death is precisely the supreme name for that to which no one can testify, what no one can see, because no one can claim to have experienced it. No one, then, can bear witness to death because for this to be possible it would be necessary to satisfy two contradictory conditions: being actually dead, hence having experienced it, and, on the contrary, coming back from it in order to talk about it. Only a dead person having returned from death would be able to speak of it. From this follows the *logical* futility of alleged limit-experiences of impending death—not because these experiences should be impugned as illusory, but because they do not concern death itself, as they allow their witness to return to life. Undergoing the limit-experience of death, coming all the way up to its limit, literally means *not* having experienced it, *not* knowing *anything* about it, precisely due to having been able to return from it. Only those who have never reached death return from it. We, who have not yet gone to it and who in spite of that mistakenly believe ourselves still able to speak of it as we speak of everything else (by saying something about it, even though it is precisely not some thing), we can consequently say nothing about it. At best, we can imagine it, and thus our opinions, our views, our presumed doctrines about death remain perfectly arbitrary, know nothing about it, and reflect only our fantasies. Whether one thinks of death as horror or as rest and solace, as nothingness or as anesthesia, says nothing about death but refers purely and simply to our dreams and nightmares. By right, we could just as legitimately imagine death as a release, an enraptured bliss, an insupportable joy. The fact that these sorts of imaginings do not often come to mind only proves our despair and our lack of ambition; but even that has no more relevance than negative or neutral fancies.

One cannot stare death in the face, we say, any more than the sun. In point of fact, we cannot see death at all, not its face, not its side, and especially not its back.[5] It remains invisible to us because, in order to see it, the potential viewer[6] would have to disappear. Or, rather, it would be necessary that the same viewer *both* disappear in experiencing death *and* return from it in order to tell us the truth (if there is any to be found). This contradiction can only be overcome on one condition: that someone resurrected would bear witness. Only one who would have experienced death fully would be able to say something about it. Thus only Christ, if he is truly raised, can witness to death.

III

The guiding thread of these analogies leads to Christ. Is this more than an analogy? Before responding to this question, if that is possible, it is advisable to consider that the paradox of death (that no one can really experience it and say anything about it at the same time) is reproduced in the paradox of holiness. Indeed, as the history of religions teaches, holiness in general defines the setting apart that distinguishes what belongs to the divinity in opposition to what remains in the world, what stays in the temple in opposition to what remains on the threshold (the *pro-fane*, *profanum*); in short, it sets a limit that one cannot transgress without danger or without precise and complicated practices of purification. Yet in biblical Revelation, holiness is not limited to distinguishing areas of experience; it characterizes the absolutely singular and inamissible[7] uniqueness of God. For God gives himself to be praised precisely as the Holy One. "And they [the seraphim] called to one another and said: 'Holy, holy, holy, is the Lord God of hosts. The entire universe is filled with his glory'" (Isa. 6:3). Or also, "They [cf. the living creatures] did not cease to repeat 'Holy, holy, holy the Lord and Master of all (*pantokrator*), who was and who is and who is to come'" (Rev. 4:8). God is distinguished from the world and from other gods inasmuch as he is "glorious in holiness, awesome in splendor" (Exod. 15:11). Thus he reveals himself inasmuch as no one—no one other than Him—can enter into the vicinity of his holiness, which separates him from any other [*tout autre*] as the Wholly Other [*Tout Autre*]. "God called to him out of the bush: 'Moses, Moses!' And he said, 'Here I am.' Then he said: 'Come no closer! Remove the sandals from your feet, for the place on which you are standing is holy ground.' God said further: 'I am the God of your father, the God of Abraham, the God of Isaac, and the God of Jacob.' And Moses hid his face, for he was afraid to look at God" (Exod. 3:4–6). God's alterity imposes itself as absolute precisely as the alterity of holiness. And this alterity of holiness is manifested only as it remains invisible [*invisible*]. Or, more precisely, inasmuch as it is only manifested as what cannot be aimed at [*invisable*],[8] inasmuch as it cannot become an object for the intentionality of a gaze: "Moses said: 'Show me your glory, I pray.' And he said: 'I will make all my splendor pass before you . . . you shall stand on this rock and while my glory passes by I will put you in a cleft of the rock, and I will cover you with my hand until I have passed by; then I will take away my hand, and you shall see my back; but my face cannot be seen.'" Precisely, "you cannot see my face; for no one can see me and remain alive" (Exod. 33:18–23). God's glory, that is to say, God's holiness, is manifested as such and consequently is manifested as invisible. Holiness marks the realm of God's very phenomenality as unreachable invisibility.

Without any doubt, the election of the people as people of God requires that this people enter into God's very holiness, as "holy nation" (Exod. 19:6): "You shall be holy, for I the Lord your God am holy" (Lev. 19:2). Yet the real history of the covenant unfurls as the growing contradiction between the manifestation of God's unreachable holiness and the people's powerlessness to become themselves holy. The Law of holiness makes sin obvious, demonstrates in counterproof the non-holiness, the profanation of the people. In this way, "through the Law comes knowledge of sin" (Rom. 3:20). Therefore it was necessary for God's holiness, which had remained invisible among humans and even (indeed above all) among the "holy nation," that an absolutely new man would make it manifest. "The Law indeed was given by God through Moses; grace and truth came to us through Jesus Christ. No one has ever seen God. It is the only Son, who is in God's bosom, who has made him known" (John 1:17–18). Christ carries God's holiness all the way into the world, summing up in himself alone the whole people presumed holy. God's holiness is only shown to the world in the face of Christ, who, having come before Abraham and before Moses, alone can say, "Whoever has seen me has seen the Father" (John 14:9). But this manifestation of holiness, even and above all in the Word's flesh, literally respects its fundamental characteristic—its invisibility [*son invisibilité*] from the world's point of view, the fact that it cannot be reached [*son invisabilité*] as object available to intentionality. What is called the messianic secret does not consist in a voluntary concealment, which would retain a possible visibility, reserved for a privileged few and denied to the crowd. It results from the fact (by right) that holiness cannot give itself to be seen to what is not (yet) itself holy: manifestation can only be fulfilled to the extent of what the eyes can bear—"I still have many things to say to you, but you cannot bear them now" (John 16:12). The impossibility for humans, not only the crowd, the soldiers and the Roman leaders, the priests and the scribes, but (especially) the disciples themselves, to bear the visible will increase with the extent of the manifestation, more and more radical and hence dazzling, of the holiness with which the Son and the Father glorify each other reciprocally in the Spirit. This contradiction reaches its peak in Christ's silence and disfiguration at the time of his passion, where the maximum of holiness is swallowed up by the maximum of invisibility, of death. The paschal glory itself remains in a sense invisible, because its triumphant holiness can still not be reflected in the world that it renders void all the same. Therefore, it can only be manifested to believers themselves to the extent to which they can "bear" it. Because "their eyes were kept from recognizing him" (Luke 24:16) and the "disciples did not know that it was Jesus" (John 21:4), at Emmaus holiness must resort to the semi-clarity of the sacrament, visible sign of the thing as such invisible, in the breaking of the bread.

Thus holiness, even that of Christ, even that of the resurrected, remains by definition invisible.

IV

One thinker has understood and formulated such a paradox more than anyone else. Pascal distinguished between what he called three orders, classified in hierarchical fashion: First the order of the flesh that characterizes bodies but also the power of the world in general, in particular the power of princes who govern in the visibility of the senses. Then comes the order of minds that concerns people of knowledge, their sciences and their truths, in particular the logic of scholars and philosophers, as it appears in the light of reason. Finally appears the order of hearts—where only charity rules—its activities [*commerce*] and its holiness, in the light of Christ that encompasses precisely also those we call the saints. Yet Pascal posits a law that governs the respective phenomenalities of these three orders: each of the orders sees the one or both of the orders inferior to it, but remains invisible to them. That is, no order sees superior order(s) appear, whereas the invisibility of a superior order sees the order(s) it dominates perfectly. "The greatness of clever men is invisible to kings, to the rich, to chiefs, and to all the worldly great. / The greatness of wisdom, which is nothing if not of God, is invisible to the carnal-minded and to the clever. These are three orders differing in kind." Consequently, the saints "are recognized by God and the angels, and not by bodies or by curious minds. God is enough for them."[9] Saints remain invisible to all that does not belong to holiness, exactly as scholars and thinkers remain invisible to the world of the flesh (what today we call in a trivial manner the media and publicity—in short, the world reduced to what the television screen can grasp of it as so many material objects). This law does not suffer any exception, and must not. Otherwise, holiness would revert to the world and its profanation. Likewise, incidentally, great minds, scholars, and thinkers must, in order to remain themselves, remove themselves absolutely from the intrusive and destructive curiosity of the body.

The holiness of saints remains and must remain invisible to all that does not belong itself to holiness. There is no modern mythology at stake here, which would add itself to the figures of the *poète maudit* [lit., the cursed or outcast poet], the wandering Jew, the poor and the humiliated (even if it illuminates them with a new and benevolent light), but "our life hidden with Christ in God" (Col. 3:3). In short, at stake is the realm of phenomenality proper to holiness, which can only be manifested for those who have experienced it, that is to say, who have passed into it and who do not come back from it, thus disappearing for the eyes of those who have not yet passed into it. It certainly is a phenomenality suitable to Christian and Jewish Revelation, as the first letter of John formulates it rigorously: "See what love the Father has given us, that we should be called children of God; and that is what we are. The reason the world does not know us is that it did not know Him. Beloved, we are God's children now; what we will be has not yet been revealed" (1 John 3:1–2). But this is no less a matter of a rule of strict phenomenality, worthy of certain phenomena that are just as visible in this very invisibility as all those in the rest of the world.

Notes

Preface

1. Eleven of the French chapters had been previously published; six have been previously published in English translation. Previous publication information is provided in the first note to each chapter.

2. Emmanuel Levinas, *Notes philosophiques diverses*, in *Oeuvres 1*, ed. R. Calin and C. Chalier (Paris: Grasset, 2009), 287.

3. "Intellectus enim merces est fidei. Ergo noli quaerere intelligere ut credas, sed crede ut intelligas, quoniam 'Nisi credideritis, non intelligetis.'" Augustine, *In Evangelium Iohannes tractatus*, 29.6, translated by John W. Rettig as *Tractates on the Gospel of John 28–34, Fathers of the Church* vol. 88 (Washington, DC: Catholic University Press, 1993), 18. The verse quoted in the citation comes from an ancient translation of Isaiah 7:9.

1. Faith and Reason

First published as "La foi et la raison," in *Dialogue entre la foi chrétienne et la pensée contemporaine*, ed. Jean-Marie Lustiger, 11–30 (Paris: Parole et Silence, 2005). Previously published in English in *The Visible and the Revealed* (New York: Fordham University Press, 2008), 145–54.

1. Saint Augustine, *De civitate Dei*, 8.1, trans. Gerald G. Walsh and Grace Monahan as *City of God, Fathers of the Church*, vol. 14 (Washington, D.C.: Catholic University Press, 1952), 21.

2. Saint Thomas Aquinas, *Questiones disputatae de Potentia*, Q. 7, A. 5, ad. 14, trans. as *On the Power of God* (Westminster, Md.: Newman Press, 1952), 33.

153

3. Friedrich Nietzsche, "Von den Verächtern des Leibes" ["On the Despisers of the Body"], *Also sprach Zarathustra: Ein Buch für Alle und Keinen*, 1.4, in *Nietzsches Werke: Kritische Gesamtausgabe*, ed. Giorgio Colli and Mazzino Montinari (Berlin: Walter de Gruyter, 1967–91), trans. Walter Kaufmann as *Thus Spoke Zarathustra: A Book for None and All* (New York: Penguin, 1954), 34; trans. mod.

4. René Descartes, *Discours de la méthode*, part 6, in *Œuvres de Descartes*, ed. Charles Adams and Paul Tannery, 11 vols. (Paris: Vrin, CNRS, 1964–79), henceforth abbreviated AT, trans. John Cottingham, Robert Stoothof, and Dugalf Murdoch as *Discourse on Method*, in *The Philosophical Writings of Descartes*, vol. 1 (Cambridge: Cambridge University Press, 1984).

5. [Most English translations say "full of grace and truth"; the Greek is *pleireis charitos kai aleitheias*. *Charis* is usually translated as "grace," but the Latin term *caritas*, normally translated as "love" or "charity," is related to it. Marion's somewhat idiosyncratic French rendering is here preserved because of the importance of the terms he uses. Most standard French translations translate this verse (like the English) as *pleine de grâce* and not *saturé d'amour*.—Trans.]

6. Saint Augustine, *De fide rerum quae non videntur*, c. 2 and 4, trans. C. L. Cornish as *Concerning Faith in Things not Seen*, in *Nicene and Post-Nicene Fathers*, 1st ser., vol. 3 (1887; repr., Peabody, Mass.: Hendrickson , 1995), 338; trans. mod.

2. In Defense of Argument
First published as "Apologie de l'argument," in *Revue Catholique Internationale Communio* XVII.2/3 (1992): 12–33; previously unpublished in English.

1. Among an abundant and uneven literature, the clear synthesis by J.-M. Ferry stands out: *Habermas: L'éthique de la communication* (Paris: Presses Universitaires de France, 1987).

2. On this point, see my note, "L'idéologie ou la violence sans ombre," *Communio* V.6 (1980): 82–92.

3. [Another, more literal, way to translate the title of this piece would be "Apology for Argument"—Trans.]

4. This is why I am here consistent with other positions that I have taken in "Droit à la confession," *Communio* I.1 (1975): 17–27, and "L'avenir du catholicisme" (Chapter 6 in this book).

5. Allow me to allude here to a paradox that Jean d'Ormesson, who shows himself here a good historian of dogma, developed recently on television. At an entirely different level one would have to take up again the history of rational methods of discussion elaborated by Christian theology, whether understood as a "science" or as "doctrine." It has perhaps already provided many elements of a response to the question that we are beginning to rediscover.

6. [Molière, *"The School for Wives" and "The Learned Ladies,"* trans. Richard Wilbur (New York: Harcourt, Inc., 1978), 246.]

7. *Grundlegung zur Metaphysik der Sitten*, AA IV, 429, trans. H. J. Paton as *Groundwork of the Metaphysic of Morals* (New York: Harper and Row, 1964),

96. See also the *Critique of Practical Reason*: "Act in such a way that the maxim of your will would always be able to be valid at the same time as principle for a universal legislation." In regard to the relation between the Gospel precept and its critical formulation, Kant himself maintains a very balanced position from which the hasty critics should draw inspiration: "the Christian principle of morals is not in itself theological, that is, the character pertaining to it is not that of heteronomy. On the contrary, what is being advocated here is the principle of the autonomy of pure practical reason, the principle, that is, of reason operating by itself. The Christian moral doctrine does not suppose that knowledge of God and his will is that in which the laws in question are grounded. It merely supposes that God and his will are grounds for the attainment of the *summum bonum*, while, at the same time, laying down the condition that these laws are to be obeyed. Indeed, even though the question be what is, strictly speaking, the *motive force* prompting obedience, the Christian doctrine does not assign this to the thought of desirable consequences resulting from obedience being rendered to these laws. On the contrary, what it looks upon as the motive force is solely the representation of duty, its being the faithful observation of that duty which alone constitutes the worthiness to acquire a share in the *summum bonum*." *Kritik der Praktischen Vernunft*, I. AA V, 129; trans. H. W. Cassirer as *Critique of Practical Reason* (Milwaukee: Marquette University Press, 1998), 162. On the unity of the "Golden Rule," I take up the remarkable demonstration of Paul Ricoeur in *Soi-même comme un autre* (Paris: Seuil, 1990), 8.2, 254ff., trans. Kathleen Blamey as *Oneself as Another* (Chicago: University of Chicago Press, 1992), 218–27, despite certain ideological critiques, as for example that of C. Bouchindrome, "Limites et présupposés de l'herméneutique de Paul Ricoeur," in *Temps et récit de Paul Ricoeur en débat* (Paris: Cerf, 1990).

8. It is the real merit of the overall very beneficial book by Paul Valadier, *L'Église en procès* (Paris: Calmann Lévy, 1987, 1992), to have firmly recalled this evidence: "Speaking in the name of its convictions and without claiming thereby to dictate the only possible solution, the Church plays the game of pluralism; in so doing, it also provokes other religious, ethical, and philosophical traditions to intervene in the debate and to proclaim what makes sense for them" (140). Furthermore, Valadier had provided a perfect example of this work of argumentation in a very balanced contribution to *Communio*: "Contestées et nécessaires: Les interventions sociales du magistère," *Communio* VI.2 (1981): 6–16. The insufficiencies of the work of this journal nevertheless did not escape him: "theological production coming from the laity today (as from the journal *Communio*) shines neither by its openness to concrete ecclesial problems nor by its concern for intellectual confrontation with current rationality" (*L'Église en procès*, 201). I will retain this brotherly correction for the future. But basically, one must also once and for all agree among Catholics on what are "concrete ecclesial problems." It is in fact possible that the laity (more exactly the baptized) do not recognize the same "concrete ecclesial problems" as the

clerics; in other words, it is possible that the problems of power in the Church (even and especially of the "power of the laity," which has become such a typically clerical concern!) are not priorities for us, for us the simple baptized, who expect first and foremost only the sacraments from the Church, which make us sufficiently strong to live in the world without being of the world. Besides these sacraments (and instruction), the rest seems to me often very abstract in the Church. "Concrete" debates in regard to the powers in the Church probably remain legitimate, or even beneficial; but for the simple baptized, they have no priority at all, all the more as what is at stake in the matter of these quarrels as old (and completely inextricable) as the Church itself, is in short often an abstruse combat. As to "current rationalities," the simple baptized experience far less pain in "opening themselves" to them since, by formation and profession, they constantly use them in the firms, administrations, and universities where they work on a daily basis. Besides, the most basic good faith would have to lead us to recognize that in regard to the "concrete" and "lay" problems, *Communio* has collected (certainly since 1985, the date on which I gave up directing its publication) a very consequential number of theologians, philosophers, historians, specialists in the social and the exact sciences, economists, high functionaries, jurists, writers, artists, etc. In short, unless one were not reading it, one would have to concede that *Communio* has worked on this, and not merely at a mediocre level. Everyone knows that more and better things have to be done. But this work will be accomplished more easily if such unjust clichés no longer have currency, so that a reasonable discussion could begin even *within* the Church.

9. This is what Valadier has underlined magnificently: "The Christian life is not a quiet accommodation to the world: It is the role of the pastors in the Church to recall this. In so doing—and this is yet another argument—the Church can certainly be misunderstood (but can one understand God's requests?), but it plays its prophetic role no less for all that. Contesting the utilitarianism that reduces human relations to the rank of commercial banality, as well as the individualism that defines the human by his immediate needs, the moral message of the Church, notably in the matter of sexuality, strikes head-on against obvious facts. By doing this, it saves modernity from itself, because it sets up a barrier to a process of the banalization of the human itself and accelerated indifferentiation. Thus, far from being backward, the position of the magisterium anticipates against obvious facts, the illusory and noxious character of which we will quickly see" (*L'Église en procès*, 207).

Here, as is often the case, his accord with Jean-Marie Lustiger is obvious: "Really, where sexual morality is concerned, I would be inclined to adopt a point of view inherited from the past, because what it does basically is remind us of a fundamental requirement of moral behavior, which is that a general norm eventually frees even those subject to particular failings. I think that there is a similarity here with the position taken up by the Church on problems of labor. In his encyclical letter *Laborem Exercens* the pope said that we must put human beings back at the center of the economic system; many people are returning to that point of view. On the question of sexuality and attitudes to the body, society is today more or less where it was a hundred years ago in social matters. In the nineteenth century capitalism was rampant and factories were exploiting child labor. In the twentieth century it is being exploited for sexual ends. There has been a kind of erotic explosion which justifies that sort of behavior and it comes from the application of modern science to sexuality. This produces excesses in sexual matters that are rather like the excesses produced at the beginning of the industrial revolution. So it seems as though the Church, in its attitude to the human body, is not lagging behind but is well ahead." Jean-Marie Lustiger, *Osez vivre* (Paris: Bayard, 1985), 31, trans. M. N. L. Couve de Murville as *Dare to Live* (New York: Crossroad, 1988), 18.

3. The Formal Reason of the Infinite

First published as "La raison formelle de l'infini," in C. Michon, ed., *Christianisme: Héritages et destins* (Paris: Livre de Poche, Biblio-Essays, 2002), proceedings from a conference called "2000 Après Quoi?" ["2000 Years after What?"], held at the Sorbonne in December 1999. See the more detailed development in *In Excess: Studies of Saturated Phenomena*, trans. Robyn Horner and Vincent Berraud (New York: Fordham University Press, 2002), chap. 6, §§3, 5–6; and *Negative Certainties*, trans. Stephen E. Lewis (Chicago: Chicago University Press, 2015), chap. 2, §§10–13; previously published in English as "The Formal Reason of the Infinite," in *The Blackwell Companion to Postmodern Theology*, ed. Graham Ward (Oxford: Blackwell, 2001), 399–412. It appears by permission of Blackwell, © 2005 by Blackwell Publishing Ltd. The original English translation has no footnotes.

    1. Aristotle, *Metaphysics* E 1, 1026a27.
    2. *Metaphysics* Z 13, 1039a7, "*hē entelechia khōrizei.*"
    3. Plato, *Philebus* 17e.
    4. Plotinus, *Enneads* II 4.15, "*hē hulē to apeiron.*"
    5. René Descartes, *Meditations on First Philosophy* III, AT VII, 45, lines 23–29, trans. John Cottingham, Robert Stoothoff, and Dugald Murdoch as *The Philosophical Writings of Descartes*, vol. 2 (Cambridge: Cambridge University Press, 1984), 31.
    6. Immanuel Kant, *Reflexionen zur Metaphysik*, §4192, *Nachlass, Akademie Ausgabe* VII (Berlin: De Gruyter, 1926), 451; emphasis added. Cf. Descartes, Second Replies: "sed me istam vim concipiendi majorem numerum esse cogitabilem quam a me unquam possit cogitari, non a meipso, sed ab aliquo alio ente me perfectiore accepisse" (AT VII, 139, lines 19–22); "but that I have the power of conceiving that there is a thinkable number which is larger than any number that I can ever think of, and hence that this power is something which I have received not from myself but from some other being, which is more perfect than I am" (*Philosophical Writings*, 100).

7. Descartes, *Meditations on First Philosophy* III, AT VII, 46, lines 19–23; *Philosophical Writings*, 32. Cf. *Principia Philosophiae* I, §19: "est de natura infiniti ut a nobis, qui sumus finiti, non comprehendatur."

8. Descartes, *Meditations on First Philosophy*, AT VII, 46, lines 8 and 12; *Philosophical Writings*, 31–32.

9. Ibid., Fifth Replies, AT VII, 368, lines 2–4; Descartes, *Philosophical Writings*, 253, in response to an objection that seems right (but is actually false) by Gassendi: "But if you do not grasp the infinite, but merely the finite, you do not have a true idea of the infinite, but only of the finite. You can at most be said to know part of the infinite; but this does not mean you know the infinite itself." Fifth Objections, AT VII, 296, line 26–27; Descartes, *Philosophical Writings*, 206. Gassendi makes two mistakes: (a) limiting any *cogitatio* only to the comprehension of finite objects; thus, (b) to attain the infinite on the conditions of knowledge of the finite—so there is nothing surprising in his concluding from this that the infinite cannot be comprehended, because in this formulation it is a matter of a contradiction in terms—the one that the Cartesian paradox precisely tries to get beyond.

10. "Rationaliter comprehendere incomprehensibile esse." Saint Anselm, *Monologion*, vol. 1, §64, ed. Franciscus Salesius Schmidt (Edinburgh: Apud Thomam, Nelson et Filius, 1938), 75.

11. "Non ea disputatio comprehendit, sed sanctitas: si quo modo tamen comprehendi potest quod incomprehensibile est." Bernard de Clairvaux, *De consideratione* V 14 PL 182, 805d, trans. John D. Anderson and Elizabeth T. Kennan as *Five Books on Consideration: Advice to a Pope* (Kalamazoo, Mich.: Cistercian Publications, 1976), 177.

12. "De Deo loquimur, quid mirum si non comprehendaris? Si enim comprehenderis, non est Deus." Augustine, Sermo 117.3, 5 *Patrologiae cursus completus. Series Latina*, ed. Jacques-Paul Migne (Paris: Migne, 1857–1866), vol. 38, 663, henceforth abbreviated PL; trans. R. G. MacMullen, in *Nicene and Post-Nicene Fathers*, 1st ser., vol. 6 (Peabody, Mass.: Hendrickson, 1995), 459.

13. Michel de Montaigne, *Essais* II, 12 "Apologie de Raymond de Sebond," ed. Pierre Villey (Paris: Presses Universitaires de France, 1965, 1988), 500, trans. Roger Ariew and Marjorie Grene as *Apology for Raymond Sebond* (Indianapolis: Hackett, 2003), 61.

14. Augustine, *De ordine*, book 2, Second Debate, 16.44; PL 32, 1015, trans. Solvano Borrusco as *On Order* (South Bend, Ind.: St. Augustine's Press, 2007), 109.

15. Thomas Aquinas, *De potentia*, Q. 7, A. 5, ad. 14, trans. as *On the Power of God* (Westminster, Md.: The Newman Press, 1952), 33. Similarly, "Deus est qui sola ignorantia mente cognoscitur." *Book of the XXIV Philosophers*, §23, ed. and trans. Françoise Hudry (Grenoble: J. Millon, 1989), 164.

16. Dionysius, *Divine Names*, VII, 3 PG 3, 872a, trans. C. E. Rolt as *The Divine Names* (London: SCPK Press, 1977), 152.

17. Basil of Caesarea, Letter 234.1, "aiesthesis autou thes akatalepsias," *Patrologiae cursus completus. Series Graecae*, ed. Jacques-Paul Migne (Paris: Migne, 1857–1866), vol. 32, 869; henceforth abbreviated PG.

18. Gregory of Nyssa, *Life of Moses*, II, §163, PG 44, 377a, ed. J. Danielou, *Sources Chrétiennes* 1 (Paris: Cerf, 1968), 210, henceforth abbreviated SC; trans. Abraham J. Malherbe and Everett Ferguson (New York: Paulist Press, 1978), 95.

19. Blaise Pascal, *Pensées*, ed. Louis Lafuma (Paris: Flammarion, 1973), §149; trans. A. J. Krailsheimer (New York: Penguin Books, 1966), 78; trans. mod. See also §230.

20. [This piece was originally delivered at a conference entitled "2000 Years after What?" Marion refers to the title of the conference here and again at the end of the essay.—Trans.]

21. Gregory of Nyssa, *On the Creation of Man*, XI, PG 44, 156b, trans. H. A. Wilson as *On the Making of Man*, in *Nicene and Post-Nicene Fathers*, 2nd ser., vol. 5 (Peabody, Mass.: Hendrickson, 1995/1893), trans. mod. (supported, among others, with the *Homilies on Ecclesiastes* VII, PG 44, 732c–d). See also Basil of Caesarea, *Against Eunonimus*, III.6, PG 29, 668a, and Cyril of Jerusalem, *Catechetical Lectures* VI.6 PG 33, 548b.

22. Descartes, *Meditations on First Philosophy*, IV, AT VII, 57, 13–15; *Philosophical Writings*, 40.

23. Dionysius, *Divine Names* IX.6, PG 3, 913c, trans. Rolt, 166 (trans. mod.).

24. Pascal, *Pensées*, ed. Lafuma, §130; trans. Krailsheimer, 62.

25. Michel Foucault says, "As the archaeology of our thought easily shows, man is an invention of recent date. And one perhaps nearing its end . . . [one can certainly wager that] man would be erased, like a face drawn in sand at the edge of the sea." *Les mots et les choses* (Paris: Gallimard, 1971), 398, trans. as *The Order of Things* (New York: Random House, 1970), 387.

26. Edmund Husserl, *Ideen zu einer reinen Phänomenologie und phänomenologischen Philosophie: Erstes Buch, Allgemeine Einführung in die reine Phänomenologie*, ed. W. Biemel, vol. 3 of *Husserliana: Edmund Husserl Gesammelte Werke* (The Hague: Martinus Nijhoff, 1950–),§42, 77, trans. Daniel O. Dahlstrom as *Ideas for a Pure Phenomenology and Phenomenological Philosophy. First Book: General Introduction to Pure Phenomenology* (Indianapolis: Hackett, 2014), 74.

27. Jean Chrysostom, *De l'incompréhensibilité de Dieu*, V, 259, ed. A. M. Malingrey, R. Flacelière, J. Daniélou, SC 28 (Paris: Cerf, 1970), vol. 1, 294, trans. Paul W. Harkins as *On the Incomprehensible Nature of God*, vol. 72, *Fathers of the Church* (Washington, D.C.: Catholic University of America Press, 1984), 149.

28. See my article "Substance and Subsistence," in *On the Ego and on God: Further Cartesian Questions* (New York: Fordham University Press, 2007), 80–99.

29. "Mens se ipsam non conoscit, nisi quatenus corporis affectionum ideas percipit." Baruch Spinoza, *Ethica* II, §22; trans. R. H. M. Elwes as *Ethics* (New York: Dover, 1955), 103 ("The human mind perceives not only the modifications of the body, but also the ideas of such modifications").

30. Nicolas Malebranche, *Recherche de la vérité*, Éclaircissement XI: "We hence have no clear idea about either the soul or its modifications." In *Oeuvres complètes*, vol. 3, 168, trans. Thomas M. Lennon and Paul J. Olscamp as *The Search after Truth* (Cambridge: Cambridge University Press, 1997).

31. Immanuel Kant, *Kritik der reinen Vernunft*, A346/B404, trans. Norman Kemp Smith as *Critique of Pure Reason* (New York: Palgrave Macmillan, 2003), 331.

32. The positive inversion is in 1 Cor. 15:10: "But by the grace of God I am what I am." Bernard de Clairvaux echoes this exactly: "Ego quidem, cum adhuc veritatem non nossem, aliquid me putabam esse, cum nihil essem." (*Degrees of Humility and of Pride* IV.15). The pride of thinking myself something takes me, in fact, to the rank of a simple being among others, which I am not; "I am nothing" means not only that I am not what I believe myself to be by myself, but that I do not reduce myself to the rank of a being, however privileged one would like it to be.

33. Ludwig Wittgenstein, *Tractatus logico-philosophicus*, §6.44, *Schriften*, vol. 1 (Frankfurt am Main: Suhrcamp, 1980), 81.

34. Gregory Nazianzen, *Theological Oration* 27.5, PG 36, 17b, trans. Frederick Williams as *On God and Christ: The Five Theological Orations and Two Letters to Cledonius* (Crestwood, N.Y.: St. Vladimir's Theological Seminary Press, 2002), 29.

35. "Mens humana adaequatam habet cognitionem aeternae et infinitae essentiae Dei." Spinoza, *Ethica* II, §47; trans. Elwes, 118.

36. [Marion's play on words "*le garder sous la garde de notre regard*" here cannot really be recreated in English. Literally, it means something like "guarding it under the guard of our gaze"—Trans.]

37. Pascal, *Pensées*, ed. Lafuma, §131, trans. Krailsheimer, 65.

4. On the Eminent Dignity of the Poor Baptized

First published as "De l'éminente dignité des pauvres baptisés," *Revue Catholique Internationale Communio* IV.2 (1979): 27–44; previously unpublished in English.

1. [Both "baptized" and "lay" can stand as independent singular nouns in French and are used in that way throughout this article. In consultation with the author, the translation has added "person" or switched to the plural as necessary to make grammatical sense in English. The title of the chapter plays on the title of a famous sermon by Bossuet on "the eminent dignity of the poor."—Trans.]

2. [The English translation of this and other ecclesial documents mentioned in this chapter can be found on the Vatican website: http://www.vatican.va/archive/hist_councils/ii_vatican_council/documents/vat-ii_const_19641121_lumen-gentium_en.html.—Trans.]

3. [The term "leadership" is in English in the original.—Trans.]

4. Cf. Heinrich Denziger, *Enchiridion Symbolorum: Definitionum et declarationum de rebus fidei et morum* (Barcinone: Herder, 1960), 960; and Gervais Dumeige, *La foi catholique* (Paris: Éditions de L'Orante, 2000), 894.

5. [The phrase Marion is using here, "*avec fracas et (sans doute) perte,*" can also be used idiomatically (*avec perte et fracas*) to mean "unceremoniously."—Trans.]

5. The Service of Rationality in the Church
Previously unpublished in both French and English, this text was originally written in response to a journal exposé on "Catholic Intellectuals Today" but was withdrawn by the author.

6. The Future of Catholicism
First published as "L'avenir du catholicisme," *Revue Catholique Internationale Communio* X.5/6 (1985): 38–47; previously unpublished in English.

1. In this sense, I remain faithful to my editorial of the first issue of the Francophone edition of *Communio*, "Droit à la confession," *Communio* I.1 (1975): 17–27, and to my contribution to number VIII.6, "La crise et la Croix" (1983): 8–22, included as chapter 5 under the title "La crise cruciale," in *Prolégomènes à la charité* (Paris: Edition de la Différence, 1986, 2007), trans. Stephen E. Lewis as "The Crucial Crisis," in *Prolegomena to Charity* (New York: Fordham University Press, 2002), 102–23.

2. [The French *l'esprit* can mean both "mind" and "spirit." In Hegel it is usually translated as "spirit," following the German *Geist*, which has a similar ambivalent connotation, but "mind" often seems more appropriate in this context, so both terms are used here to translate one French term.—Trans.]

3. Kant, respectively, *Kritik der Fakultät der Urteilskraft*, §84, trans. J. H. Bernard as *Critique of Judgment* (New York: Hafner Press, 1951), 284, trans. mod.; *Kritik der Praktischen Vernunft*, AA vol. 5, 131, trans. H. W. Cassirer as *Critique of Practical Reason* (Milwaukee: Marquette University Press, 1998), 166.

4. [Literally, "final goal." Kant's German *Zweck* (which means end, goal, or purpose) is usually translated as "end" into English and *but* (goal) into French. As Marion uses both "end" (*la fin*) and "goal" (*le but*) in this paragraph, I have for the most part employed standard translations of the French rather than the common way of translating Kant's German.—Trans.]

5. Nietzsche, *Thus Spoke Zarathustra*, passim, Preface 53; I, §5, "Of the Despisers of the Body"; I, §14 "On the Friend"; III, §14 "On the Thousand and One Goals," etc., trans. Walter Kaufman as *Thus Spoke Zarathustra: A Book for None and All* (New York: Penguin Books, 1954), 12.

6. [Throughout this paragraph Marion employs *connaître*—to know—for the mode of knowing relating to objects, and *reconnaître*—to recognize or acknowledge—for the different mode of knowing that goes beyond it.—Trans.]

7. [The tradition of iconography refers back to "the image not made by human hands" according to a story in which the gravely ill king of Edessa requested an image of Christ who—not having the time to sit for a painting—supposedly wiped his face on a cloth that became imprinted with his features,

thus forming an image "not made by human hands." The story is often taken as an endorsement of portraying Christ in an icon and its image is a popular icon in its own right.—Trans.]

8. Blaise Pascal, *Pensées*, ed. Louis Lafuma (Paris: Flammarion, 1973), §131, trans. A. J. Krailsheimer (New York: Penguin Books, 1966), 65.

9. Gregory of Nyssa, *On the Creation of Man* XI.3–4, PG 44, 156b, trans. H. A. Wilson as *On the Making of Man*, in *Nicene and Post-Nicene Fathers*, 2nd ser., vol. 5 (Peabody, MA: Hendrickson, 1995/1893), 396–97.

10. See Claude Bruaire's analyses in *L'être et l'esprit* (Paris: Presses Universitaires de France, 1983), 29–83.

7. Nothing Is Impossible for God

First published as "À Dieu, rien d'impossible," *Revue Catholique Internationale Communio* XIV.5 (1989): 43–58. See on this point the fuller developments in *The Visible and the Revealed* (New York: Fordham University Press, 2008), chapter 1, and *Negative Certainties*, trans. Stephen E. Lewis (Chicago: University of Chicago Press, 2015), chapter 2; this article previously unpublished in English.

1. Paul Claudel, *Tête d'or*, 2nd version, 2nd part, in *Theatre I*, ed. J. Madaule, "Pléiade" (Paris: Gallimard, 1956), 210.

2. [The term *effectivité*, used heavily in this essay, is throughout Marion's work usually translated as "actuality," although it really means something more like "effectiveness," "efficaciousness," or even "efficiency" (from the German *Wirklichkeit*). *Effectif* does, in fact, mean "real," "actual," or "effective," and *effectuer* means to carry out or perform something, thus making it real or actual in a certain sense. The English term "actuality" most closely corresponds to *realité* in French (*actualité* designates something quite different, namely, that something is up to date or is the latest news, although it is employed to translate Aristotle's *energeia*). In either case, in this essay "actuality" does not always seem the best translation of *effectivité*, which here designates more something that is really taking place and occurring, although one believes it to be impossible, so I have tried to adjust the translation depending on the context. This term is very important in Marion's work and would profit from closer examination. Its various translations should not be taken for granted (including translating it as "actuality").—Trans.]

3. Note that the Jerusalem Bible [in French] does not translate the entire text, but merges the two final statements without detaching "*a panta gar dunata para Theōi*." Yet, this formulation (that Mark also cites exactly) admits a different translation besides the one that we have privileged, provided one implies the article *ta dunata*: "All possibilities are with God." It hence appears to take a position by anticipation on the metaphysical question of the relation between God and the possibilities [lit., "the possibles"]: the possibilities are in God, but precisely because they constitute the possibility of what for humans amounts to the impossible; God appears then not as place of possibilities (in the metaphysical

sense) but as the *place of impossibilities* (which become in him only possibilities), far from becoming the protector of what humans take to be their possibilities.

4. Aristotle, *Metaphysics* Θ 8, 1049b5, in *The Basic Works of Aristotle*, ed. Richard McKeon, trans. W. D. Ross (New York: Modern Library, 2001), 828.

5. Gottfried Wilhelm Leibniz, *Monadologie* §31, trans. Robert Latta and George R. Montgomery as *Discourse on Metaphysics and Other Philosophical Writings: Discourse on Metaphysics, The Principles of Nature and of Grace, The Monadology* (Peterborough, Ont.: Broadview Press, 2012).

6. Leibniz, *Monadology* §32.

7. Leibniz, *Monadology* §38.

8. Leibniz, *Principles of Nature and of Grace*, §7.

9. Martin Heidegger, *Sein und Zeit*, §7, trans. John Macquarrie and Edward Robinson as *Being and Time* (New York: Harper and Row, 1962), 63.

10. Edmund Husserl, *Ideen I*, §24, trans. Daniel O. Dahlstrom as *Ideas for a Pure Phenomenology and Phenomenological Philosophy. First Book: General Introduction to Pure Phenomenology* (Indianapolis: Hackett, 2014), 43, trans. mod.

11. I have since called this the *saturated* phenomenon. See *Being Given: Toward a Phenomenology of Givenness*, trans. Jeffrey L. Kosky (Stanford: Stanford University Press, 2002), §21–23, and the clarification in *The Visible and the Revealed* (New York: Fordham University Press, 2008), 119–44.

8. The Phenomenality of the Sacrament

First published in Italian as "La fenomenalita del sacramento: Essere e donazione," in *Il mondo del sacramento: Teologia et filosofia a confronto*, ed. Nicolas Reali (Milan: Editions Paoline, 2001), published in French as "La phénoménalité du sacrement," *Revue Catholique Internationale Communio* XXVI.5 (2001); previously published in English as "The Phenomenality of the Sacrament—Being and Givenness," in *Words of Life: New Theological Turns in French Phenomenology*, ed. Bruce Ellis Benson and Norman Wirzba, 89–102 (New York: Fordham University Press, 2010).

1. Session XII, c. 3, canon 3, Heinrich Denzinger, *Enchiridion symbolorum: Definitionum et declarationum de rebus fidei et morum* (Barcinone: Herder, 1960), note 876.

2. Augustine, *De civitate Dei*, 10.5, trans. William Babcock as *City of God* (Hyde Park, N.Y.: New City Press, 2012), 309.

3. Thomas Aquinas, *Summa theologiae*, IIIa, q. 61, a. 3, reply, trans. David Bourke as *Summa theologiae* (New York: McGraw-Hill, 1974), 56:45. See also q. 60, a. 4, reply.

4. Thomas Aquinas, *Summa contra gentes,* IV, c. 56, trans. Charles J. O'Neil as *On the Truth of the Catholic Faith* (New York: Image Books, 1957), 247.

5. According to Duns Scot *(Ordinatio,* I, d. 3, p. 1, q. 3, n. 139, *O.o.,* ed. C. Balic, t. 3, p. 87), Suárez *(Disputationes Metaphysicae,* XXXVIII, s. 2, n. 8, *O.o.,* ed. C. Berton, t. 26, p. 503), and Descartes *(Principia philosophiae* I, §52:

"*non potest substantia primum animadverti ex hoc solo, quod sit res existens, quia hoc solum nos non afficit,*" trans. John Cottingham, Robert Stoothoff, and Dugald Murdoch as *Principles of Philosophy*, in *The Philosophical Writings of Descartes*, vol. 1 [Cambridge: Cambridge University Press, 1984], 210); see my analysis in *Questions Cartésiennes II* (Paris: Presses Universitaires de France, 1996), III, §3, 99–108, trans. Christina M. Gschwandtner as *On the Ego and on God: Further Cartesian Questions* (New York: Fordham University Press, 2007), 89–94.

6. In this sense, the process explained by the Thomistic theory of the Eucharist (real accidents of sensible substances are replaced by the body and blood of Christ) does not differ formally from Cartesian eucharistic physics (numerical identity of the space is initially attributed principally to the physical body, then transferred to the body from Christ). See J.-R. Armogathe, *Theologia cartesiana: L'explication physique de l'Eucharistie chez Descartes et dom Desgabets* (The Hague, Martinus Nijhoff, 1977).

7. Descartes, *Discours de la méthode*, AT VI, 76, lines 16–22; trans. John Cottingham, Robert Stoothoff, and Dugald Murdoch as *Discourse on Method*, in *The Philosophical Writings of Descartes*, vol. 1 (Cambridge: Cambridge University Press, 1984), 150.

8. Aquinas, *Summa theologiae*, IIIa, q. 62, a. 5, reply; Bourke, 67.

9. Augustine, *De civitate Dei* 10.5, Babcock, 309. Aquinas, *Summa theologiae*, IIIa, q. 60, a. 1, reply.

10. *Summa theologiae*, IIIa, q. 60, a. 6, reply, Bourke, 21–25.

11. Ibid., IIIa, q. 60, a. 3, reply, Bourke, 11–13.

12. [Here and in the title of the next section, "*se donner, se montrer*" can also be translated "to be given, to be shown"—the construction is both passive and reflexive in French. Although the terms have been translated throughout the text as reflexive, the French holds both meanings together, which ought to be kept in mind.—Trans.]

13. Immanuel Kant, *Kritik der reinen Vernunft*, A109, trans. Norman Kemp Smith as *Critique of Pure Reason* (New York: Palgrave Macmillan, 2003), 137.

14. Edmund Husserl, *Ideen zu einer reinen Phänomenologie und phänomenologischen Philosophie: Erstes Buch, Allgemeine Einführung in die reine Phänomenologie*, ed. W. Biemel, vol. 3 of *Husserliana: Edmund Husserl Gesammelte Werke* (The Hague: Martinus Nijhoff, 1950–), henceforth Hua., §10, 21, trans. Daniel O. Dahlstrom as *Ideas for a Pure Phenomenology and Phenomenological Philosophy. First Book: General Introduction to Pure Phenomenology* (Indianapolis: Hackett, 2014), 22; trans. mod.

15. Martin Heidegger, *Sein und Zeit*, §7, respectively, "das Sich-an-ihm-selbst-zeigende" (31), and "Das was sich zeigt, so wie es sich von ihm selbst her zeigt, von ihm selbst her zeigen lassen" (34), trans. John Macquarrie and Edward Robinson as *Being and Time* (New York: Harper and Row, 1962), 54, 58.

16. Martin Heidegger, *Prolegomena zur Geschichte des Zeitbegriffs*, §32, 423, trans. Theodore Kiesel as *History of the Concept of Time: Prolegomena* (Bloomington: Indiana University Press, 1985), 307.

17. Edmund Husserl, *Idee der Phänomenologie,* Hua. II, 14, trans. Lee Hardy as *The Idea of Phenomenology* (Dordrecht: Kluwer, 1999), 69.
18. Ibid., 11; Hardy, 67.
19. *Summa theologiae,* IIIa, q. 62, a. 1, ad 1m; Bourke, 55.
20. Ibid., IIIa, respectively, q. 64, a. 1, reply, Bourke, 103–5; and a. 2, reply, Bourke, 107: "The power of the sacrament is derived from God alone" (*virtus sacramenti sit a Deo solo*).

9. Transcendence par Excellence

First published as "La transcendance par excellence," *Revue Catholique Internationale Communio* XXX.5/6 (2005): 11–18. Previously unpublished in English.

1. The same is true in regard to the ordinary teaching of the magisterium, as Vincent Carraud has recently shown: "Apparuit caritas. L'image de Dieu: Banalité et originalité d'une encyclique," *Revue Catholique Internationale Communio* XXXIV.5 (2009): 87–100.

10. The Recognition of the Gift

First published as "La reconnaissance du don," *Revue Catholique Internationale Communio* XXX.1 (2008): 169–82. The argument was further developed in *Negative Certainties*, trans. Stephen E. Lewis (Chicago: University of Chicago Press, 2015), chapter 4, §§19–21. Previously published in English as "The Recognition of the Gift," special issue, *Studia Phaenomenologica* (2009): 15–28. It appears by permission of Zeta Books, © 2009 Zeta Books.

1. Augustine, *De fide rerum quae non videntur*, c. 4, trans. C. L. Cornish as *Concerning Faith of Things Not Seen*, in *Nicene and Post-Nicene Fathers*, 1st ser., vol. 3 (Peabody, Mass.: Hendrickson, 1995/1887), 338.
2. Martin Heidegger, *Sein und Zeit* (Tübingen: Max Niemeyer Verlag, 1926/1993), 35; trans. John Macquarrie and Edward Robinson as *Being and Time* (New York: Harper and Row, 1962), 59.
3. Either Mount Gerazim or Jerusalem (John 4:21), both of them rejected by Christ in favor of worshipping in spirit and truth (John 4:23), i.e., in him.
4. Also: "Even if I testify on my own behalf, my testimony is valid because I know *where* I come from and *where* I am going, but you do not know *where* I come from or *where* I am going" (John 8:14).
5. Or going from seeing to knowing: "If you knew me, you would also know my Father" (John 8:19).
6. Irenaeus, *Contra haereses*, 4.6.6, trans. as *Against Heresies* in *Ante-Nicene Fathers*, vol. 1 (Peabody, Mass.: Hendrickson, 1995/1867), 469. See Saint Augustine: "Cum Pater ostenditur, et Filius ostenditur qui in illo est; et cum Filius ostenditur, etiam Pater ostenditur, qui in illo est—when the Father is manifested, the Son also, who is in Him, is manifested; and when the Son is manifested, the Father also, who is in Him, is manifested." Or, "visibilem namque Filii solius personam, invisibilis Trinitas—For the invisible Trinity

wrought the visible person of the Son." But the relation is here to some extent set apart through the doubling of the Son in the invisible and visible Son. Augustine, *De Trinitate*, 1.9.18; 2.10.18; 2.5.9, trans. Arthur West Haddan as *The Trinity* in *Nicene and Post-Nicene Fathers*, 1st ser., vol. 3 (Peabody, Mass.: Hendrickson, 1995/1887), 27, 46, 41, respectively.

7. "Zeit und Sein," in *Zur Sache des Denkens* (Tübingen: Max Niemeyer Verlag, 1969), 8, trans. Joan Stambaugh as *On Time and Being* (New York: Harper and Row, 1972), 8.

8. [*L'abandon* is etymologically related to *don* (gift) and refers to both abandonment/rejection and to abandon, freedom, even excess. Marion frequently plays on the link between *don*/gift and *abandon*/giving to the point of abandon(ment), in the sense of both abundance and total loss.—Trans.]

9. Confirmed by Luke 22:21: "The hand of him who is going to betray me (*tou paradidontos me/tradentis me*)" and Matt. 26:16: "opportunity to betray Him (*hina auton paradō/ut eum traderet*)."

10. See "For even the Son of Man did not come to be served, but to serve, and to give his life as a ransom for many" (Mark 10:45); or, "For there is one God and one mediator between God and men, the man Christ Jesus, who *gave himself* as a ransom for all men" (1 Tim. 2:5–6); "the glorious appearing of our great God and Savior, Jesus Christ, who *gave himself* for us to redeem us from all wickedness" (Titus 2:13–14).

11. See also the beginning of the same chapter: "I commend you because you remember me in everything and maintain the traditions just as I handed them on to you (*kathōs paredōka humin, tas paradoseis katechete/et sicut tradidi vobis, praecepta mea tenetis*)" (1 Cor. 11:2).

12. Absent from 1 Cor. 11, but used in Matt. 26:28, Mark 14:24, and Luke 22:20.

13. We understand in this context how a gift in the Temple can be condemned, which will be understood in relation to what is due to one's father or mother (Matt. 15:1–9 and Mark 7:1–13): this is not a "liberal" interpretation of the imperative to honor your father and your mother, but refers to redirecting toward the Temple what is due to natural solidarity and which, for this reason, is almost *unnoticed* and makes the gift become *visible*, which from then onward focuses all the attention on itself and thus disappears *as* gift. On the contrary, the apostles sent on a mission must only accept gifts that are unnoticed: "You have received freely (*dōrean*), give freely (*dōrean*)" (Matt. 10:8), in the pure transparency of the gift offered, "*in ratione dati et accepti*" (Phil. 4:15).

11. "They Recognized Him and He Became Invisible to Them"

First published as "Ils le reconnurent et lui-même leur devint invisible," in *Demain l'Église: Hommage au cardinal Lustiger*, ed. J. Duchesne and J. Ollier (Paris: Plon, 2001). Previously published in English as "They Recognized Him; and He Became Invisible to Them," *Modern Theology* 18, no. 2 (2002): 145–52. It appears by permission of Blackwell, © by Blackwell Publishers Ltd., 2002.

1. With Mark 16:12–13 as sole parallel.

2. *Paroikeis*, word for word: a foreign inhabitant, passing through Jerusalem (see the Septuagint Gen. 17:8). But in this case they are dealing with what we might call "a funny sort of pilgrim."

3. A formulation that takes up Luke 7:16, Acts 7:22, and Luke 1:6 and 20:26, respectively.

4. Same situation, at least at the outset, for Mary at the tomb: "she . . . saw Jesus standing, but she did not know that it was Jesus" (John 20:14). Likewise for the disciples at the Sea of Tiberias: "the disciples did not know that it was Jesus" (John 21:4).

5. Paul Claudel, "Emmaüs," in *Œuvres complètes*, vol. 23 (Paris: Gallimard, 1964), 76.

6. Third day, not the second (against the Jerusalem Bible and Osty), according to *The Gospel According to Luke I-IX*, ed. Joseph A. Fitzmeyer, *The Anchor Bible* (Garden City, N.Y.: Doubleday, 1979), vol. 28, 1564.

7. See: "For I tell you that this scripture must be fulfilled in me, 'And he was reckoned with transgressors' [Isa. 53:12]; for what concerns me (*to peri emou*) finds its fulfillment" (Luke 22:37—see also 4:21).

8. The same or nearly the same formulation is found at the multiplication of the loaves (Luke 9:12): already then the Christ had begun to teach the Kingdom of God (9:11), in order then to distribute to them, after have said the blessing (9:15, as in 24:30), bread (as in 24:30), and fish (24:43).

9. This is often translated "Where do you live?" (for example, in the Vulgate or the Jerusalem Bible), but it would be better to render it, "Where do you stay?," and to hear this said as one still hears it in the countryside—"to stay" signifying "to live." And in fact they "stayed," lived at his home that day (John 1:39).

10. As in the short ending of Mark 16:8: "They went out and fled from the tomb; for they were all trembling and beside themselves. And they said nothing to anyone, for they were terror-stricken." Already and completely, the issue here is the experience of the inexpressible, of the unthinkable, of the resurrection. At once the debate about the authenticity of the long ending (with the explicit accounts of the resurrection, Mark 16:9–20) appears objectless—here again, the Christ must speak, say his words, and give his significations so that the phenomenon may at last become tolerable and visible. The phenomenal continuity between the two texts coincides perfectly with that of the two accounts in Luke.

12. The Invisible Saint

First published in English as "The Invisibility of the Saint," trans. Christina M. Gschwandtner, *Critical Inquiry* 35, no. 3 (2008): 703–10, later in French as "Le saint invisible," *Revue Catholique Internationale Communio* XXXIV.5 (2009): 77–86. English version reprinted in *Saints: Faith without Borders*, ed. Françoise Meltzer and Jaś Elsner (Chicago: University of Chicago Press, 2011), 355–62. It appears by permission of the University of Chicago Press, © 2009 by The University of Chicago.

1. [The French word *saint* that is at the center of this article can mean both "holy" and "saint." *Sainteté* similarly can mean "sanctity," "saintliness," "sainthood," "godliness," or "holiness." Marion is assuming all of these connotations, and they should be kept in mind whenever the term "saint" or "holy" appears in English.—Trans.]

2. [The essay begins with a triple invocation of the term *saint* (similar to the trice-holy, which Marion will quote later) separated only by articles or qualifiers: *Le saint, quel saint? Un saint*, a structure difficult and awkward to re-create in English, especially as translating *saint* as holy in this context would not make much sense.—Trans.]

3. Molière, *Tartuffe*, 1.1.69.

4. Primo Lévi, among others, explains this clearly: "I must repeat: we, the survivors, are not the true witnesses . . . we survivors are not only an exiguous but also an anomalous minority: we are those who by their prevarications or abilities or good luck did not touch bottom. Those who did so, those who saw the Gorgon, have not returned to tell about it or have returned mute, but they are the 'Muslims,' the submerged, the complete witnesses, the ones whose deposition would have a general significance. . . . We speak in their stead, by proxy." Primo Lévi, *Les naufragés et les rescapés* (Paris: Gallimard, 1989), 82, trans. Raymond Rosenthal [from the Italian] as *The Drowned and the Saved* (New York: Simon and Schuster, 1988), 83–84.

5. [Marion again plays on words here: *en face* means in front of, *de biais* means from the side, tangentially, or indirectly, *de dos* means from the back, but here really from the "other side of" or from "beyond" death.—Trans.]

6. [In addition to being the substantivization of the verb *voir*, to see, a *voyant* is a seer, visionary, or clairvoyant. The term can also mean indicator or mark, as in the recipient who becomes the indicating screen for the incoming saturated phenomenon.—Trans.]

7. [*Inamissible*, rarely used in English, means "incapable of being lost."—Trans.]

8. [Marion repeatedly uses *invisible* and *invisable* together in this text. *Invisable* designates what cannot be reached or that for which one cannot aim, but it can also mean that something is inconceivable or that one cannot look at it. I mostly translate it as "unreachable" here, which seems the least awkward, but all connotations should be heard in the term.—Trans.]

9. Blaise Pascal, *Pensées*, ed. Louis Lafuma (Paris: Flammarion, 1973), §308; trans. A. J. Krailsheimer (New York: Penguin, 1966), 124.

Index

Anselm, Saint, 34, 158*n*10
Apel, Karl Otto, 22
Aquinas, Thomas, Saint, 35, 116, 153*n*2, 158*n*15, 163*nn*3–4, 164*n*8, 164*n*9
Aristotle, 15, 31, 78, 94, 116, 157*n*1, 162*n*2, 163*n*4
Armogathe, Jean-Robert, 164*n*6
Augustine, Saint, xiii, 5, 12, 34, 35, 103, 125, 153*nn*3,1, 154*n*6, 158*nn*12,14, 163*n*2, 164*n*9, 165*n*1, 165–66*n*6

Basil of Caesarea, Saint, 35, 159*n*17, 159*n*21
Bernanos, Georges, 68
Bernard of Clairvaux, Saint, 34, 82, 158*n*11, 160*n*32
Bloy, Léon, 68
Bonnety, Augustin, 68
Boudon, Raymond, 22
Bruaire, Claude, 162*n*10
Bultmann, Rudolf, 87

Carraud, Vincent, 165*n*1
Celsus, 87
Cézanne, Paul, 39, 82
Chateaubriand, François Auguste René, 68
Chrysostom, John, Saint, 40, 159*n*27

Claudel, Paul, 139, 162*n*1, 167*n*5
Clavel, Maurice, 100
Cyril of Jerusalem, Saint, 159*n*21

Darwin, Charles, 5
Dionysius the Areopagite, 35, 39, 61, 158*n*16, 159*n*23
Denziger, Heinrich, 163*n*1
Descartes, René, 7, 17, 32, 33–35, 39, 40, 43, 78, 94, 116, 154*n*4, 157*nn*5,6, 158*nn*7–9, 159*n*22, 163–64*n*5, 164*nn*6,7
Duns Scotus, John, 32, 116, 163*n*5

Erasmus of Rotterdam, 5

Fichte, Johann Gottlieb, 78, 95
Foucault, Michel, 39, 159*n*25

Galileo, Galilei, 5, 6, 32
Gregory Nazianzen, Saint, 41, 160*n*34
Gregory of Nyssa, Saint, 35, 38, 82, 159*nn*18,21, 162*n*9

Habermas, Jürgen, 20, 22, 154*n*1
Hegel, Georg Wilhelm Friedrich, 19, 29, 78, 94, 95, 116, 117, 161*n*2

169

Heidegger, Martin, 8, 17, 78, 95, 97, 98, 109, 110, 116, 127, 131, 163*n*9, 164*nn*15,16, 165*n*2
Henry, Michel, 98
Hölderlin, Friedrich, 29
Hugo, Victor, 66
Hume, David, 95
Husserl, Edmund, 25, 40, 95, 96, 98, 100, 103, 109, 110, 116, 159*n*26, 163*n*10, 164*n*14, 165*n*17

Irenaeus, Saint, 131, 165*n*6

John Paul II, 27
Justin Martyr, Saint, 4, 29

Kant, Immanuel, 25, 26, 32, 35, 40, 42, 79, 94, 95, 96, 108, 109, 116, 155*n*7, 157*n*6, 160*n*31, 161*nn*3,4, 164*n*13
Kepler, Johannes, 32
Khomeini, 27

Leibniz, Gottfried Wilhelm, 15, 78, 87, 94, 95, 116, 163*nn*5–8
Lévi, Primo, 168*n*4
Levinas, Emmanuel, xii, 98, 100, 153*n*2
Locke, John, 95
Lustiger, Jean-Marie, 27, 156–57*n*9

Malebranche, Nicolas, 40, 87, 95, 117, 160*n*30
Maritain, Jean, 17
Maximus the Confessor, Saint, 4

Merleau-Ponty, Maurice, 98, 100
Molière, 145, 154*n*6, 168*n*3
Montaigne, Michel de, 35, 158*n*13

Nicholas of Cusa, 32
Nietzsche, Friedrich, xiv, 7, 14, 15, 17, 78, 79, 116, 154*n*3, 161*n*5

Ockham, William of, 55
Ormesson, Jean de, 154*n*5

Pascal, Blaise, xiv, 31, 39, 67, 81, 150, 159*nn*19,24, 160*n*37, 162*n*8, 168*n*9
Péguy, Charles, 24
Piero della Franscesca, 39
Plato, 31, 67, 116, 157*n*3

Renan, Ernest, 87
Ricoeur, Paul, 155*n*7
Rousseau, Jean-Jacques, 95

Sartre, Jean-Paul, 66, 67, 81
Schelling, Friedrich Wilhelm Joseph von, 95
Spinoza, Baruch, 40, 116, 117, 159*n*29, 160*n*35
Suárez, Francisco, 32, 94, 95, 116, 163*n*5

Valadier, Paul, 155*n*8, 156*n*9
Verlaine, Paul, 68
Veuillot, Louis, 68
Voltaire, 66, 87

Wittgenstein, Ludwig von, xi, 41, 160*n*33

Perspectives in Continental Philosophy
John D. Caputo, series editor

Recent titles:

Emmanuel Alloa, *Resistance of the Sensible World: An Introduction to Merleau-Ponty*. Translated by Jane Marie Todd. Foreword by Renaud Barbaras.

Françoise Dastur, *Questions of Phenomenology: Language, Alterity, Temporality, Finitude*. Translated by Robert Vallier.

Jean-Luc Marion, *Believing in Order to See: On the Rationality of Revelation and the Irrationality of Some Believers*. Translated by Christina M. Gschwandtner.

Adam Y. Wells, ed., *Phenomenologies of Scripture*.

An Yountae, *The Decolonial Abyss: Mysticism and Cosmopolitics from the Ruins*.

Jean Wahl, *Transcendence and the Concrete: Selected Writings*. Edited and with an Introduction by Alan D. Schrift and Ian Alexander Moore.

Colby Dickinson, *Words Fail: Theology, Poetry, and the Challenge of Representation*.

Emmanuel Falque, *The Wedding Feast of the Lamb: Eros, the Body, and the Eucharist*. Translated by George Hughes.

Emmanuel Falque, *Crossing the Rubicon: The Borderlands of Philosophy and Theology*. Translated by Reuben Shank. Introduction by Matthew Farley.

Colby Dickinson and Stéphane Symons (eds.), *Walter Benjamin and Theology*.

Don Ihde, *Husserl's Missing Technologies*.

William S. Allen, *Aesthetics of Negativity: Blanchot, Adorno, and Autonomy*.

Jeremy Biles and Kent L. Brintnall, eds., *Georges Bataille and the Study of Religion*.

Tarek R. Dika and W. Chris Hackett, *Quiet Powers of the Possible: Interviews in Contemporary French Phenomenology*. Foreword by Richard Kearney.

Richard Kearney and Brian Treanor, eds., *Carnal Hermeneutics*.
Aaron T. Looney, *Vladimir Jankélévitch: The Time of Forgiveness*.
Vanessa Lemm, ed., *Nietzsche and the Becoming of Life*.
Edward Baring and Peter E. Gordon, eds., *The Trace of God: Derrida and Religion*.
Jean-Louis Chrétien, *Under the Gaze of the Bible*. Translated by John Marson Dunaway.
Michael Naas, *The End of the World and Other Teachable Moments: Jacques Derrida's Final Seminar*.
Noëlle Vahanian, *The Rebellious No: Variations on a Secular Theology of Language*.

A complete list of titles is available at http://fordhampress.com.

www.ingramcontent.com/pod-product-compliance
Lightning Source LLC
Chambersburg PA
CBHW020110020526
44112CB00033B/1129